MODERN BANKING

MODERN BANKING

BY

R. S. SAYERS

CASSEL PROFESSOR OF ECONOMICS
IN THE UNIVERSITY OF LONDON

SEVENTH EDITION

OXFORD
AT THE CLARENDON PRESS
1967

Oxford University Press, Ely House, London W. 1

GLASGOW NEW YORK TORONTO MELBOURNE WELLINGTON
CAPE TOWN SALISBURY IBADAN NAIROBI LUSAKA ADDIS ABABA
BOMBAY CALCUTTA MADRAS KARACHI LAHORE DACCA
KUALA LUMPUR HONG KONG TOKYO

FIRST EDITION 1938
REPRINTED FIVE TIMES
SECOND EDITION 1947
REPRINTED TWICE
THIRD EDITION 1951
REPRINTED THREE TIMES
FOURTH EDITION 1958
FIFTH EDITION 1960
SIXTH EDITION 1964
SEVENTH EDITION 1967

PRINTED IN GREAT BRITAIN

PREFACE

IN the preface to the first edition of this book, I claimed that it presented 'an exposition of modern banking in the light of current theory . . . addressed primarily to the university student who wishes to include in his honours course a study of banking sufficient to enable him to understand how this important part of the economic system really works nowadays'. I repeated this claim when in 1963 I substantially rewrote the book for its sixth edition. The seventh edition now offered is in the main a reprint of the sixth, to which is added a Note outlining some of the more important changes in the English monetary scene in the 1960's. For this Addendum the main printed sources are the (quarterly) *Midland Bank Review*, the *Quarterly Bulletin* of the Bank of England, and *Financial Statistics* (a monthly publication of H.M. Stationery Office). All these sources I strongly recommend to the student who wishes to keep himself up to date.

In the main text, I have made fairly considerable amendments in Chapter 11, with generous help from Professor Ernest Bloch of New York University and Dr. George Garvy of the Federal Reserve Bank of New York; they are not responsible for any errors that remain.

The theoretical chapters are almost untouched, except that Chapter 10 has a new opening paragraph. Even the kindest readers of the earlier version complained of the chapter's first sentence, and I have tried to clarify by reconstructing and expanding the entire paragraph.

In other chapters there are numerous small amendments to bring figures and other points of detail up to date. In general, the facts may now be assumed to relate to the latter part of 1966, but for some matters—especially the London money market—it is important to remember that the new Addendum offers a serious corrective.

68-03660

In the course of 29 years the readers who have discussed with me points in this book must number hundreds, and it would be invidious at this stage to make a short enough list for individual acknowledgement by name. I can only emphasize, with warm thanks, my awareness that the present edition owes much to many many readers of its forerunners.   R. S. S.

London School of Economics
January 1967

CONTENTS

1

INTRODUCTORY

1. *The Economic Importance of Banks*

BANKS are institutions whose debts—usually referred to as 'bank deposits'—are commonly accepted in final settlement of other people's debts. The transfer of a bank deposit from one person to another, by the handing over of a cheque, is a common method of payment. The cheque itself is merely the instrument by which the bank is given instructions, and the cheque itself cannot reasonably be described as money; but the deposit that can be so transferred does serve as money, 'money' being the word we apply to anything ordinarily used in settlement of debts.

The word 'debts' is here used in the broad sense of any obligation fixed in terms of money, whether that obligation is established by some long-term contract, some governmental order, or by the purchase over the counter of a shop. The taxpayer has a debt imposed on him by the taxation law, a debt that is assessed by the tax official and then has to be discharged by payment of money of some kind. When a householder signs a lease for his house, he incurs debts in the form of the obligation to make a series of payments at future dates, as rent of his house, and these payments have to be made in some form of money acceptable to the landlord. When a child buys an ice-cream from the ice-cream van in the street, the child incurs a debt which has to be settled by the immediate payment of sixpence to the ice-cream vendor. In the last of these three examples the use of a bank deposit would not be appropriate and a coin would be expected; but in the other two, the transfer of a bank deposit, by cheque or some other kind of order to the bank, would in England be readily accepted. For all large payments, and for many small payments, bank deposits are accepted in final settlement of debt; for most small payments notes or coin, which can be described as subsidiary money, are used. The position is similar in the United States and in Canada, but in many other countries of the world bank deposits are less widely used and notes are more prominent; in Western European countries there is also an important Post Office system, the Giro, whereby both large and small debts are commonly settled.

In explaining why bank deposits are described as money, no reference has been made to the term 'legal tender'. Whether an instrument of payment—a coin or note, for example—is legal tender is not, in a highly developed financial system, of any economic importance. Legal tender status is, as the words imply, conferred by the law of the country; its substantial meaning is that a creditor to whom legal tender has been offered suffers certain restrictions if he refuses to accept the payment and thereafter seeks by legal process to enforce payment. It cannot be too strongly emphasized that for economists this is a matter of no importance in a country such as England: for what matters and what does not matter from an economic point of view depends upon the actual practice of people in the ordinary business of life, and it is by what they ordinarily do and what they ordinarily think that people effectively determine what is and what is not 'money' in an economic sense.

The special interest of economists in the activities of banks is due to the monetary nature of the deposit liabilities of the banks. Like any other business undertaking, the activities of banks are of direct personal interest to the people who use them and to the people who work in them: both customers and employees want the banks to be efficiently run. People use the banks for the purpose of making payments and as sources of loans, and efficiency in both these functions is desirable; the latter involves society's interest in the distribution, between different uses, of the resources that can be devoted to adding to the real capital of the nation. Thus far, however, the community's interest in banking is much the same as in any other form of business. Beyond this, there lies the community's interest in banks because by their operations they can affect 'the monetary situation', in the sense of the availability of purchasing power. This can most readily be understood by reference to the ordinary lending business of a bank. When a bank makes an advance, by allowing a customer to overdraw his account, the bank in effect exchanges its own promise to pay immediately against the customer's promise to pay off the advance later on; the economic importance of this exchange is that the bank's promise to pay immediately is absolutely *effective purchasing power*, whereas the customer's promise to make a payment later is, at best, purchasing power of a dubious and limited nature. By a mere exchange of obligations—the essence of bank lending—there has been an increase in the effective purchasing power at the disposal of the persons and corporations (including 'companies') who do the spending that constitutes the *total demand* for goods and services. In so far as the amount of this spending is affected by the amount of purchasing power people have at their disposal, operations in the banks will influence the total spending that is going on: that is to say, the activities of banks will influence the pressure of total demand.

The extent to which the community's productive resources are employed, and to some extent the prices (wages &c.) at which they are employed, and the general level of prices of the products, are all to greater or less extent influenced by the pressure of total demand being exerted at any time. Hence the banks' activities, because they have effect on the monetary situation, have some bearing on the broad functioning of the economy, in the sense of the degree to which its productive resources are employed and the behaviour of price levels. Just how great or how little this influence is in an economy such as that of modern Britain, is not self-evident; the question of how much or how little lies behind much of the discussion in parts of this book (particularly Chapters 9 and 10). That there is *some* influence is generally accepted, and this is why economists have an interest in banking beyond their general interest in any form of business activity.

Aside from the routine work of effecting payments for people by allowing the transfer of bank deposits from one name to another, the important economic aspect of banking is in the *creation* of readily available purchasing power by the exchange of the banks' promises against the promises of other people. From the point of view of the bank, the debt into which it has entered (its liability to pay when the borrower draws a cheque) is matched by an asset (the claim it has against the borrower). Equally, from the point of view of the borrower, the debt into which he has entered (the liability to repay the bank advance) is matched by the asset he now holds, in the shape of the power to draw on the bank, a power that is effective purchasing power. But though on a balancing of assets and liabilities, neither the bank nor the customer is any 'richer' than before, *something has been added*. This something is the difference between the effective purchasing power inherent in a bank deposit and the very questionable purchasing power inherent in an individual's own promise to pay at some future time; and economists have got into the habit of referring to this something as 'liquidity'. They say that the exchange of promises between the bank and the borrower, though it has increased total financial assets by no more than it has increased total financial liabilities, *has increased liquidity in the economy*.

'Liquidity' is a word that came into common use in the discussion of financial affairs originally in the sense of *capacity for being exchanged for money immediately and without loss.* It continues often to be used in this strict sense, but economists have found it convenient to extend its meaning to cover *degrees of exchangeability* and, in a loose way, to summarize certain qualities in a balance-sheet statement of assets and liabilities.[1] Most important in economic theory has been its increased use in monetary theory where, in close relation to the original financial usage, it is used in the sense of degree of exchangeability for the means of final payment. In this sense liquidity is an attribute of a great variety of claims on other financial institutions—building societies, savings banks, and hire-purchase finance companies, among many others—and the activities of these 'non-bank financial intermediaries' can thus also affect the liquidity of the spending units who have, among their financial assets, claims against such intermediaries as well as the bank deposits which are 'liquid' in the extreme sense. Just how close these other financial claims are to bank deposits is partly a matter of business practice in dealing with them (how readily for instance they are exchanged for bank deposits) and partly a matter of how their owners think of them. If people come to think of them as very readily exchangeable, without appreciable loss, into bank deposits, then these financial claims (e.g. 'shares' in building societies) will satisfy the need for liquidity, and will be important substitutes for money, even though they may not actually be used for making final payments.

In a community that has reached this high degree of financial sophistication, and where credit is elastic and fear of a general financial collapse is absent, it may well come about that the community's willingness to spend—the total pressure of demand—will be influenced more by the activities of the whole range of financial institutions and by the credit practices of other businesses than by the much narrower circle of banks. The Radcliffe Committee,

[1] The concept of liquidity, especially with reference to its use by bankers, is further examined in Chapters 2 and 8.

which investigated the working of the British monetary system in 1957–9, was persuaded by the witnesses it heard that the British economy had developed in this way. But even in such a system the activities of the banks, because they are such important lenders, are of great influence over the whole structure of financial claims. Moreover, since the liabilities of the banks are the 'money' with which payments are actually made, a failure of the growth of bank liabilities (deposits) to match a growth in the volume of transactions can set up a chain of reactions that may eventually check the growth of total demand. Some economists, and more especially those who have found it difficult to accept the Radcliffe Committee's judgement of the facts of the British economy, lay heavy stress on this power of the banks, a power resting on their control of bank deposits, whereby the banks can influence the behaviour of total demand.

Thus although a full discussion of the 'monetary' influences on the country's economic activity would have to include an examination of the behaviour of a very wide range of financial intermediaries, the business of the banks, in the ordinary narrow sense, must remain at the centre of such a discussion. In this book it is with their behaviour —the activities of these basic financial businesses called banks—that we shall be mostly concerned; but at times— and particularly when we try to trace the influence of the banks on the level of total demand—it will be necessary to pay some regard to the great web of other financial claims that serve nearly but not all the purposes of money.

II. *The Process of Creation of Money*

For the actual payments made in final settlement of all the debts that arise in everyday life, bank deposits are overwhelmingly important in Britain, in North America, and in Australia, and in only slightly less degree in many other countries. Notes (often called 'bank-notes') and coin serve for a large proportion of the smaller transactions, particularly for the payment of wages and in retail trade. Precise figures for some of the important items in British banking are difficult to find, as the British banks are only very gradually accepting the desirability of publication, but we may take certain figures shown in a new Government publication, *Financial Statistics*, as indicative of the more important quantities. In the issue of September 1966 the *Current* and *Deposit Accounts* of the London clearing banks and the Scottish banks are shown totalling £9,317 millions. This figure may be compared with the total of notes (issued by the Bank of England) and coin (issued by the Royal Mint) in circulation (outside the banks), estimated at £2,713 millions. Thus three-quarters of the total supply of the means of payment consists of the liabilities of the banks to the public.

What induces the banks to get into debt to the public on this colossal scale? The banks have voluntarily entered in their books I O U's to all sorts of people, to an aggregate running into thousands of millions of pounds. What has induced them to do so? They are profit-seeking corporations. They are induced to become debtors to other people by these others offering in exchange certain claims that equal the capital value of the bank's liability and bear interest. It is from the interest payment on these claims that the bank derives much of its income. Provided that it is successfully managed, the bank's assets always equal its liabilities. The bank deposits—i.e. the debts of the bank to the public—are always covered by the assets people have offered to the bank in exchange for deposit claims against the bank. The process of 'creation' of bank deposits is essentially an exchange of claims. The member of the public offers a claim of some sort—such as legal tender State money, or a government bond, or a mere promise—and the bank offers a book debt called a bank deposit. The claims the bank takes from its customers, in exchange for the deposits entered in the books, are the bank's *assets*, and these assets bring the bank much of its income.

The standard assets of a commercial bank are overdrafts and loans, bills discounted, investments, and cash.[1]

The overdraft system of the banks is well known. In return for an undertaking on the customer's part, an undertaking often reinforced by the handing over to the bank of some negotiable security of which the bank may dispose if the customer fails to meet his obligations, the bank allows the customer to 'overdraw' his account. That is to say, the customer is allowed to draw cheques beyond the amount previously standing to his credit in the bank's books, up to the limit set in the overdraft arrangement. (This limit will be fixed after the banker has considered the customer's needs and prospects of profit.) This overdraft facility is equivalent to a bank deposit in representing part of the supply of money with which individuals can buy goods and services, and it becomes part of the visible supply of money as the right to overdraw is exercised and other people (recipients of the borrower's cheques) acquire claims against the lending bank. These claims are money, because people are prepared to accept them in settlement of debts. The borrower undertakes that by the end of, say, three months he will have acquired from other people various kinds of money—State-issued money or claims against this and other banks—to the amount of his overdraft. These claims he hands over to the bank, thus paying off his accumulated debt. In addition he is obliged to pay interest—i.e. he has to provide additional money, so much per cent. on his overdraft, as a payment for the use of the money for the given period. This additional money (the interest charge) provides the bank with a large part of its living. As far as giving and receiving claims in loan and deposit transactions are concerned, it will, if everyone

---

[1] The following pages serve to introduce these standard assets and to explain how bank transactions in them affect the supply of money. More detailed discussion will be found in later chapters (particularly 2 and 10).

meets his obligations, finish 'all square'. The income of the bank depends on the additional claims (the interest and other charges) it makes against people who incur debt to the bank, either directly by loan or overdraft arrangements, or indirectly when the bank acquires the claims from previous creditors of those people.

When the system by which banks lend to individuals and firms is not the overdraft system but the loan system, the process is even simpler in its effects on the supply of money. The borrowing customer gives certain undertakings and also perhaps provides 'collateral security' to protect the bank. The bank at once places the sum of the loan to the credit of the customer: its debts are increased by that amount, and, since its debts constitute money, the supply of money is increased by the amount. At the same time the assets of the bank have increased by the amount of the loan. Its liabilities and its assets have increased by equal amounts. Were the amount £1,000 and were this the sole operation of the bank the balance sheet would be:

Liabilities	£	Assets	£
Deposits (i.e. credit balances of customers) . .	1,000	Loans to customers .	1,000

The gross income of the bank would be increased by whatever interest charge it made for the loan. Out of this gross income it might pay a lower rate of interest on customers' credit balances, and it would have to meet its costs of administration. Any remainder would be a net profit.

As the borrowing customer pays away the £1,000 by cheques drawn in favour of other people, the liabilities of the bank become liabilities not to that customer but to the payees of the cheques. What happens next depends on what those payees choose to do with their claims against the bank.

An alternative procedure, which used to be very common but is now mainly confined to a few branches of overseas trade, is that in which the borrower finances himself by drawing a bill of exchange. The bill of exchange is in effect a written promise to pay a sum at some future date, usually guaranteed by some reputable finance house.[1] Then a person with funds to spare can 'discount' the bill, which means he can pay a sum of money for it now, the sum being slightly less than the sum promised in the bill. When a bank discounts a bill of exchange it in fact acquires the bill as an asset, giving in exchange a deposit—i.e. incurring a debt to a customer. Its liabilities and its assets are increased by the same amount. Its balance-sheet still balances, but its gross income is increased by the difference between the sum it pays for the bill and the sum which the bill says is payable at the named date ('maturity'). This difference is called the 'discount'.

Another way in which a bank may add to its debts is by the purchase of securities, such as government bonds. The bank pays for the bonds by a cheque on itself,[2] i.e. it gives a debt in exchange for the bonds that become part of its assets. The balance-sheet shows change on both sides:

Liabilities		£	Assets			£
Deposits (i.e. debts to customers) .	.	. 1,000	Investments (Government bonds)	.	.	. 1,000

The process is precisely the same when the bank acquires land or buildings for its offices.

A bank will also give a credit balance (i.e. incur a debt) to anybody who offers it a claim against another bank. This happens, for example, when Smith, who banks with Barclays, draws a cheque in favour of Jones, who pays it into his own account at the Midland. In this instance

[1] For detailed account of bills of exchange see Chapter 3.
[2] Or it may give a cheque on its balance with the central bank. The effect is precisely the same, for the payee at once exchanges this claim for one against his own bank (he pays the cheque into his account) and aggregate public claims against the banks are increased by the given sum. The settlement of any inter-bank indebtedness which may arise is discussed later.

there has merely been a transfer of indebtedness between banks—no increase. The original balance-sheet positions of the two banks may be supposed to have been thus:

MIDLAND BANK		BARCLAYS BANK	
Liabilities	*Assets*	*Liabilities*	*Assets*
£	£	£	£
Deposits (Jones) 1,000	Bills dis- counted and invest- ments, &c. 1,000	Deposits (Smith) 2,000	Loans, &c. 2,000

Smith then draws a cheque for £500 in favour of Jones who pays it into his own account. The immediate effect on the position of the two banks is shown below:

MIDLAND BANK

Liabilities		*Assets*	
	£		£
Deposits (Jones) . .	1,500	Bills discounted and invest- ments, &c. . . .	1,000
		Claims against other banks (Barclays) . . .	500
	1,500		1,500

BARCLAYS BANK

Liabilities		*Assets*	
	£		£
Deposits (Smith) . .	1,500	Loans, &c. . . .	2,000
Claims of other banks .	500		
	2,000		2,000

This will not be the final position, as Barclays and the Midland will settle their inter-bank indebtedness by some transfer of assets from Barclays to the Midland. Barclays' assets will go down by £500 whilst the Midland's assets go up by £500. Which particular assets are transferred we shall see later. But it is clear that there has been no increase in the supply of money. All that has happened has been that the composition of the supply has changed, in that more of it is now Midland Bank debts and less is Barclays Bank debts, and, of course, the ownership of the money has passed from Smith to Jones. The banks are less in debt to Smith and more in debt to Jones than before. Jones has more purchasing power at his disposal than before, Smith has less. The aggregate supply of purchasing power is unchanged.

One very important kind of asset the banks may acquire in exchange for a deposit liability has not yet been mentioned. This is 'Cash'. Cash consists of State money (in Britain now only 'silver' and copper coin) and of liabilities of the central bank, or bankers' bank (in England, the Bank of England). The liabilities of the central bank may be either book liabilities—i.e. deposits with it—or bank notes. When a customer 'pays in' a wad of notes and some odd silver and copper coins, say, £31. 17s. 9d. he acquires a deposit to that amount. The bank, that is to say, becomes indebted to the customer to the amount of £31. 17s. 9d. Its balance-sheet will have the following items added:

Liabilities				Assets			
	£	s.	d.		£	s.	d.
Deposits . . .	31	17	9	Cash in hand . .	31	17	9

When a customer draws a cheque to 'self' and takes it to the bank for cash, or receives a cheque from somebody else and goes to the bank to 'cash it', the process is precisely reversed—Deposits go down and Cash in hand goes down. As, for reasons we have seen above, individuals sometimes prefer to use cash and sometimes cheques, cash is continually crossing the bankers' counters. Retail tradesmen are continually paying it in (exchanging cash for bank deposits) and employers of labour and spenders of incomes paid by cheque are continually drawing out cash (exchanging bank deposits for cash). Passing cash across a bank's counter is essentially changing one kind of money for another—the proximate result is no change in the aggregate supply of money in the hands of the public. That further results may follow any decided net change in its composition is shown in Chapter 2.

The book claims against the central bank, i.e. the deposits at the central bank, are another form of cash. Ignoring, for the time being, the fact that the central bank may act as banker to the Government and to other people, we consider solely the central bank's operations as the bankers' bank. The other banks choose to hold deposits at the central bank because it is convenient to settle inter-bank indebtedness by transferring their deposits at one bank—the central bank. If, as we saw above might happen, one bank becomes indebted to another, the debt can be settled by a book entry at the central bank, the deposit there of the creditor bank (the Midland in our example) being raised and the deposit of the debtor bank (Barclays) being reduced. The aggregate debts of the central bank have not changed; but it now owes more than before to the Midland and less than before to Barclays.

As transactions between members of the public are always leading to a flux and reflux of cash to and from the banks, and to inter-bank indebtedness, every bank finds it essential to hold, as part of its assets, cash in hand (till money) and at the central bank (Bankers' Deposits). This cash holding is called the 'cash reserve', and we shall have much more to say about its significance in succeeding chapters. The cash reserve is, to the banker, less attractive than the other assets because it brings him no income. He is obliged to hold it owing to the monetary habits of the public and the structure of the banking system.[1] But once any important section of the public has developed the banking habit the cash reserve need not bear a high ratio to aggregate assets. Consequently, in the world as we know it, bankers have ample inducement to create debts to other people, and that means creating purchasing power.

The ability of the banks to create purchasing power in this way depends on their conducting their business in such a way as to inspire and maintain public confidence in their reliability as debtors. The scale on which bank

[1] In some countries the obligation to hold a cash reserve is a legal obligation.

deposits will be held by the public will depend on this confidence, on the competing attractions of alternative financial assets, and on the money values of both the stock of wealth and the flow of incomes. These money values, in their turn, can be influenced by the banks' activities in creating deposits. In short, the amount of bank deposits, the level of prices and the flow of money incomes are all in some degree interdependent, and it will be the purpose of the remaining chapters of this book to show how the banks' conduct of their business affects the nature of this interdependence.

It is not our purpose to trace the entire chain of consequences of the behaviour of the banking system; we shall confine ourselves to showing how the behaviour of the banking system influences the pressure of total demand, and we shall throughout the book assume that it is through the pressure of demand that the banking system influences the general level of prices and money incomes. This is not to suppose that prices and incomes are *determined* by the behaviour of the banking system. Our assumption is rather that it is one of the relevant factors: we accept the view of the National Economic Development Council, that

the rate of increase of money incomes depends on many things, including the cost of living, the state of industrial relations, the rate of increase to which people have become accustomed in the past, the rate of growth of productivity, import prices, the state of competition at home and from foreign producers. But past experience suggests that it is also dependent to a considerable extent on the pressure of demand and is higher the higher this pressure.

So, without assuming any regular quantitative connexion between the volume of bank deposits and the movement of prices, we do assume that banking behaviour is *relevant*, through the pressure of total demand, and in the light of this we may consider how the Government and its agencies can use the banking system to influence the working of the economic system.

2

COMMERCIAL BANKING

1. *Structural Questions*

THE banking systems of different countries vary substantially from one another, but there has been during the present century a universal tendency for each nation to develop a wide network of banks centred upon the chief trading centre of the country, with the largest banks themselves established in that centre and grouped round a quite different institution referred to as the 'central bank'. The English system had already assumed this shape more than a century ago, though the banks were then much smaller and more numerous than they are today. The systems of many other countries, including underdeveloped countries, have shown some tendency to gravitate towards the English pattern, but all have their peculiarities. Especially the banking system of the United States has characteristics all its own, and requires separate study in Chapter 11.

In general, each country has its own structure of banks and other financial institutions. This is, at least in its present degree, a novelty: until quite recently large tracts of the world were served predominantly by outposts of the City of London or of other great financial centres. Such areas lacked 'central banks' of their own. Gradually the activity of the London outposts has declined in relative importance, while local banks have grown up and central banks have been established in one country after another. As in England in the past, within the frontiers of each country the banks and other financial institutions have been growing bigger, and becoming more definitely centred on the major trading centre in which the central bank is established. Because trade and other business transactions cross frontiers in huge volume, many banks—especially the large banks in great trading centres—have important international business; nevertheless, the banking business of the world is organized in the main on national lines, and in the present century this has been becoming more rather than less true. Some of the great British overseas banks remain, and there are other international banks as well; but banking organization does not easily straddle national frontiers.

Most of the descriptive material in this book is drawn from the contemporary English system. But, because similar systems have been developing in many other countries, much of what is said of the English system is broadly applicable to other countries. Moreover, however different the forms and the organizations may appear, bankers think in much the same way the world over. They get into the same habits, they adopt the same attitudes to their customers, and they react in much the same way to changes in the economic climate. The principles of banking therefore have world-wide validity, and what is said of English bankers and the working of the English system can often be said with almost equal truth of other countries. Not quite equal truth: differences of law, differences of national character, differences of history, even differences of language, do make for national peculiarities in banking. As we study the English system, we shall sometimes glance at the different ways of other systems; in Chapter 11 we leave the English system and study the U.S.A., and then in Chapter 12 we look at some of the problems special to less 'developed' countries.

The more developed financial systems of the world characteristically fall into three parts: the central bank, the commercial banks, and the other financial institutions. These are now often referred to by economists as 'financial intermediaries', because in effect they mediate between people who save (and therefore have money to lend or invest) and people who want to secure the use of money for the purpose of spending, particularly (but not exclusively) on capital goods. It must be emphasized at once that in this sense commercial banks are 'financial intermediaries', for they also borrow from those who are not immediately spending all their current receipts and they lend to those who have intentions of immediate spending on goods beyond the range of their own current receipts. We shall therefore do well to think of *all* financial institutions, including banks, as in the business of borrowing and lending money; and we must attach to our miscellaneous collection outside the banks the inelegant label, 'non-bank financial intermediaries'.

Central banks, with special reference to the Bank of England, are discussed in Chapters 4 and 5, the commercial banks in this chapter, and some of the more important non-bank financial intermediaries in Chapters 3 and 7.

In appearance the main distinction between a central bank and a commercial bank is that nowadays the central bank does not do much banking, but the more fundamental difference is one of aim. The commercial bank thinks primarily of making a profit, whereas the central bank thinks of the effects of its operations on the working of the economic system. If the commercial bank is taking a long view it will sometimes forgo immediate profits for the sake of stability; but it is competing with other banks and cannot afford degrees of far-sightedness and altruism far beyond those of its competitors. It has its shareholders, and is expected to do the best it can for them even if (as in England) it does not have to tell them just how well it is doing for them. The central bank, by contrast, is usually owned by the government. A few of the central banks of the world have, for historical reasons, some shareholders, to whom they pay dividends; but though cases have occurred of central banks altering their course in order to avoid a loss of income, these have been departures from central banking principles, and the universally accepted practice is for any shareholders' dividend to be as fixed as payments on a government bond. The commercial banks may be few or many, and they are to be found doing business with the general public all over the country. There is only one central bank in each country. It has few offices and it does little if any business for the general public. Its market operations are mainly impersonal and are confined to what is necessary for influencing the country's financial business in the directions dictated by economic policy.

In England the commercial banks used to be referred to as 'the joint-stock banks', and this term is still often found in the literature of the subject. Recently the term 'the clearing banks' has become common usage, and we shall sometimes use this term, interchangeably with 'commercial banks' when only England is in question. The term 'clearing banks' has its origin in the fact that the commercial banks which have absorbed almost all of the ordinary banking business of the country are the members of the London Bankers' Clearing House, an organization (described in Appendix 1) that greatly increases the efficiency of the cheque system and so has enabled 'the clearing banks' to provide for their customers a service unrivalled by those outside the Clearing House. The Clearing House system has its parallels in other countries' banking systems, of course, but the term 'clearing banks' is not used elsewhere. In the United States the term 'commercial banks' is commonly used, though sometimes they are referred to as 'the member banks'. The latter usage is not strictly correct, for many commercial banks (some of the 'State banks'—banks registered under State, as opposed to Federal, laws) are not member banks; but in many ways the operations of non-member banks and those of member banks are subject to the same influences, and for this reason confusion of the two categories is often pardonable enough. In Western Europe commercial banks are often referred to as 'credit banks', in distinction from the investment banks, though the distinction between these two types of institution is sometimes in practice blurred.

Although there are exceptions in some parts of the world, the typical commercial bank in most countries is a very large institution having a large number of branches scattered over much if not all of the country. Simple examples of this 'branch-banking' are in England, Scotland, Canada and Australia. In England there are in form eleven clearing banks conducting the ordinary banking business of the country. Of these eleven, one is an Irish bank, having scarcely any business domestic to England and only by historical accident still a member of the London Bankers' Clearing House. Of the other ten, five are often described as 'The Big Five' and have about six-sevenths of the business; of these five, Barclays, the Midland and Lloyds might well be described as 'The Big Three', each of these being much bigger than the other two, Westminster and National Provincial. But the National Provincial has recently bought one of the smaller branch banks, the District, although the process of absorption is apparently going to be slow, so that the District Bank will in appearance remain like two others (Martins and Williams Deacons) as a rather large regional bank, traditionally established in the north-west of England but pushing out new branches into the south and east during the last twenty years. The last-named, Williams Deacons, is with Glyn Mills (the tenth of the Clearing Banks) owned by the Royal Bank of Scotland; this group is called 'The Three Banks Group' but the two English members of the group have considerable independence in their rather specialized fields of operation. The eleventh member of the Clearing House is Coutts, which is owned by the National Provincial but is maintained as a separate establishment because of the special nature of some of its principal accounts.

Thus, ignoring the one Irish member, the London Clearing Banks—the group that conducts the ordinary banking business of England—may be listed as follows:

Short Name	Deposits, &c. in November 1966 £ millions	
Barclays	2,256	
Midland	2,031	
Lloyds	1,709	
National Provincial	1,065	
District	318	1,440
Coutts	57	
Westminster	1,262	
Martins	444	
Williams Deacons	157	
Glyn Mills	70	

In the U.S.A. the picture is very different. Although branch banking is on the increase, banking in that country is still predominantly of the opposite type—the 'unit banking' system such as existed in England in the middle of the nineteenth century. In this system the bank's operations are confined in general to a single office, though some have branches limited to a small part of the country. The persistence of the unit banking system in the United States is in conformity with legal restrictions; these reflect a traditional American fear of a 'Money Trust' and particularly the resistance of the Middle and Far West to dominance by New York financiers. (Even central banking in the United States has been affected by this strong historical force; the central bank there is in form a federation of twelve banks, each with its own region.) Like the English unit banks of a century ago, the unit banks of America are linked together by a 'correspondent bank' relationship. A country bank deposits some of its cash reserves with a bank in the nearest big city, and the city banks themselves send funds to the great centres of New York and Chicago. Remittances of funds from one part of the country to another are made through the correspondent banks—i.e. by transference of the deposits in the

books of a city bank from the name of one country bank
to that of another country bank, or (through the clearing
organized among the city banks) from the account of a
country bank with one city bank to the account of another
country bank with another city bank. Besides these convenient arrangements whereby payments can be made
across the network of correspondent banks, the banks in
the great cities sometimes provide other important services
for their 'country correspondents'. They provide, for
example, facilities for transacting foreign business, and
there are often standing arrangements for consultation on
lending risks, and even for sharing loan business. By
arrangements of these various kinds the unit banks in
a correspondent network are enabled to enjoy some of the
advantages of a branch banking system. In comparing
branch banking with unit banking we must accordingly
remember that unit banks are not entirely independent of
each other but are connected by the correspondent links.

Where there are no impediments of law or of strong
political tradition the unit banking has tended to give way
to branch banking on a nation-wide scale, and to few
rather than many banks. This movement for fewer and
bigger banks, each with more and more branches spread
more widely over the country, seems to be continuing, and
clearly there are deep-seated reasons for it. These reasons
are not difficult to find. They are essentially the advantages
of spreading risks and the advantages of large-scale
organization; but sometimes the disadvantages of large-
scale organization are evident enough to keep some of the
smaller and more localized banks alive.

The advantages of spreading risks are of great importance in the ordinary business of banking, as it has
been practised for generations, and the advantages of
large-scale organization are apparent both in this 'ordinary
business of banking' and in the accretions of ancillary
services that have become important in the twentieth
century.

'Ordinary banking business' consists of changing cash for bank deposits and bank deposits for cash; transferring bank deposits from one person or corporation (one 'depositor') to another; giving bank deposits in exchange for bills of exchange, government bonds, the secured or unsecured promises of business men to repay, &c. The 'bank deposits' are merely I O U's written in the books of the bank, and the customer's willingness to take such an I O U in exchange for either cash (or for some promise of value) is based on his confidence in the bank and on the convenience the bank can offer to its customers. This convenience is, above all else, the convenience of using the bank deposits for settling debts—the convenience of paying one's landlord or builder or grocer or bookseller by sending a cheque. The general acceptability of bank deposits as a means of payment depends on complete confidence in the ability of the bank to exchange its own promises (the deposits) for other means of payment (directly or indirectly cash) on demand. The basis of the customer's willingness to hold bank deposits thus all boils down to his complete confidence in the bank's ability to pay cash on demand, and this is what is meant when it is said that a bank must be *liquid*. 'Liquidity' is a word that has become an economist's pet, besides undergoing the ordinary English process whereby the metaphorical becomes the normal and then breeds further metaphor. We shall have to return to Liquidity at a later stage;[1] but meanwhile we must note that in practical banking liquidity means capacity to produce cash on demand in exchange for deposits. To retain its customers, a bank must so conduct its business as to maintain liquidity.

The basic requirement is relevant to our immediate problem of the structure of banks, because the maintenance of liquidity is a costly burden that can most economically be met by a large bank. It is costly in the sense that the more cash the bank holds in relation to

[1] See especially Section II of Chapter 8.

a given amount of deposits, the less can the bank hold in assets that bring a yield in interest charged. The large bank can afford to hold a lower cash reserve in each office, for one office can draw on another far more readily than one unit bank can draw on another unit bank. The system of 'correspondent' relationships does modify the disadvantage of the unit bank, but only slightly, for deposits with a correspondent bank are relatively unremunerative. In English banking today this economy of the larger bank has, in this simple form, disappeared because, as we shall see later, the cash requirement has become a matter of official regulation, every bank being required to hold its cash reserve at 8 per cent. of its deposits. It did, however, have some influence on the earlier trend away from small-scale banking, and remains important in other countries where the cash ratio is not fixed by governmental requirements. And everywhere a closely related factor remains important: the efficiency with which the larger bank can arrange that a margin of its earning assets can be turned into cash if customers' demands for cash are unexpectedly large.

Another kind of advantage of the large bank with many branches is in minimization of the 'bad debts' that are incurred in its business of lending to customers ('giving bank deposits in exchange for the promises of business men to repay'). The wider the area covered by a bank, the more varied, in terms of industries and trades, is its business likely to be. It is true that there are times of universal good trade and times of universal bad trade, but some industries—those producing 'consumer durables' for example—are likely to suffer more than others in general depression. Beyond the more general ups and downs of trade, particular industries are subject to secular rise and decline as a result of changes in taste or changes in technique. In so far as declining industries are strongly localized, unit banks depending on small areas may incur severe losses and actual collapse may follow, whereas

losses incurred by branch banks in depressed areas can be
offset by profits earned by branches of the same banks in
more prosperous areas. For example, the chronic depression of some sections of American agriculture in the
1920's was one of the causes of the hundreds and hundreds
of small-bank failures that seemed so incompatible with
the general prosperity of the United States at that time.
In the same years the English branch banks were incurring
heavy losses in the Lancashire cotton industry, but those
which had branches all over the country were able to
shrug off their Lancashire losses without difficulty, while
even the more localized banks of the north-west were able
in one way or another to conceal their troubles. If, in the
inter-war period, the stricken towns of the industrial
north-west had had their own unit banks, it is incon-
ceivable that the English banking system would have
escaped serious internal crisis.

When the local banks of nineteenth-century England
were absorbed in the great branch banks, it was often said
that both the banks and their customers would suffer from
the loss of personal contact between banker and customer,
and this argument against large-scale branch banking is
heard in many other countries today. It is said that the
local banker, with his direct personal knowledge of the
local business men, will know which of them have, and
which have not, the aptitude for business and the soundness of moral principles desirable in a borrower. The old
English private banker, it was sometimes asserted, knew
all the family histories and would therefore know which
young business men were worthy of assistance. Against
this it may be suggested that family history is not an
invariably good guide to credit-worthiness, and the individual banker may have been reluctant to refuse a loan to
the incompetent or dishonest scion of a family with which
the father and grandfather had been on intimate social
terms. The English branch banks of today have perhaps
learned to get the best of both worlds in this matter. They

encourage their employees to mix with the local customers on the golf course, and select and pay them accordingly. The local manager may then acquire personal knowledge of his customers and their families. At the same time the remoteness of Head Office, to which he is known to be responsible, enables the manager, when he has to refuse a loan, to do so without the social awkwardness that might arise if he alone had the responsibility.[1]

These advantages of large banks have long been evident, and were the main factors behind the amalgamation movement that gathered speed in the early years of the twentieth century and led to the present concentration of business in a few great banks in England and Wales. There are other advantages that have become important only in the middle decades of the century, and these have given a fresh impulse to the concentration of business. First, the application of electronic methods to the huge volume of routine work has put a premium on organization on the largest possible scale. Secondly, partly because the banks have operated as a price cartel but have competed with each other in the provision of services to customers, elaborate ancillary services are now expected not just by a few wealthy customers but by a great number in every town, and it has become necessary to include in the staffs of many branches some clerks who have a modicum of specialist knowledge in investment business, foreign exchange, and other services the banks advertise as available. These specialist services can be more economically provided by two or three very large bank branches in a town, than by six or seven smaller branches. Moreover, both

---

[1] I should perhaps add that the ideal branch manager will leave his customer neither with the impression that he (the manager) has himself been so odious as to refuse the advance, nor with the impression that it is useless to talk to the local manager when the advance will in the end be refused by a remote and unsympathetic Head Office. Rather the local manager should persuade the customer that his projected enterprise (occasioning the request for a loan) is too risky and that the whole matter should, in the customer's own interest, be dropped.

for the routine work with the latest machines and electronic devices, and for the ancillary services the man behind the counter is expected to provide, the training of bank employees inside the banks has itself become an important and specialized task. The bank employee cannot now learn his work by learning arithmetic and writing at school and then listening to occasional hints from the Chief Clerk: he has to be trained in a specialist job, and this training is most economically organized on a considerable scale.

In all these ways the economies of large-scale organization have undoubtedly been extending in banking during recent decades, and it is not surprising that further steps in bank amalgamation have, for the first time for many years, come into prospect. Since 1918 governments have, in the interests of preserving adequate competition, had a settled policy of preventing any further merging of the great English banks, but as banking changes its shape, and new possibilities of economies in large-scale organization are opened, this policy may be ripe for revision. It may become necessary to weigh opportunities for more economical organization against the arguments for preserving such elements of competition as still remain in the system. If the competitive element is to be yet further reduced, a question bound to arise is whether the banking service is one for public administration instead of for private profit-maximizing corporations. This is a question that should be answered in the light not only of the way banking services and technical methods develop but also of how the banks compare with other businesses in their influence on the working of the economic system. It is to this more immediate problem, rather than to the ultimate choice between public and private administration, that we address ourselves in this book.

11. *The Bankers' Clearing House*

Among the functions of the commercial banks enumerated above there was an item, the transfer of bank deposits from one person to another. If there is a system of branch banking, the transfer of a deposit of a Mr. A in London to the account of Mr. B in the Oxford branch of the same bank is simple enough: the entire transaction is internal to the bank concerned. A system of unit but corresponding banks manages to achieve almost as great simplicity—provided, of course, that the banks in the two places are corresponding banks. But when the debtor and creditor—the drawer and the payee of the cheque—bank with unconnected banks this simplicity disappears. When A, who banks with Barclays, writes a cheque in favour of B, who banks with the Midland, how is the deposit actually transferred from one to the other?

The connexion between the two banks is made by the *Bankers' Clearing House*. The business of 'clearing' inter-bank indebtedness in London is distributed between two parts of the London Clearing House, which deal with Town (i.e. City financial district) and General (i.e. remainder). There are Clearing Houses in the great industrial towns in the provinces, dealing with local cheques, and less formal arrangements in every other large town. We may, however, confine our attention to the London Clearing House, and ignore its internal divisions.[1]

Every day individuals all over the country are sending cheques drawn on their accounts at one bank to people who bank with other banks. There will be a continual stream, into each bank, of cheques drawn on each of the other banks. These cheques constitute claims to deposits in these other banks, and the bank receiving the cheques is, therefore, becoming a creditor of each of the other

[1] These paragraphs give the general principles only. For a detailed account see Appendix 1.

banks. At the same time, each of the other banks will have been receiving cheques, paid in by its own customers to be added to their own accounts, drawn on the bank we have been considering. To the amount of these cheques, the first bank will be running into debt with the other banks. They have claims against it to the amount of the cheques. All these cheques that have found their way into the other banks are collected twice a day and taken to the Clearing House. There Barclays Bank, for example, will find itself in debt to each of the other banks as they present cheques drawn on Barclays and paid over their counters; and Barclays will, on the other side of the account, be presenting each of the other banks with cheques drawn on them. The various amounts are added up and offset against each other. Barclays may then find that it has paid a million pounds more on Lloyds cheques than Lloyds has paid on Barclays cheques. They exchange cheques and Lloyds remains a million pounds in debt to Barclays. Suppose with all other banks both these banks find their debits and credits equal, then Lloyds settles the account by drawing a cheque on its own deposit in the books of the Bank of England. Actually each day's transactions will be rather more complicated than this; but the essential process is clear enough—inter-bank indebtedness arising from the transfer of deposits from one person to another is offset as far as possible and any remaining balances are covered by transfer of Bankers' Deposits at the Bank of England.

In our example the position after the particular clearing will be that Lloyds' deposit liabilities to the public will have decreased by one million pounds (its customers having received a million pounds less from customers of other banks than they have paid to them), and on the assets side its 'cash at the Bank of England' will also have gone down by one million pounds. Barclays' deposit liabilities to the public will have risen by one million pounds and so will Barclays' 'cash at the Bank of England'. The *aggregate* bank deposits in the country will not have been affected by the operation; nor will the aggregate of 'cash at the Bank of England' ('Bankers' Deposits' as these balances are generally called). The entire process is a transfer having no monetary significance. The general run of banking business in the country will normally lead to these transfers being small and purely temporary; but if there arises a pronounced tendency for people to bank less with Lloyds and more with the Midland, there will be a continued decline in Lloyds' deposit liabilities and equally in its cash reserve. The equal absolute fall in the two figures implies a fall in the ratio of cash to deposits in Lloyds Bank. Such a fall in the 'cash ratio', if it persists, will call for corrective action by Lloyds Bank; the nature of this corrective action, and its consequences, are for examination later in this book.

III. *The Liabilities and Assets of Commercial Banks*

Bank deposits are, as we have seen in Chapter 1, simply entries in the books of the banks, showing that persons and corporations have such and such claims against the banks. These promises are considered by the holders to be general purchasing power: they are useful for the purpose of making payments of all but the smallest kind. A bank 'creates' a deposit simply by acquiring assets, whether these assets be cash, or other proper claims on the government, or the promises of customers to pay in the future (these appear as 'Advances' in the bank's books), or even the buildings in which the bank conducts its business. Some of the deposits so created may at once be paid over to customers of other banks; to the extent that there is a net transfer of this kind, the original bank will have to pay cash (part of its assets) to other banks, but the effect remains that, taking all banks together, the expansion of assets by the action of the first bank will have increased the total liabilities of all banks and their total assets, by the amount of the original operation. (A full account of this operation of 'expansion of bank credit' would take account of certain 'leakages'; to this we return in Chapter 10.)

The result of the past actions of the banks, in the creations of liabilities and assets, can be seen in their balance-sheets. These balance-sheets are published twice-yearly, in conformity with requirements of the Companies Acts, but interim statements are published every month, and these, by arrangement with the monetary authorities, now show the items of most interest from the point of view of the working of the monetary system. These 'monetary items', liabilities to the public and assets acquired in the banking operations, do not balance; a full balance-sheet includes on the assets side such items as the office-buildings owned by a bank, and on the liabilities side the shareholders' capital with reserved and undistributed profit. These items reflect the fact that the banks are constituted as joint-stock companies of the ordinary kind, and in England and the U.S.A. (but not in Italy or France) they are in fact owned by ordinary people and other bodies who like this type of investment. The principal purpose of bank capital was historically to bear the brunt of exceptional losses and thereby to inspire the confidence of customers. Nowadays, in England at least, capital has ceased to be necessary, especially as the banks are, by special dispensation under the Companies Acts, allowed to conceal their profit experience, and do in fact leave their shareholders and their customers almost completely ignorant of their trading experience. Nevertheless, in traditional reaction to the growth of their deposit liabilities but also because some of their individual advances to customers have become so huge, the English banks did in the 1950's increase the capital items shown in their formal balance-sheets. What the true 'net worth' of their business may be is of course quite another matter, since they freely exercise their right to conceal reserved profits.

This does not matter to the working of the monetary system, though it does matter to bank shareholders when an amalgamation of banks is proposed.

In some other countries, where the banks are less firmly established and public confidence could be more easily shaken, the capital of banks naturally retains its original significance. In many countries there is a legal requirement relating the minimum capital to the deposit liabilities of a bank. Ten per cent. has been a commonly required ratio, this being a figure that should cover even an unlucky year in bad debts and still leave a good margin to maintain confidence.

Leaving aside these 'capital' items, the general nature of the liabilities and assets of the English banks is shown in the top of the following table, taken from a monthly statement. The lower half shows the comparable figures for the United States, taken from the monthly returns shown in the *Federal Reserve Bulletin*.

SUMMARY OF LONDON CLEARING BANKS' FIGURES
16 Nov. 1966
(£ millions)

Liabilities		Assets		
Current Accounts	4,892	Cash in hand at the Bank		
Deposit Accounts	3,620	of England .		778
		Money at call		1,145
		Bills discounted		1,083
		Advances		4,759
		Investments .		1,163

UNITED STATES—ALL COMMERCIAL BANKS
28 Sept. 1966
($ millions)

Liabilities		Assets	
Demand Deposits	148,000	Loans .	212,000
Time Deposits	157,000	Investments .	102,000
		Cash Assets .	56,000

In these statements, the English *Current Accounts* are parallel to the American *Demand Deposits* in the sense that these are the deposits against which the customer has the right to draw cheques or to demand cash on the spot. They are therefore the most immediately available purchasing power, and they do not bear any interest. In England the *Deposit Accounts* bear interest which is fixed by the bankers' cartel and is normally 2 per cent. less than Bank Rate; to the customer these deposits are almost as useful as current account balances, since they are subject to only 7 days' notice of withdrawal and are in fact, though not in law, transferable in reasonable amounts without notice though on penalty of some loss of interest. The American *Time Deposits* are less immediately available: they are by law subject to not less than 30 days' notice, and are thus much more nearly parallel to such English claims as Building Society shares or deposits. They carry interest at rates fixed by the individual bank, subject to maxima governed by statutory regulation. Because of this difference, American economists commonly exclude Time Deposits when they are adding up the supply of money (in the sense of means of final payment) although it is usual in the English context to include Deposit Accounts as well as Current Accounts. The difference is only one of degree, and may serve to illustrate the difficulties that arise when economists seek tidy figures to fit into their models.

The distinction between Current Accounts (or Demand Deposits) on the one hand and Deposit Accounts (or Time Deposits) on the other is also of interest if we are thinking of people's financial assets not as the instruments with which they make payments but as the form in which they hold part of their stock of wealth: the 'store of value' rather than the 'medium of exchange' aspect. Most Current Accounts are regarded by their owners ('the depositors') as primarily balances to be turned over continuously as income is received and spent, or as a business firm has sales receipts and pays out its current costs. Other balances—and these in a rough way fit the Deposit Account category—are regarded rather as *investments* or *savings*. They are held not to meet the certain needs of the near future, but as part of their total wealth which individuals call their 'savings' or private capital. This however is another distinction of degree only. All deposits—and many other assets as well—are held against contingent excesses of payments over receipts. There is no sharp line between the balance I hold in case I have to go on an unexpected long railway journey next week and the balance I hold because I may want to visit my daughter across the Atlantic next year. But there is a difference of degree, which is reflected in the terms on which I am prepared to hold each kind of balance. From one part I look primarily for convenience and do not expect the bank to pay interest; from the other—my 'savings deposits'—I look not only for the convenience of having it quite easily available but also for some small interest payment. Moreover, I may be prepared to 'invest' these savings elsewhere if attractive opportunity arises; as a store of value, a bank deposit may be closely rivalled by 'deposits' or similar claims on other financial institutions, including government agencies.

On the *Assets* side, *Cash in hand* means Bank of England notes and coin in the tills and vaults of the commercial banks. *Cash at the Bank of England* means a book entry (a deposit) in the Bank of England in favour of each bank. The combined cash item, *Cash in hand and at the Bank of England*, thus consists of liabilities of the Bank of England, together with a relatively small amount of coin, which is issued through the Bank of England by another government agency, the Royal Mint. As the coin is in fact exchangeable into Bank of England notes on demand, the position is basically that the cash 'reserve' of the commercial banks consists of central bank I O U's, and this is substantially the case also in the U.S.A. *Money at call* means loans to the Discount Houses; these Discount Houses are certain highly specialized financial intermediaries, in the City of London, whose function is explained in Chapter 3 below. The loans are repayable nominally when demanded on any day, though there is some variety in the precise arrangements. The Discount Houses, when they have borrowed these sums from the banks, will have at once paid away the sums to other people; if the banks call upon them to repay, they must in some way or other obtain command of deposits now standing in other people's names, or induce the Bank of England to provide them with cash. *Bills discounted* are I O U's (or post-dated cheques) which the banks have bought, the process of buying a bill being traditionally described as 'discounting'. The banks hold these pieces of paper, in exchange for which they will have given claims against themselves. At the due date the debtors who have signed the pieces of paper are under obligation to provide bank deposits (at the Bank of England or at some other bank) to the face value of the bills. A large part of the total consists of *Treasury Bills*,[1] issued by the Government as borrower. Of the remainder, most are *Bills of Exchange* issued by commercial businesses of various kinds, which have found this a convenient way of raising money. Treasury Bills and most Bills of Exchange are payable in three months or less. Also included under *Bills discounted* is a part of certain government guaranteed loans for export business: to the extent that these loans are repayable within eighteen months, they are counted as *Bills discounted*.[2]

The remainder of these loans to exporters are included in the very large and important item, *Advances*. These are loans, normally in England on the overdraft system, to industrialists, professional men, and others. The banks allow the business men to pay deposits to other people on the understanding that they will, within a fairly short period, obtain deposits for repaying the bank if called upon to do so. The advance appears in the books of the bank (and so in the published statistics) only as the borrower draws cheques in accordance with the permission the bank has given; likewise the deposits created by this

---

[1] For details of Treasury Bills, see pp. 54–58 below.
[2] Cf. pp. 192–6 below.

operation appear only as the payees of the cheques pay them into their accounts. The lending bank usually sets, at least in a broad way, a limit to the overdraft permission granted, and it is often remarked that the 'unused' over-draft facilities—the margin between the amounts already drawn and the agreed limits—are just as effectively pur-chasing power as are the deposits that have already appeared through the actual exercise of permission to overdraw. The English banks have, however, maintained that any statistical summary of these unused overdraft rights would be unrealistic. It is nevertheless important, when we are assessing the factors influencing the total spending in the country, to remember that business men often take decisions depending on the fact that they have unused overdraft facilities. In handling American banking statistics the problem does not arise in quite the same way, because there the lending bank credits the full amount to the borrower at once, leaving the borrower to draw cheques against the credit balance now at his disposal, but having also entered in a Loan Account an amount to the debit of the customer, who has the obligation to pay off that sum at the agreed time. Thus in the American system the full agreed amount appears at once in the balance-sheet, both as an increase in Deposits and as an increase in Loans; nevertheless American business men may still be influenced by the belief that they could easily get more loans at their banks, just as English business men may be influenced by their unused overdraft facilities.

Investments are securities, especially British Govern-ment, British local government authority, and other Commonwealth securities marketable on the Stock Ex-change and having longer lives to maturity (repayment date) than the three-months' Treasury Bills. When a bank buys a *new* government security it places at the disposal of the Government a part of its own balance at the Bank of England (cash). When it buys an *old* security through the Stock Exchange, or from an issuer other than the British

Government, it places a deposit at the disposal of the person or other body selling (or issuing) the security.[1]

iv. *The Elements of Policy in Commercial Banking*

On the deposit side of its business, the aim of a bank is simple enough: to maximize the total of deposits, because the bigger its deposits the bigger its opportunities for earning profits. Its deposit business brings in its train opportunities for various services to customers and, though some services may be provided at a loss to attract customers, others earn commissions that help profits. More importantly, the bigger the volume of its deposits, the bigger can be both the lending business it does for its customers and the total of securities it holds in its securities portfolio, and these two items earn interest rates higher (in general) than the rates that need be paid on Deposits—especially as no interest at all is paid on those standing on Current Account. Every bank therefore likes to attract deposits, and the success of a new branch is judged partly by the amount of deposits it has attracted from new customers.

Nevertheless, the banks do not try to attract deposits by bidding higher prices, in the shape of higher rates of interest. The rate allowed on deposit accounts and the no-interest rule for current accounts are both the subject of agreement among the banks, which apparently consider

---

[1] As this is sometimes a point of difficulty it may be as well to summarize the proceeding. Lloyds Bank buys a bond through the Stock Exchange paying, say, £1,000 for it with a cheque on its balance at the Bank of England. Mr. A. has sold the bond and directly or indirectly receives the cheque for £1,000, and pays it into his account at Barclays Bank. Barclays Total Deposits go up by £1,000, and when Barclays present the Lloyds cheque to the Bank of England, through the Clearing House, Barclays cash goes up by £1,000, Lloyds going down by the same amount. Lloyds investments have gone up by the amount its cash has gone down, the deposits at Lloyds are unchanged, and Barclays are up by £1,000. If Mr. A. banks with Lloyds then there is no redistribution of cash; but Lloyds investments and Lloyds deposits both go up by £1,000.

that more would be lost than gained if they offered better interest terms either in competition with each other or in competition with other financial intermediaries. In the short run this is probably a good business view, but the narrow view taken by the cartel has, at any rate when taken in conjunction with other practical banking rules, undoubtedly had the effect of narrowing the bank's share of the total credit business of the country. (This policy, however, has been modified in the 1960's. Competitive rates are negotiated for large deposits, though these deposits are actually placed with subsidiary or connected institutions and not in the books of the clearing banks themselves.)

Thus far we have, however, been limiting our view to a bank's attempts to attract to itself a larger share of the total business. It is now necessary to consider what limits the total business all the banks can do; for, as has appeared in Chapter 1, when banks make advances or acquire other assets, they create deposits. Why do not the banks, acting in step with each other, create more and more deposits, so enlarging both sides of the balance-sheet and their earning power? What does in fact restrain them?

The answer lies in the *liquidity rules*. These vary from one country to another. They have their origin in the rules of thumb bankers evolved for themselves in their endeavour to reconcile the competing incentives of immediate profit and long-term command of customers' confidence. In England the rules have long lost touch with any realistic assessment of the risks, the ins and outs, of a bank's business; flexible rules evolved in a haphazard way by generations of bankers were gradually conventionalized until in the nineteen-forties and fifties they became official requirements. In many other countries the rules have legal force; the lack of legal sanction in England does not make any substantial difference, but perhaps saves the English banks from the necessity for finicking adjustments that would be of no economic significance.

The simplest liquidity rule, and that most commonly

operating in the outside world, is the requirement of a minimum ratio of cash to deposits: a minimum cash ratio. In England requirements are more complicated. A *fixed* cash ratio is required: 8 per cent. against total deposits.[1] This is different from a minimum ratio, which allows a bank to have a higher cash ratio if it so chooses. The second rule is that the 'liquid assets', defined to include 'cash', 'money at call', and 'bills discounted' in the comprehensive senses described above, should not in the monthly statements fall below 28 per cent. of total deposits. There is a seasonal movement in the liquid assets of the banks, with a high point in the late months of the year and a low in February–March; the banks aim at not less than 31 or 32 per cent. in November–December, to allow for the regular run-down which will then leave them on the right side of the 28 per cent. line in the following quarter.

In current English conditions the second rule—the '28 per cent. liquid assets rule'—is the effective restraint on the deposit-creating activities of the London Clearing banks. Within the 28 per cent. (or 31–32 at the seasonal high) the Bank of England and the clearing banks see to it between them (strictly, via the discount market, as is explained in later chapters) that other liquid assets are exchanged for cash, or cash for other liquid assets, in sufficient amount to correct any disturbance of the cash ratio. This neutralization of the cash ratio as a restraining rule is not an inevitable part of English institutional arrangements. It may be changed in the course of time; it is therefore necessary to emphasize that it is a matter of choice, implicit in the policy nowadays followed by the English authorities in relation to short-term rates of interest. For the present the reader must take it as one of the facts of the current situation, that the operative

---

[1] The figure of 8 per cent. refers to the mid-week position. Within the week some variation may be allowed; the withdrawal of notes on Fridays (for wage-payments) and their return on Mondays and Tuesdays are thus equally irrelevant to the banks' estimate of their position in relation to the required cash ratio.

restraint on expansion of bank credit is the 28 per cent. ratio, while within the total of liquid assets the operators see to it that 8 of the 28 shall consist of cash.

This liquidity rule, which the Bank of England expects the London Clearing Banks to observe, is *the effective restraint* on the deposit-creating activities of the banks. The liquid assets covered by the rule include some claims of commercial origin—bills of exchange and the approved export credits within 18 months of maturity—but variations in these are now relatively small and can easily be compensated, deliberately or otherwise, by changes in the total of Treasury Bills that nowadays form the most important part of the total of liquid assets. The same argument applies to the Money-at-call which is the other main segment of the liquid assets. This Money-at-call consists of loans to the discount market, and this market uses the loans to enable it to hold bills of exchange, Treasury Bills and other short-term government paper, and the amount of Money-at-call needed by the discount market depends upon the availability of these liquid assets. In a sense, Money-at-call in the balance-sheets of the clearing banks represents bills of exchange and short government paper *held indirectly* by the banks. The availability of liquid assets for the banks thus depends upon the total availability of bills of exchange, approved export credits near maturity, and short government paper, this last consisting largely of Treasury Bills.[1] The dominant element is the great mass of Treasury Bills, including both those held directly by the banks and those held by the discount market.

Treasury Bills are created by the will of the Government, just as cash—equally a 'liability' of government (including the central bank as a State institution)—is created by the will of the Government. In countries which

---

[1] A complication of some importance is the short-bond holding of the discount market; another less disturbing factor is the non-clearing bank money borrowed by the discount market. These complications are discussed in Chapter 3 below.

have a simple cash-ratio requirement for their commercial banks, the cash created by the authorities sets a limit to the amount of deposits that can be created by the banks; similarly in England the amount of Treasury Bills created by the authorities sets a limit to the amount of deposits that can be created by the banks. The universal rule is that the imposition of a requirement of a minimum ratio of certain state liabilities to bank deposits gives the state, as creator of the State liabilities, power to limit the creation of bank deposits. The element that makes England odd man out in the application of this rule is that in England the prescribed state liabilities are effectively the Treasury Bills (although other paper is included in the 28 per cent. requirement), whereas in other countries cash is the prescribed state liability.

The rule operates as the *effective restraint* and not as the *determinant* of the creation of deposits. This distinction has to be made because, although the Government can fix the total of Treasury Bills it creates, there are possibilities of 'leakage' of Treasury Bills to holders outside the banking system (in 'the banking system' we here include the clearing banks and the discount market, but not 'foreign' banks). The leakage arises from the purchase of Treasury Bills by (1) the large industrial and commercial companies, (2) non-bank financial intermediaries such as insurance companies, and (3) foreign holders (including in 'foreign' all overseas banks). When, by the operations of the Government and the central bank, additional Treasury Bills (say £10 millions) are issued (without, we are assuming, a compensating cancellation of cash), the initial effect may easily be that the clearing banks find their liquid assets (cash, bills, and money-at-call) increased by the full amount of the addition. On the basis that they have to hold a liquid assets ratio of 30–34 per cent. against their deposit liabilities, it might be supposed that the addition of £10 millions to their liquid assets would allow them to add £20 millions to their other

assets (investments and advances) and, corresponding to
the £30 millions increase in assets (£10 millions liquid
and £20 millions other) their deposit liabilities would
equally be increased by £30 millions. But, as will be
explained in Chapter 10, the process of expansion of the
assets and liabilities of the banks will set in motion a series
of developments in the economic system that culminate
in a rise in the total of money incomes and in the total of
privately owned assets. As this happens, various 'drains'
on the liquid assets of the banks begin to show themselves:

1. As incomes rise, a larger total of notes may be required for circulation; unless the central bank is
   willing to 'offset' this, there is a loss to the liquid
   assets of the commercial banks.
2. As the incomes rise, the demand for imported goods
   rises, and the profitable opportunities of export sales
   are curtailed. The adverse balance of trade causes
   a net balance of bank deposits to pass into foreign
   ownership; the foreign holders will ordinarily want
   to use these to buy foreign currency from the reserves of the central bank, or at least to buy
   Treasury Bills. In either case, there is a loss of liquid
   assets to the commercial banks.
3. As the total of privately held assets increases, people
   will seek to redistribute the total in such a way as to
   restore their 'normal' selection of various classes of
   assets (case (1) above is really a special case of this).
   This may involve a desire to hold more Treasury
   Bills directly (in large industrial corporations, for
   example). Indirectly, the expansion of total liabilities
   of non-bank financial intermediaries may cause them
   to hold more Treasury Bills. In such ways, the total
   of liquid assets available to the banks is diminished.

The central bank may choose to 'offset' any of these
drains, but it can only do so by creating for injection into
the system a further supply of liquid assets (cash or

Treasury Bills). It will thus remain true that the amount of deposit-creation that can be sustained is *less than* three times the original injection of liquid assets, despite the fact that the banks' liquid assets ratio is about one-third. *How much less* will depend upon a number of factors such as the comparative importance of bank deposits, cash, and other financial assets in the wealth-holding habits of the public. The more fully the banks provide the public with every kind of facility the public values, the more important will bank deposits be and the more nearly will the deposit-expansion multiplier approach the reciprocal of the reserve ratio. (In our example, the reserve ratio is about one-third, but the injection of £10 millions of liquid assets provides a basis for *less than* £30 millions; i.e., the deposit-expansion multiplier is less than 3.)

Because of this complication of the 'leakages'—a complication only partially described above—we cannot say that the amount of deposits the banks will create is fixed by the required liquidity ratio and the absolute amount of liquid assets created by the monetary authorities. But any divergence because of the leakages can ordinarily be counted in one direction only: the deposit-creating power of the banks falls short of

$$\text{(liquid assets created by monetary authorities)} \times \frac{1}{\text{Required liquidity ratio.}}$$

We *can* therefore say that the volume of bank deposits, though not *determined* in this way, is *limited by* the action of the monetary authorities in (*a*) creating liquid assets and (*b*) fixing a minimum ratio of liquid assets to be held by the commercial banks.

Our next step is to consider the activities of the discount market, which in London complicates the connexion between the commercial banks and the central bank. We shall then be ready to look at the central bank itself, and consider how it operates on the liquid assets that are available to the commercial banks.

3

THE DISCOUNT HOUSES, THE ACCEPTING HOUSES, AND THE LIQUID ASSETS OF THE BANKING SYSTEM

1. *The London Money Market*

THE activity of the commercial banks in making advances to their customers and in buying securities, and so in creating bank deposits, is substantially governed by the amount of liquid assets available to them. Liquid assets become available to them largely through the operation of the monetary authorities, that is to say, by the operations of the Government (as a tax-collector, a borrower, and a spender) and of the Bank of England which is the Government's banker. In the English setting, however, the contact between the Bank of England and the commercial banks is complicated by the existence of the London Money Market and certain conventions that govern operations in that market. These institutional arrangements in the City of London are unique, and have their origin in historical circumstances that have largely disappeared. We need not here concern ourselves with the history, but some attention to the current working of the institutions is necessary, if we are fully to understand the working of the banking system, and particularly if we are to assess the methods whereby monetary policy is implemented.

Apart from the Bank of England—to whose interest in the money market we shall return in Chapter 5—there are four classes of businesses operating in the London Money Market. These are (1) the London Clearing Banks, (2) the overseas and foreign banks, (3) the Accepting

Houses and other merchant bankers, and (4) the Discount Houses. All these are concerned in the market's business of buying and selling (discounting and rediscounting) bills of exchange and (more importantly) Treasury Bills, and the first three are engaged in the making of very short-term loans to the fourth group, the Discount Houses. It will be noticed that the Stock Exchange is not reckoned as part of the money market: it is a market, a very active market, in longer-term loans, and it has certain points of contact with the money market, but it does not impinge seriously on the mechanism of banking policy, and we may safely leave it aside from our immediate purposes.

Of the four groups in the money market itself, the first has already been described in Chapter 2. In the present chapter we describe the Accepting Houses and the Discount Houses. There remain the overseas and foreign banks. These are banks whose main banking business is for customers in other countries, even though a few overseas banks have their head offices in London. Originally the main business of these banks was, and sometimes their main business today remains, the financing of overseas trade; some of them are therefore of great importance in the foreign exchange market. As their principal business arises from foreign trade, the flow of payments to and from any one of these banks is highly fluctuating, the fluctuations reflecting seasonal movements of crops, weather variations from year to year, the ups and downs of world demand for particular commodities—and on top of all these, there may be major irregularities in the international flow of capital. These banks therefore, against deposits that are largely liabilities to people in other countries, prefer to hold assets that are highly liquid. They hold some balances with the clearing banks, but much larger amounts (between £100 and £200 millions) are lent to the Discount Houses. Beyond this, they hold £200 millions or more in Treasury Bills and other sterling bills, and another £100 millions or so in very short government bonds. Besides being in these ways important lenders in the money market, they have some importance on the borrowing side in that they sell some of their bills of exchange, which have originated in their customers' trading business.

From the point of view of money market operations, the Scottish banks are more properly classed with the overseas banks than with the London Clearing Banks. The banking business of the Scottish banks is overwhelmingly domestic, in the sense that it is with (Scottish) residents in the United Kingdom; they operate on similar (but not identical) principles as the London Clearing Banks, and they are subject to some measure of control by the Bank of England. But in the London Money Market they operate independently, they do not consider themselves bound to follow the practices of the clearing banks, and (more importantly from the point of view of the daily working of the market) they are not in the London Bankers' Clearing House. In day-by-day terms therefore, the market thinks of them as lenders and buyers of bills 'outside the clearing'. Along with the overseas and foreign banks and the Accepting Houses, the Scottish banks are 'outside lenders'.

We have still to describe two very important money-market groups—the Accepting Houses and the Discount Houses—but first the reader must be told more of the paper—the 'bills' that are such an important item in their business. These are the bills of exchange and Treasury Bills which have already intruded themselves as assets held by the various classes of banks. It was business in ordinary bills of exchange that provided the foundation and shaped the ways of the discount market, and the bill of exchange therefore takes first place in this account.

II. *The Bill of Exchange*[1]

A cheque of the ordinary kind is technically a Bill of Exchange payable at sight; but the layman can most readily grasp the nature of the Bill of Exchange if he considers it as a post-dated cheque. This is in effect what is used when a creditor, accepting a cheque, promises not to present it at the bank for a few days. Then John Brown has a claim against my bank on my account and receives payment on the due date. If he should want the money earlier he must find someone who will take the cheque (after he has himself endorsed it) to hold until the due date, and the man who provides the money may deduct a small amount to compensate him for waiting till the due date.[2]

When our post-dated cheque is called a Bill of Exchange the due date is called 'maturity'. The process of handing round the endorsed bill in exchange for ready money before maturity is called 'discounting the bill of exchange'. The margin between the ready money paid and the face value of the bill (which is the amount payable by the debtor at maturity) is called the 'discount', and is calculated at a rate per cent. per annum on the maturity value.

Suppose that Thomas Debtor buys goods from John Creditor. Creditor wants his money now, but Debtor wants to postpone payment until he has resold the goods. They may agree to settle the transaction by Creditor 'drawing a three months' bill' on Debtor.[3] The form will be something of this kind:

---

[1] The reader may find further details on the subject of this section in *The Bill on London*, prepared by Messrs. Gillett Bros. Discount Co. Ltd., and published by Chapman & Hall, London, 3rd ed., 1965.

[2] This paragraph is essentially a layman's description for other laymen; the commercial lawyer will find a looseness of expression which I think is defensible in this context. And the word 'waiting' in the last sentence will offend the post-Marshallian economic theorist. Strictly I should have written 'parting with liquidity'.

[3] Actually bills in the London market vary in currency from one to

London, 27 July 1957.

To Thomas Debtor,

Three months after date please pay to John Creditor or Order, the sum of One Thousand Pounds for Value received.

Signed: John Creditor.

Then Creditor is the Drawer of the bill and Debtor is the Drawee of the bill. Creditor sends the bill to Debtor who acknowledges his responsibility for payment of the thousand pounds at maturity by writing on the bill his 'Acceptance'. When the bill has been 'accepted' Debtor has for the time being closed the transaction. He simply has to be ready to pay a thousand pounds to anyone who happens to own the bill three months hence.

As Creditor prefers immediate cash to a thousand pounds in three months' time, he takes the accepted bill to someone who has money to lend on such security. But Creditor does not *borrow* on security of the bill. He *sells* the bill—parts with all his interest in it—outright. Creditor has to endorse the bill to show that he has parted with his claim. His endorsement incidentally renders him liable to meet the bill at maturity should Debtor fail to do so. When Creditor sells the bill the financier who takes it from him pays not £1,000 but, say, £990. The £10 difference represents the interest on £990 for the three months which must elapse before maturity—the rate of discount would then be quoted as 4 per cent.[1] The financier has in fact exchanged £990 now for £1,000 (due from Debtor) three months hence, the £10 is his price for doing so, and the bill is legal evidence of his claim to the £1,000.

The bill is a convenient instrument because, like a government bond, it can change ownership conveniently during its currency. If the financier who took the bill from

six months; but throughout the following pages the three months' bill has been taken as typical: the great majority of London bills are three months' bills.

[1] The arithmetician will notice here the difference between 'true discount' and 'commercial discount'—the rate of the latter being calculated on the sum payable at maturity.

Creditor decided after, say, a month, that he needed cash he could raise cash by *rediscounting* the bill. The bill would now represent a claim to £1,000 *two* months hence, and the spot cash price for it would (if the relevant interest rate is again 4 per cent.) have risen to £993. 6s. 8d. He would have to endorse the bill and would be responsible for meeting it at maturity should the other names on it fail. But, supposing all goes well, the transaction has closed as far as he is concerned and he has secured interest at 4 per cent. per annum for one month's loan of £990.

III. *The Work of the Accepting Houses*

The trade bill described above is a device for securing in a convenient form, and with clearly understood legal safeguards, the financing of a transaction in goods that takes some time to complete. The importation of foodstuffs and raw materials into England are transactions of this kind and some of these are financed by the discounting of bills. Neither exporter nor importer has to go without his money while the goods are in transit, the money for the exporter being in fact provided by the *discount market*, until the importer has had time to resell the goods. If, as will generally be the case, neither the exporter nor the importer is a man whose name is recognized in the discount market as a credit-worthy name it may be difficult to secure money for the bill unless some firm of repute can be induced to guarantee the bill. It is worth paying some commission to secure a good name on the bill, for this greatly increases the ease of discounting, and the appropriate rate of discount is lower. The specialist firms called the *Accepting Houses* provide these guarantees, for which they charge commission. They maintain agencies in important trading centres abroad and make it their business to know the credit-standing of various traders. Having ascertained that an American importer is credit-worthy the Accepting House is willing to open an *Accep-*

tance Credit for him. The size of the acceptance credit will depend on the size of the importer's transactions and the Accepting House's estimate of his ultimate resources. Suppose the credit to amount to £20,000. Then the American importer buys goods in England from an English merchant, the latter agreeing to take as payment a three months' bill for £15,000. The price of the goods may be called £15,000, but it is understood that three months' credit is given. Then the English merchant is advised by the American that the latter has a credit with such and such an Accepting House. The English merchant then draws a bill, not on the American importer but on the Accepting House. The Accepting House has made itself liable to meet bills on the American's account up to the £20,000 limit. The bill is then sent to the Accepting House in London, which acknowledges its obligation by 'accepting' it. The bill can then be discounted readily by the English merchant (or his agent). It has a first-class British name on it and will be discounted at one of the lowest rates in the market. The Accepting House has its own arrangements with the American importer, whereby the latter promises to meet the debts which he incurs. The bill itself is payable on maturity by the Accepting House. For the use of its name in this way the Accepting House charges a commission, and its receipts from commissions enable it to maintain in various commercial centres the credit intelligence service that is essential to the avoidance of bad debts. The Accepting House must be recognized in London as having ample resources of its own for meeting all the obligations it incurs—otherwise its name on a bill would have no value and there would be no advantage in drawing bills on the Accepting House.

Sometimes the arrangement between the debtor who has to pay ultimately and the Accepting House is made indirectly through the debtor's bank. If the debtor is, say, an Argentine importer, he can induce his own bank in the Argentine to secure an acceptance credit for him in

London, enabling him to tell his creditor to draw the bill on a great London Accepting House. The Argentine bank makes itself responsible for the debt to the Accepting House and makes its own arrangement with the final debtor, the Argentine importer. An acceptance credit of this type is called a 'Reimbursement Credit'. The Accepting Houses and banks grant these reimbursement credits at particularly low rates (frequently $\frac{1}{2}$ per cent.) as all they have to do is to satisfy themselves about the soundness of the Argentine bank—a very much simpler matter than looking into the credit-worthiness of an individual Argentine importer. The Argentine bank will itself naturally make some charge to the Argentine importer; but the division of labour in seeking credit information, between the London Accepting House and the Argentine bank, may well lead to some reduction in the total cost.

The function of accepting bills of exchange has been described above as performed by the Accepting Houses. In fact some of this business is now handled by the London Clearing Banks, which in this century have increasingly developed banking services for foreign trade, especially that in which their own domestic customers are engaged. As part of this service, they have gone into acceptance business on a large scale, now amounting to something like a quarter of the acceptance business done in London. The remainder is largely in the hands of the traditional Accepting Houses, though the overseas banks in London also have a share.

These Accepting Houses are seventeen in number, and form a distinctive (and distinguished) group within a much larger number of firms describing themselves as 'Merchant Bankers'. Historically the term 'merchant banker' was used of a wealthy merchant who developed a banking side to his business; in London this banking business would often be largely connected with foreign trade. The general run of merchant bankers in London do not now engage in commodity trade, but have a miscellaneous financial business, including a little banking and a lot of work in connexion with the issue and placing of securities. The Accepting Houses are merchant banking firms that have acquired a very high repute as acceptors of bills of exchange, and submit themselves to informal surveillance by the Bank of England. They bear names that have become almost household words—Barings, Rothschilds, Kleinworts, Erlangers, Lazards, &c. Each is a very small business by comparison with a Big Five bank, but in the particular lines of business in which they specialize they are powerful bodies.

The acceptance business that gives a description to this group of firms does not itself directly involve either borrowing or lending. Essentially it is the sale of the use of a name, as effective guarantor that there will be no default on the bill of exchange. This guarantee can only be effective, however, if the Accepting House is known to have substantial assets, including some so highly liquid that bills will invariably be not merely paid but paid at the proper moment. On the other side of the balance-sheet, an Accepting House has deposit liabilities, including some to customers for whom it is doing acceptance business. (As a way of protecting itself against default by the customers to whom it is selling its name, it expects those customers to make deposits with it.) The Accepting Houses are thus banks, with deposit liabilities and with assets a good proportion of which are highly liquid. But this banking business arises mainly from their acceptance business or other work they do for customers, and it is only marginal in the English domestic banking scene. The Accepting Houses are not included in the cartel of the clearing banks; their rates for deposits and advances are similar to those ruling in the clearing banks, but they are less rigid. They are nevertheless not seriously competitors with the clearing banks for ordinary banking business, although they could sometimes become a nuisance if they were left uncontrolled when the authorities forced a credit squeeze on the clearing banks. This possibility has been recognized, in that the Accepting Houses have received the same sort of 'requests' from the authorities as have been addressed to the clearing banks.

The more serious interest taken by the Bank of England in the business of the Accepting Houses arises from the privileged position accorded by the Bank of England to bills that have been accepted by the select houses. The Bank of England's approval of an Accepting House—approval contingent on an annual review of the House's business—implies that a bill accepted by that House can be rediscounted at the Bank of England. If a bill is re-discountable in this way—i.e. it is 'eligible'—it will be discounted in the London market at a lower rate (it will command a *higher* price) than a bill not carrying such an approved name. Acceptance by an approved accepting house (and similarly by a clearing bank) therefore has a cash value—a value that stands behind the acceptance commission the Accepting House can charge, a value that could be knocked down overnight if the Bank of England withdrew its approval.

The Accepting Houses contend that both as bankers and as acceptors they are *passive*: that the volume of their business depends upon the total volume of business coming to London, the activity of international trade, and of the particular commodity trades in the finance of which some of them are specialists. They strive to compete with each other—and with the Clearing Banks and competitors in other international centres—by the quality of service they provide, but the total volume of business available is insensitive to changes in the ruling level of commissions and interest rates.

Partly as an historical sideline to their acceptance business but partly also because the decline of the bill of exchange left them looking round for more to do, the Accepting Houses (and other merchant bankers in some degree) have other quite different functions. One such function is the issue of new securities, which will, once issued, be traded on the Stock Exchange. They act as 'issuing houses', negotiating with would-be raisers of capital and then inviting public subscription by the publication of a 'prospectus'. The Accepting Houses have for this purpose an important clientele in the great industrial companies. Secondly these Houses have in recent decades developed a huge business as trustees and investment advisers for charitable foundations, colleges, and corporations of other kinds having large sums to invest. As trustees they directly control huge investments, but as advisers their influence may be even greater, for the bodies they advise have hundreds of millions of pounds to invest and the investments are constantly being changed. For some of the Accepting Houses this has become almost their major activity, and it is certainly one that gives them influence on the working of the domestic economy.

Nevertheless, they remain important in the finance of overseas trade and other international banking business in which London shares. Their acceptance business greatly exceeds that of the clearing banks and is not far short of the amount done by the overseas banks, although the latter have the lion's share of 'non-resident' deposit business.

IV. *The Treasury Bill*

The Bill of Exchange described in the second section of this chapter had its origin—and substantially remains —as a device for raising money on goods during their transit from one place to another. The ease with which money could be obtained by discounting of bills of exchange, once a good market in bills had developed, encouraged extension of the device to allow people to borrow money without any goods being in transit at all. By arrangement between one firm, which is anxious to borrow money, and another firm, which is for some reason willing to participate in the transactions, a bill can be drawn by the first firm on the second firm. Once the second firm has 'accepted' the bill, the bill can be discounted and effectively a loan is thus obtained for the period of the bill, the lender having as security the two names on the bill he holds. Such a bill, when not arising from any genuine transaction in goods, is called a 'finance bill'. Finance bills vary greatly in quality, according to the standing of the borrowers. One particular kind of finance bill put out by a first-class borrower is nowadays the most common bill in the market: this is the Treasury Bill, on which the British Government borrows, and which has its parallels in many other countries.

The Treasury Bill, being issued by the British Government, does not need to be 'accepted' because no one can add security to that already given by the word of the British Government. It is thus a mere promissory note of the British Government. In exchange for deposits at the Bank of England the Government gives a written promise to pay ninety-one days later a sum of £5,000, £10,000, £25,000, £50,000, or £100,000. The form of the Treasury Bill leaves a space for the creditor's name; but the sum is payable to 'Bearer' if no name has been entered, and most of the bills the market handles remain Bearer Bills. This would be unthinkable with ordinary commercial bills where the addition of each signature adds to the security. But the Treasury Bill is a promise of the British Government, and no discount house or bank signature can add to that security. The unquestionable security makes it possible for them to pass round the market as Bearer Bills without anyone hesitating to take them up if he has money to lend.

The principal advantage of the Treasury Bill to the Government as the borrower is that it is on the average cheaper than long-term borrowing. This cheapness to the borrower reflects the advantage the lender enjoys in having his money certainly available very soon. The creditor lends his money knowing that the exact sum will be paid to him three months hence. For such highly 'liquid' security the lender is in general willing to lend at rates appreciably lower than those he expects when he ties up his money for years (or can retrieve it only by sale on the Stock Exchange, perhaps at a big capital loss). Even when, as happened in 1956, Treasury Bill rates are as high as, or even higher than, long-term rates, the Government sees advantage in borrowing on Treasury Bills in order to limit its sales of bonds that commit it to paying high rates of interest over a long period of years. The Treasury Bill has in fact been a boon to both parties: the Government, whose borrowing needs have been swollen by two great wars, and the discount market, which since 1929 has found the supply of commercial paper[1] uncomfortably small. The central bank also finds advantage in the existence of a substantial volume of Treasury Bills for, as we shall see in Chapter 5, the Treasury Bill is an ideal security for the central bank to buy and sell.

The Treasury Bills are issued partly by 'tender', partly 'through the tap'. The tap issue is to government departments that have funds in hand and to certain overseas monetary authorities. The government departments include, besides the ordinary departments of State, the government savings banks, the statutory insurance funds, the Bank of England Issue Department, and the Exchange Equalization Account. The rate of discount at which the bills are issued through the tap is unknown and is irrelevant to the discount market. The tender issue is offered to London bankers (including many Commonwealth and foreign banks), discount houses, and brokers. Anyone else wishing to tender must apply through one or other of these channels. The Government invites these firms to offer a price, to be paid on some day in the following week, for

---

[1] 'Commercial paper' is here used in the London sense of any bill having its origin in a commercial transaction, in contrast to 'government paper'. In New York and therefore in Chapter 11 the term 'commercial paper' has another connotation.

every £100 that the Government will pay to them at the
Bank of England exactly three months later. If a discount
house is willing to take Treasury Bills at, say, £4. 10s. 8d.
per cent. per annum, it tenders on Friday for the amount
it is willing to take (not less than £50,000) at a price
£98. 17s. 4d. per cent., specifying that it will take up
the bills on, say, Tuesday. On Tuesday it must pay
into the Government account at the Bank of England
£49,433. 6s. 8d. Thirteen weeks after that Tuesday the
Government will pay to the discount house £50,000 against
surrender of the Treasury Bills.[1]

The tender issue is made every week and the amount
offered is usually between £150 and £200 millions each
week; the amount is varied continually in order to offset
variations in other government receipts and disbursements.
At the peak revenue season (January to March), for example, the Treasury Bill issues are reduced, maturities of
old bills being allowed to exceed the weekly offer; on the
other hand, a big bond maturity or excess government
expenditures may occasion a temporary expansion of the
Treasury Bill issue, new bills issued exceeding maturities
of old bills.

The procedure has now become highly conventionalized
and is the subject of close understandings between the
banks, the discount houses, and the authorities. The clearing banks—the ordinary English commercial banks—tender for Treasury Bills only on behalf of their customers.
They do not tender on their own account but obtain all the
bills they want from the discount houses after the latter
have held the bills for at least a week. The discount houses
are formed into an Association, and members of the Association tender on the basis of an agreed price.[2] The total

---

[1] The above details apply to ninety-one-day bills. In the years 1956–62,
sixty-three-day Treasury Bills were also issued; they did not suit market
needs as well as had been expected, and were dropped.

[2] The concerted tender is recognized by the Bank of England. It is
often referred to as tender by 'the syndicate', the use of this word originating in successive arrangements between a number of discount houses in

amount of bills tendered for by the discount houses corresponds more or less to the total offered in each week, but there is always also a large 'outside' tender, by certain overseas banks and others outside the London Clearing Banks' group, and by the Bank of England (operating both as an agent for others—e.g. the Federal Reserve Bank of New York—and on account of its own Banking Department). To obtain bills the outside tenders have therefore to be at prices equal to or a shade above the Association's price. In so far as they are at a price favourable to the Treasury, the outside tenders are accepted in full, and the associated discount houses get the rest (their price being a shade lower—i.e. their discount rate a shade higher). Every discount house finds that its allotment bears the same proportion to its tender—sometimes a high proportion, sometimes a low one, according to whether the outside tenders (at the cheaper rate) are small or large. The Treasury each week announces the *average* price at which it has placed the week's offer of Treasury Bills—and the higher the proportion allotted to the discount houses, the nearer is this average price to the Association's price.

On the day a Treasury Bill has been issued—when it still has three months to run—it is called a 'hot' bill. Hot bills are often in demand for the customers of the banks. Any time after it is seven days old one of the big banks may buy it (at the ruling market rate, which will usually be a few pence less than the original tender rate), but most of the bills stay with the discount houses for at least three or four weeks. After that the banks more and more eagerly buy them, and few of them remain in the portfolios of the discount houses right to maturity. While they are held by the discount houses, the bills are used by the discount houses as security for the money that they borrow at call, &c., from the banks. For this money they have to pay

the 1930's. The internal arrangements of the syndicate are highly complex and do provide for a far stronger element of competition between members than the word 'syndicate' implies.

rates of interest varying from day to day and from hour to hour; on the average these rates are below the Treasury Bill rates and therefore allow the discount houses a 'running profit' on the bills in their portfolios.

v. *The Discount Houses as Holders of Short Bonds*

In the Great Depression of the nineteen-thirties the total value of commercial bills outstanding at any one time dwindled to a hundred millions or so, and the market's margin on Treasury Bills became insignificant or even negative. In these circumstances the discount market turned, in an attempt to earn a reasonable living, to operating in short-term government bonds. Some of these bonds are issued originally with short lives—one-, two-, or five-year Exchequer Bonds, for example. Others are bonds that have originally had a much longer life—a twenty-year War Loan or Conversion Loan, perhaps—but become 'short bonds' as they approach maturity. When these longer-term bonds are within a year or two of maturity, and particularly if they stand at a premium, they have little appeal to the ordinary investing public, as new purchases; and though some holders will continue to hold them until maturity, the majority of the bonds will always through various circumstances (death, bankruptcy, alternative investment attractions, &c.) be coming on the market. As maturity approaches it is worth the while of financial institutions such as discount houses to offer an attractive price to obtain securities which, while not as liquid as three-months' bills, are absolutely firm claims to cash payment in a reasonably short time and will at such a price yield a definite return.[1] This return is often appreciably above the rates at which the discount houses could borrow the money to enable them to hold the bonds (which were

---

[1] The price offered by a discount house will be higher than that offered by any 'ordinary investor', since the latter cannot finance his holding by cheap 'money at call' and is differently taxed.

pledged as security), and the discount houses are therefore able to earn a comfortable 'running profit' on their bonds.

When it first developed this activity of the discount houses was thought dangerous, and it depended much on the funds that discount houses were able to borrow from the 'outside' banks—the foreign and colonial banks, and other financial institutions not primarily concerned with banking in England. But with the growing weight of government debt operations after the middle nineteen-thirties, the authorities realized that this new business of the discount market could facilitate the big official operations in course and in prospect. The chief objection to the business was that, the bonds being much less liquid than bills, there was a risk (if only remote) of large loss if the discount houses had to sell their bonds before maturity in a period of rising interest rates.[1] The Bank of England therefore took the view that the capital structure of the discount market should be strengthened, and that once this had been done the bond dealings of the discount houses might be benevolently regarded as long as they were confined within reasonable limits. Some of the smaller houses were amalgamated and there was a general move to increase capital; the present position is that every one of the twelve discount houses (i.e. excluding the running brokers) has capital resources of at least a million pounds.[2]

[1] Taking a crude arithmetical example: if, when a one-year 1 per cent. bond has just been bought at 100, the rate on one-year bonds rises to 2 per cent., the market price of the 1 per cent. bond will fall to about 99 and (rates continuing at the new levels) it will (ex-dividend) steadily rise to 100 at the maturity date a year later. If the discount house has to sell the bond in the early months (though not if it can hold to maturity) its capital loss will greatly exceed any net yield it has obtained. This example is only a crude one, because in practice considerations of dividends dates and taxation rules will greatly affect the arithmetic of profit and loss.

[2] The consolidation of the discount houses came in two distinct phases, the first occasioned by the recognition of the implications of the bond business in the thirties, and the second by the desire of the authorities to see the discount market playing a very special part in the operations of war finance. For the sake of simplicity these two phases have in the main

Bond dealings are regarded as a legitimate activity, the great English banks as well as the 'outside institutions' regularly lend money to the discount houses against bonds, and the Bank of England also regards these bonds as eligible security when the discount houses apply to it as the lender of last resort.

The official benevolence is entirely dependent on observance of reasonable limits. These relate to the total sum that may be used by a discount house in this way and to the length of life of the bonds that may be held by discount houses against borrowed money—both limits to which prudence in the discount houses themselves would anyway point. It is understood that the limit of amount is about eight times the true capital resources of the discount house concerned, and that this total must be very heavily weighted by the shorter bonds. As regards length of life, the rule is that a bond with a life exceeding five years should not be held against borrowed money.[1] A discount house will, however, hold only a relatively small amount of bonds having anything like as long as this to run, and very much more than half of its portfolio will ordinarily consist of bonds maturing within two years, and the remainder will have their maturities as carefully (but not evenly) spread over the remaining years as the technical availabilities of government bonds allow.

What advantages are there from a national point of view in this practice? What is the social justification for the payment of the income thus derived by the discount houses? The answer is in large part to be found in the fact that (apart from irredeemable stocks) even the longest-dated government bonds eventually become short-dated bonds, and therefore lose their appeal to the general body of investors who are looking for an investment to hold for an

text been telescoped into one. One of the twelve houses is the operator for the authorities and its capital resources are rather smaller.

[1] I add the qualification 'against borrowed money' because it is regarded as legitimate for a discount house to invest its own capital in longer-dated bonds.

indefinite period of years. Given this fact, the Government wants *some* financial institutions to act as a magnet to take up bonds that are getting near to maturity. These institutions can also serve a useful purpose by acting more generally as 'jobbers' absorbing ephemeral market gluts of short bonds. Moreover, the exigencies of public finance may occasionally drive the Government to issue bonds which are short-dated at the outset. And if, for these purposes, there are financial institutions willing to hold short bonds, then the Government may as well, as a matter of policy, choose to issue some short-dated bonds and get the benefit of lower rates when these can be had (as was the case through the nineteen-thirties and nineteen-forties). Given all these circumstances, it is very convenient to have such an adaptable and financially elastic institution as the London discount market to hold the bonds on the basis of funds that the banks like to regard as almost as liquid as cash (as indeed they are).

VI. *The Present Economic Function of the Discount Houses*

Since the mid-fifties the attitude of the discount market towards the business in short bonds has undergone a change. During the long period of stable interest rates down to 1957, the discount houses had done well on their bond business, earning a good margin of interest from the dividend yields and running very little risk. But when interest rates climbed upwards, especially in 1955-7, and the authorities became more willing to force on the market very sharp changes in the shortest rates of interest, profits shrank and occasionally severe losses were suffered. The discount houses therefore became much more reluctant both to sell and to buy bonds. In 1957 experience was particularly harsh, and there was an abrupt further change of attitude; since that date it cannot be pretended that the discount houses serve any substantial jobbing function in this market. When the jobbers in the gilt-edged section of the Stock Exchange need reinforcement of one kind or another, it is to the Government Broker (the Bank of England's operator)[1] that they have to look.

What would happen if the discount market dropped out of the short-bond market? The banks would no doubt operate more than they do nowadays in short bonds; but they would feel very uncomfortable about this and, to the extent that they failed to give adequate support to the short-bond market, the central bank as the instrument of government would feel obliged to operate a great deal in short bonds. This is more or less what happened in the U.S.A. in the nineteen-forties when the Federal Reserve System operated on a large scale in short- and medium-term bonds, absorbing them particularly when the commercial banks were shy, and unloading when the commercial banks were more tempted. In this way the American short-bond market was even more stable than the London one. And it could be done in London: there are no insuperable technical difficulties. We must remember, of course, that there would have to be a few more technical experts and a few more clerks in both the commercial banks and the central bank.

Similar considerations apply to the question whether the Treasury Bills business handled by the discount market could be eliminated. The discount houses are a great convenience to the commercial banks. By their manipulation of their call loans to the market and by the readiness with which they can buy Treasury Bills of any date from the market, the banks are able to settle inter-bank indebtedness daily and to cope with the vagaries (expected and unexpected) of government payments and receipts, and to do all this without impairing their cash ratios. But differences arising in inter-bank indebtedness could be adjusted along lines similar to the dealings in 'Federal

[1] On the Government Broker, see p. 115 below.

Funds' in America,[1] and now that the old prejudice against direct dealings between the Bank of England and the joint-stock banks has gone, the latter could be insulated from the irregularities of government payments and receipts—all without the intervention of this specialized body of discount houses. The liquidity of the commercial banks would *look* less, but since everyone understands the responsibilities of the central bank, liquidity would in fact be no less than it is now. In short, though the circumstances that gave birth to the discount market have in the main disappeared, its use for current purposes has its conveniences for all parties; and although on the score of its Treasury Bill operations there are no insuperable technical objections to the disappearance of the discount market, there is all the force of a tradition of great convenience and of adaptability to the changing needs of the times.

The operations of the discount houses in Treasury Bills have also a wider importance than is apparent when we confine our vision to the great clearing banks. The London market includes a much greater number of 'outside banks', both British and foreign, and banks all over the world are in telegraphic communication with London. As financial transactions, and particularly international financial transactions, have been gradually freed from official controls, and as interest rates have become flexible not only in London but throughout the world, the movement of balances from place to place has provided fresh activity for money dealers in London. By making a lively and sensitive market in Treasury Bills (in which foreign, Commonwealth, and domestic balances are increasingly invested), and in day-to-day deposits of sterling, the discount houses do useful business. Although many of their services could conceivably be offered by the great banks, such a concentration

---

[1] Member banks short of reserve funds (cash reserves) acquire from those with surplus reserves immediate deposits at the Federal Reserve Banks, returning them a day or so later. The process is essentially one of exchanging 'cash today' for 'cash tomorrow'. (See Chap. 11, sec. II.)

would imply a loss of competitiveness and might well limit London's activity and strength as a leading international financial centre.

Nor must we forget that the discount houses retain a modicum of the kind of business on which they grew up and which they are peculiarly well suited to handling. This is the trade in ordinary commercial bills of exchange, of which there are £850 to £400 millions of these now (1966) in the market. Many of these bills are sold in conveniently 'graded' parcels to the banks which, if there were no discount houses, would have to incur the expense of technical experts and clerks such as those now employed in the discount market. Again we find that work now undertaken by the discount houses *could* be done otherwise, but it is difficult to see that it could be done more cheaply, and the commercial banks may well be right in saying that it is work so different from their main service that they prefer to take advantage of a body of outside specialist firms. The discount houses engage the full-time services of no more than a few hundred, including typists and messengers as well as managers and specialist clerks. When allowance is made for the fact that the work would, in some way or other, have to be done anyway, perhaps this is not a high price to pay for one of the technical pillars of London's position as a leading international financial centre.

For besides its functioning at the centre of the domestic monetary system, the discount market has some importance in relation to London's work as an international financial centre. One aspect of this had already been mentioned: the facility afforded to overseas banks in London (including the British overseas banks) for pooling resources that must be kept in highly liquid form. Beyond this, at least some of the discount houses pick up useful brokerages in operating directly for banks in other countries which have no London office but choose to hold claims on London. The most usual such claims are Treasury Bills, which the discount houses are always ready to deal in for the account of overseas clients. There has also been a rapid growth of call money placed directly with discount houses by European banks having no London office. The size of this business in 1958 was underestimated by the Radcliffe Committee (in para. 178 of its Report), although it was quoting the authoritative evidence of the discount market: the business was already substantial at that date, and it has greatly increased since. Part at least of the discount market has in this way shown itself very much alive to the possibilities opened up by the gradual freeing of international short capital movements. This is not a business in which the discount houses alone are qualified: obviously the great clearing banks and the merchant banks have advantages in handling such international business, but in a period of rapid growth quite small financial intermediaries (and the discount houses are relatively small) can, by sufficiently making themselves useful, develop a new side to their business at a surprising speed.

4

CENTRAL BANKING: CONSTITUTIONAL QUESTIONS

1. *The Central Bank as an Organ of Government*

THE central bank is the organ of government that undertakes the major financial operations of the Government and by its conduct of these operations and by other means, influences the behaviour of financial institutions so as to support the economic policy of the Government. As a matter of history these functions have been developed in various countries by institutions that were more or less like commercial banks, and many of their operations nowadays are still of a banking nature; hence the inclusion of the word 'bank' in the term 'central bank' by which such an institution is described. But central banks are different from commercial banks in certain vital respects. First, they are governed by people who are more or less closely connected with other organs of government. Secondly, they do not exist to secure the maximum profit, which is the proper long-run aim of a commercial bank. Thirdly, they must have a special relation with the commercial banks whereby they are enabled to influence these in implementation of the Government's economic policy.

It follows, from the fact that the central bank is an organ of government, that it must be in some sense a part of the government machine and that its actions should be clearly co-ordinated with those of other executive branches of government. Nevertheless, traditionally high importance has been attached to the 'independence' of the central bank, even to the extent of insistence on private ownership and non-governmental appointment of its chief officers. This view was particularly influential in the nineteen-twenties, when the theory of central banking was being rapidly developed and accepted; it has been gradually breaking down since that period, but has never entirely disappeared. The case for giving to the central bank some special constitutional position rests on the fact that it is (as we shall see in the next chapter) the creator of cash, and thereby offers standing temptation to improvident governments. The advantages such governments enjoy, when they resort to easy finance at the central bank, are immediate and obvious; the disadvantages are not so readily perceived, but in the long run they are cumulative and can be disruptive to economic society. In recognition of this, most countries (including our own) have not been willing to reduce their central banks to the position of an ordinary department of government. The need to integrate the policy of the central bank with the broad economic policy of the Government is generally accepted, but the central bank retains a special status which is something rather more than freedom to conduct its daily technical operations unhindered. It is rather, in the words of an outstanding Governor of the Bank of England, that the central bank has 'the unique right to offer advice and to press such advice even to the point of nagging; but always of course subject to the supreme authority of the Government'.

The constitutions of central banks, as they exist today, reflect in varying degree acceptance of this view. To some extent the variations, from country to country, reflect national differences of view about central banking and are related to differences in the institutional environment in which their central banks have to work. But in the main, the variations reflect the world fashions about central banking which happened to prevail when the particular central banks were chartered or re-chartered. Sometimes the laws governing a central bank have become so out of accord with prevailing ideas that the central bank is re-chartered, as happened in the nineteen-thirties in the United States and many other countries. Or the power of the State to re-charter may lead to the written constitution being super-seded by unwritten conventions more in keeping with prevailing ideas, as happened in England during the de-cades preceding the nationalization of the Bank of England in 1946.

11. *The Bank of England*

The central bank in this country is the Bank of England.[1] The Bank of England was originally a joint-stock com-pany, established in 1694 by Act of Parliament, and the entire capital stock was acquired by the State under the Bank of England Act of 1946. Its affairs are regulated by a Governor, a Deputy-Governor, and sixteen Directors appointed by the Crown. The Governor and Deputy-Governor hold office for five years. The Directors hold office for four years, four of them retiring each year; not more than four of them may be full-time officers. All of these officers are eligible for reappointment and there is no provision for compulsory retirement, but it has been stated that normally no person over sixty-six years of age will be appointed. The Act of 1946 stipulates that members of the House of Commons, Ministers of the Crown, civil servants, and aliens may not be appointed to any of these offices; apart from these restrictions the Crown (acting of course on ministerial advice) is left entirely free to select people from any walk of life.

The effective managing body of the Bank now consists

---

[1] The Bank of England is in some sense the central bank not only of England but of the entire United Kingdom of Great Britain and Northern Ireland, but its control over the Scottish and Ulster banks is only indirect and these countries are to be regarded rather as the inmost members of the 'Rest of the Sterling Area' (see pp. 134–44 below). On this basis it is reasonable to think of the Bank of England as simply the central bank of England. It should be emphasized that this *is* a simplification.

of the Governor, the Deputy-Governor, and the four full-time executive Directors. The present Governor, Mr. L. K. O'Brien, appointed 1966, has been in the Bank of England throughout his career; he succeeded Lord Cromer whose career had been more varied. The holders of the other offices are professional central bankers, in the sense that they have spent a considerable part, if not the whole, of their careers in the service of the Bank. Central banking being what it is, at least in a great international financial centre, it is important that most of these six full-time people should have that familiarity with the Bank's business which can only come from long years of service in the Bank. In the appointment of the twelve part-time Directors the Crown has fairly closely followed the practice of the inter-war period, when the old (private) Court included not only City merchants and merchant bankers but also distinguished men from industry. There have been two appointments from London Clearing Banks, but it cannot be taken for granted that the tradition against such appointments has finally gone by the board. It is still sometimes argued that the special relationship between the Bank of England and the clearing banks makes any overlapping of directors undesirable; this is an argument that has lost some of its force since the central bank has come to have special relations also with other groups of financial institutions.

Under the Act of 1946 responsibility for the conduct of the Bank is placed upon the Court as a whole. This remains the formal position, and the Governor will ordinarily wish to carry the Court with him, after the event if not before, in his general control of the Bank's business. For the more urgent and secret matters (and important central banking decisions are usually of this kind) the Governor has at hand the 'Committee of Treasury'. This Committee consists of the Governor and his Deputy and five Directors chosen by all the Directors in a secret ballot. By long tradition this is the senior

Committee of the Bank,[1] and over a long period it exerted great authority; but the 'professionalization' of central banking and the closer relations between the Bank and the Treasury have tended to diminish the function of the Committee of Treasury, and indeed of the part-time Directors generally. The latter remain available for consultation; they are men whose opinions the Governor will not lightly disregard, but the daily activity and the real power are concentrated in the hands of the Governor and his full-time colleagues.

The Bank remains a corporate body whose powers are regulated by its charters, just as an ordinary joint-stock company's powers are regulated by its Memorandum of Association. The powers under the charters are very wide, and the operative restrictions on its activities were, until the Act of 1946, mainly self-imposed conventions that had grown as the Bank had developed its work as the central bank. The Government of the day for a very long time had always had some influence, and this influence grew significantly after 1914, and especially after about 1931. Treasury and Bank were already well used to working hand-in-glove before 1946, but only by Clause 4 of the 1946 Act did the relationship acquire specific statutory authority. The first two sub-clauses of Clause 4 are as follows:

(1) The Treasury may from time to time give such directions to the Bank as, after consultation with the Governor of the Bank, they think necessary in the public interest.

(2) Subject to any such directions, the affairs of the Bank shall be managed by the court of directors in accordance with such provisions (if any) in that behalf as may be contained in any charter

[1] It goes back to the very early days of the Bank, and was originally 'the Committee to wait upon the Lord Treasurer'—in the days before the Treasury went into commission—and, because in the early days business with and for its largest customer (the Government) absorbed the main energies of the Bank, the Committee soon attracted to itself all the Bank's major problems, irrespective of their relation to government business. Over a long period membership consisted of the Governor and Deputy and those Directors who were ex-Governors.

of the Bank for the time being in force and any bye-laws made thereunder.

It should be noted that the Governor has a statutory right to be consulted before a direction is issued, but he is not given power to veto it.[1] The Treasury retains the ultimate responsibility, but the provision about consultation ensures that it will not discharge that responsibility without having taken advice from the quarter technically most competent. In fact, Treasury and Bank have learned to work so closely together that these legal forms have ceased to have any practical importance, even if they ever had any.

The most important innovation of the Act of 1946 lies in the remainder of Clause 4, whereby the Bank of England is endowed with statutory powers to direct the affairs of the commercial banks. Hitherto the Bank of England had had to rely on the art of persuasion and, in war-time, on the bankers' knowledge that the Treasury could, if necessary in support of the Bank of England, issue Regulations under special war-time powers. Sub-clause (3) reads:

The Bank, if they think it necessary in the public interest, may request information from and make recommendations to bankers, and may, if so authorized by the Treasury, issue directions to any banker for the purpose of securing that effect is given to any such request or recommendation:

Provided that:

(*a*) no such request or recommendations shall be made with respect to the affairs of any particular customer of a banker, and

(*b*) before authorizing the issue of any such directions the Treasury shall give the banker concerned, or such person as appears to them to represent him, an opportunity of making representations with respect thereto.

There are thus two limitations upon the Bank of England's power. First, the compulsion must have the support of the Treasury (to which the banker under compulsion

---

[1] In short, the 'Old Lady of Threadneedle Street' retains her 'right to nag' (cf. p. 67).

has right of direct access) which is, through the Chancellor of the Exchequer, answerable to Parliament. Secondly, directions must relate to the whole business or to a whole class of business of a commercial bank, and not to its business with a particular customer. The latter restriction was imposed in protection of the traditional privacy of the banker–customer relationship and, since the central bank's aims refer to whole classes of business, this is not detrimental to central bank control of the monetary situation. The former restriction serves to emphasize the dependence of central banking upon government control and (like sub-clause (1)) ensures that the Treasury shall exercise compulsion only in full cognizance of the views of the compelled party.

What is most noteworthy is not, however, the limit set to the Bank's powers over the other banks, but the breadth of these powers. Central-bank legislation in other countries has generally set out in considerable detail the powers of the central bank and has supported them by specific statutory restrictions on the other banks, notably by compelling the latter to maintain 'fixed ratio' reserves at the central bank. Outside these specific statutory powers the central bankers have had to rely (as did the Bank of England before 1946) upon persuasion and co-operation, coupled sometimes with the knowledge that legislators would in the last resort intervene to support compulsion of recalcitrant bankers. The Bank of England is now operating under no such restrictions—it can issue directions compelling bankers, for example, to hold certain reserves with itself, to vary those reserves, to alter their charges for any class of business. It may compel the bankers to favour one industry or group of industries as borrowers.[1] In the exer-

---

[1] In the debates in the House of Commons, preceding the enactment of the nationalizing Bill, the then Chancellor of the Exchequer, referring to the exercise of these wide powers, said '. . . it may be desirable, in certain circumstances, to urge the banks to devote their resources to one or other form of investment which it was felt by the Government and by the Bank of England was necessary in the interests of a planned priority, with

cise of all these powers the initiative rests solely with the Bank of England, but the Bank cannot exercise compulsion except with Treasury support. Given Treasury support, the Bank's powers are unparalleled elsewhere. Their only limitation of general importance is in fact that imposed by the responsibility of the Chancellor of the Exchequer to Parliament, not only for the exercise of compulsory powers but also for advice tendered to the Crown on the appointment of the Governor, Deputy-Governor, and Directors.

Though its formal powers are thus very considerable, the position in fact remains that the Bank exercises its influence mainly by informal communication and persuasion behind the scenes. There are regular channels of communication between the Bank and the various groups of financial institutions. The London Clearing Banks, for example, have two Committees: one of their Chairmen, and one of their chief General Managers, and the Governor of the Bank has regular meetings with the Chairmen's Committee and will ordinarily communicate with the banks through the Chairman of this Committee or the Chairman of the Chief General Managers' Committee, according to the subject of his communication. Similarly there are the Accepting Houses Committee, the Discount Market Association, and bodies representing the finance houses, the insurance companies, and other groups of financial institutions. Through these organizations and by numerous personal contacts the Bank of England keeps its finger on the City's pulse and can secure compliance with its wishes without any resort to legal action. The general view among these organizations, and perhaps in the Bank of England itself, is that it is better to sit round a table and agree to a course of action than to stay away and force the authorities to exercise legal powers that might be awkward to administer with precision and answerability.

a view to securing full employment in the country and building up our export trade and other necessary elements in our economy'.

Like the other bodies that were 'nationalized' after the 1939–45 war, the Bank of England publishes an Annual Report. This is a formal and rather bare document, quite unlike the informative reports published by most other central banks. But since 1961 the Bank of England has published a Quarterly Bulletin which has made a substantial contribution towards enlightening the public on the nature of and reasons for the operations of the Bank. The range of financial information collected by the Bank has been widened, and much of this information is now passed on to the public in convenient form in this Quarterly Bulletin. In this and in other ways the Bank has made it clear that it accepts a duty to inform the public of the whys and wherefores as far as it can do so consistently with the temporary secrecy often essential to the successful daily conduct of operations.

III. *The American and other Central Banks*

The central bank of the United States of America is a system of twelve connected banks called the Federal Reserve Banks. The system was founded in 1913, and bears in its constitution marks both of its origin at that date and of successive phases in the development of ideas about central banking. We shall return in Chapter 11 to some discussion of the functioning of the system; here we are concerned simply to outline the system. For a more detailed account the reader must go to the extensive American literature, including the admirable publications of the Federal Reserve System itself.

The Federal Reserve System consists of twelve Federal Reserve Banks, each having one geographical section of the country as its sphere of operations. The capital of each Reserve Bank was subscribed by the 'member banks' in its region. Member banks are all those commercial banks that are obliged by law, or are induced, to attach themselves to the system, and such are the laws and the inducements that nearly all large banks and many of the small ones are member banks: member banks hold about 84 per cent. of the total deposits of all commercial banks. The member banks have a shadow of control over the functioning of the System in that they elect some of the Directors on the local Boards—the Boards of the individual Reserve Banks. But most of the fundamental central banking powers of the System are formally entrusted to a central body, the Board of Governors of the Federal Reserve System. This Board of Governors is in Washington, the political centre of the country, and not in New York, the financial centre. The Board consists of seven Governors appointed by the President of the United States, subject to Senate approval, for terms (not mutually coincident) of fourteen years. Among these seven are the Chairman and Vice-Chairman, appointed by the President (subject to Senate approval) for terms of four years; they are usually re-appointed for successive terms while within their fourteen-years' terms as Governors. This governing body, besides having the important central banking powers, controls important appointments in the individual Reserve Banks. The American central bank may thus be described as directed by men appointed for fairly long terms, and appointed ultimately by the Federal Government though the central bankers in office at any time are not necessarily appointed by the political Administration that happens to be in power.

During the middle decades of this century the effective decision-making body in the System has come to be the Open Market Committee. This consists in form of the seven Governors, together with the heads of five of the twelve Reserve Banks, the New York Reserve Bank being always one of these five. This Committee of twelve meets once every three weeks, and is attended by officers of the Board, of the New York Reserve Bank, and others bringing the total attendance up to sixty or seventy people: among them the leading economists of the System are prominent. It is in these three-weekly meetings that the policies of the System and the guiding lines for current operations are hammered out; the decisions are formulated and eventually published in the Annual Report of the System, together with a record of any voting by those who are formally members of the Committee.

Though unmentioned in the formal constitution of the System, the habits of travel and consultation that have grown up in the System, whereby the men at the centre keep themselves informed of what is going on and what is being thought throughout the country, and similarly the views of the Board in Washington are disseminated and understood far and wide, have become a vital part in the functioning of the System. The 'public relations' part of their work is given high priority by the Governors who, though they officially 'sit' in Washington, can rarely be found all there at once. Another informal development has been in relations with the Federal Treasury. In the United States the Treasury exercises some of the functions we in England have come to take for granted as the business of a central bank, and close contact and sympathy between the Treasury and the Federal Reserve System is therefore of high importance. This is a relationship that is bound to vary from one political Administration to another; it has been closer since 1951, and particularly since 1960.

The first charge on the net earnings of the Federal Reserve Banks is the payment of dividend, at the rate of 6 per cent. per annum, to the member banks as the stockholders. This capital charge has proved to be only a small fraction of the sums available, and nine-tenths of the remainder are paid to the U.S. Treasury, the other tenth being retained by the Banks as 'surplus', effectively a capital reserve. There was a time—in the first decade of the System's life—when the earning of an income was a consideration affecting policy, but the System now needs to give no thought to the matter: the operating profit piles up incidentally to the policies followed, the member banks get their dividend, and a large sum goes to relieve the Federal taxpayer.

Certain other governmental bodies, besides the U.S. Treasury, have functions that are sometimes within the province of a central bank. These are the Federal Deposit Insurance Corporation and the Comptroller of the Currency. They have powers to inspect the commercial banks and ensure observance of various legal restrictions; in exercise of these powers they are not, however, impinging on the main functions of the central bankers who operate in the Federal Reserve System.

The Bank of France had a long history as a commercial bank and only very gradually developed into a central bank. In 1945 the Government, which had long had effective control of the governing appointments, took over ownership from the private shareholders. Since this date the regulation of the French banking system has been shared between the Bank of France, the National Credit Council, and the Banking Control Commission. The Commission's duties are mainly of supervision and detailed regulation of the banks. The National Credit Council, which includes a variety of economic, financial, and government interests, is the main policy-making and consultative body, while the Bank of France is the executive body whose task is the implementation of policy. The Governor of the Bank of France, appointed by the Government but not often changing on a change of government, is the Vice-President of the National Credit Council and is its effective Chairman, normally deputizing for its Ministerial President. The Governor is also President of the Banking Control Commission. It is thus in the person of this Governor that the trinity of controlling bodies finds its unity, and likewise it is through close contacts of officials of the three bodies that this apparently elaborate machine works with tolerable smoothness to make the banking system conform with the monetary policy for which Ministers take responsibility.[1]

In Western Germany the central bank, the *Bundesbank*, has an immensely complicated constitution, reflecting both the peculiar structure that preceded it and the disagreements that prolonged the process of establishing the bank in 1957. Its capital is owned by the Federal Government. Its seat is at Frankfurt-am-Main, until the Federal Government (now at Bonn) goes to Berlin, when the Bundesbank also will go to Berlin, which had until 1945 been the financial as well as the political centre of Germany. There is, as one of many inheritances from the pre-1957 arrangements, a network of 'Main Offices' at eleven regional centres, and each of these Main Offices is represented on the Central Bank Council. This Council, which includes the President and Vice-President and not more than eight other Directors as well as the regional representatives, is the main policy-making body. The President, Vice-President and Directors are government appointees, with eight-year terms of office. The key appointment is that of President, but the elaboration of the whole system makes for some dispersion of authority. It is equally certain that the constitution, as well as the spirit in which it is worked, makes the German central bank the most autonomous in the world.

In other countries the legal provisions for the constitution of the central bank, and both its formal and its actual relationship with the political government, vary almost as much as those of the four countries just discussed. The power of the Government over the appointment of Directors is usually limited by provision that a Director hold office for a five- or seven-year period. There is often some restriction on the groups from which Directors may be chosen: a common provision is that so many Directors

[1] This paragraph and the next, on France and Germany respectively, are based on Chapters 1 and 2, by J. S. G. Wilson and R. G. Opie respectively, in *Banking in Western Europe* (ed. R. S. Sayers, Oxford, 1962).

shall be representative of commercial interests, so many of agricultural interests, so many of industrial interests, and so on. The Federal Reserve System used to have its Directors chosen largely on these lines, and vestiges of it remain in the local Boards. Sometimes the Directors must be representative of geographical sections of the country. Provisions such as these are intended to ensure that the central bank shall have due regard, in determining its policy, to all important interests of the country. Against this, it may be argued that the system of 'representatives' of different interests must tend to exaggerate disunity within the Board, as a compromise is less easy when men feel that they are there to watch the interests of different bodies of people. It is significant that changes in American law have whittled down the representation of specific interests in the government of the Federal Reserve System. A freer range of choice of Directors can still allow Directors to be chosen in practice from various fields without those appointed feeling under compulsion to stand by the interests of the industries from which they come. In this way, all sides of a case are likely to be put forward, but there is more chance of a tolerable compromise than when representation is on formal lines. One other special form of representation, still used in many countries, is for a high Ministry of Finance official to be *ex officio* Director of the central bank, though not always with a vote. The general tendency, however, is away from 'representational' methods of appointment, and towards the concentration of control in the hands of a highly professional body of Directors, while representative elements remain in wider consultative councils.

The key appointments have become, more than ever, those of Governor and Deputy-Governor of each central bank. They are almost everywhere appointed by their governments for periods of five or seven years or longer. They, usually supported by a small group of Directors who are professional central bankers, effectively rule the central bank, and the most difficult constitutional question is that of the relationship of these men with the political government and with other parts of the government machine. The ultimate obligation of the central bankers to defer to the political Ministers, or to resign, is now more openly recognized than it used to be. The real balance of power for all ordinary purposes continues, however, to escape the constitutional lawyers. No matter what the law says, sometimes the Minister of Finance has the stronger personality, and sometimes the governor of the central bank is the one who does not give way. Sometimes relations between the technicians in government departments and the technicians in the central bank can be close and friendly, because they have had similar social and educational backgrounds; but sometimes a traditional aloofness in the bankers' stronghold may prevent such a relationship. Again, some countries give more power to their central bankers because they fear (perhaps for historical reasons) that the politicians will shortsightedly 'tamper with the money'. Most of all, central bankers derive some strength from their greater continuity in office. The political system may produce second-rate Ministers of Finance: they come and they go. The governor of the central bank, by contrast, holds his place into a second or even a third decade; by sheer weight of experience and of long public recognition he can easily become the more powerful force.

Yet in the end the central banker does hold his place, and grows in public estimation, only if he can on the more fundamental measures carry public opinion with him. If he is badly out of tune, clashes with Ministers are less easily shrugged off, and no constitutional independence, no tradition of central bank autonomy, can save him. Like other parts of the governmental machine, the central bank exists as a body with a life of its own because the technicians who specialize in a particular sphere of economic policy have a special contribution to make to the evolution of that policy. If, not accepting the contributions others have to make, the central bankers get in the way, then sooner or later they have to go. The constitutional arrangements regulating the position of central banks attempt, in varying ways, to reflect these ultimate realities. On the rare occasions when they fail, a constitutional upheaval generally follows; more generally, the balance of power moves back and forth, according to the accidents of personalities and problems, within the framework established by law.

5

THE DOMESTIC OPERATIONS OF THE CENTRAL BANK

1. *The Bank of England as the Central Bank*

SOME of a central bank's work consists of telling other institutions what they may or may not do ('controlling'), and some consists of advising other institutions (mainly other organs of government) what they should do, but these functions, important as they are, derive from its fundamental task of operating in markets. The central bank is the market operator standing between 'the public sector' (to which it belongs) and 'the private sector'. Its power to operate is based on the fact that its own liabilities (its own 'promises to pay') are the 'cash' on which the entire banking structure of the country rests. The central bank makes cash payments, and receives cash, in settlement of transactions purely internal to the country; we shall discuss these transactions in the present chapter. It also makes cash payments, and receives cash, in settlement of transactions that arise from the business which firms and individuals have with other countries; this 'external' or 'foreign exchange' business we shall discuss in the next chapter. Transactions of both these classes give rise to a net inflow or a net outflow of cash to or from the central bank and it is basically by influencing these inflows and outflows—and so altering the cash basis of the banking system—that the central bank is able to influence the behaviour of banks and other financial institutions. We must therefore begin by looking more closely at the nature of cash, and at the central bank's operations in it. Through the remainder of this chapter the explanation will be in terms of the operations of the Bank of England, for it is in England that the possibilities of central banking have been most fully developed. Some aspects of central banking in the United States, and others special to countries with undeveloped financial institutions, are discussed in later chapters.

The important operations of the Bank of England must be discussed in terms of a few major headings in the Bank of England's published statement of account. This is a statutory form, known as the Bank Return and deriving its odd shape as a combination of two balance-sheets from the ideas of 1844 which have little or nothing to do with modern central banking. Of these items, *Bankers' Deposits* represents the balances held by the London clearing banks at the Bank of England; like an individual's bank balance, they can be drawn upon for transfer to another customer or for the purpose of obtaining notes and coin. Secondly, as the gateway between the public sector and private sector, the Bank of England holds the principal banking account of the Government: its balance appears among the Bank's liabilities as *Public Deposits.* (It is by transfers from Public Deposits to Bankers' Deposits, or vice versa, that residual claims against the Government, or residual claims by the Government, are settled.) Thirdly, there are *Other Deposits: Other Accounts* which are the balances of other customers. These *Other Accounts* include some that represent a vestige of ordinary banking business for private customers. Also, more importantly, Other Accounts include balances in favour of Commonwealth and foreign central banks or other more or less official bodies; changes in these have some significance in relation to external transactions, but they are generally quickly compensated by transactions in Treasury Bills and, like the rest of Other Accounts they may be ignored in our review of the Bank's domestic operations.

The only other liability of any importance consists of the *Notes* issued by the Bank—our familiar £10, £5, £1, and

10s. notes, as well as some of larger denominations which do not emerge in circulation. The issue of all these notes is subject to the Currency and Bank Notes Act of 1954, in accordance with which there is at present (9 November 1966) a *Fiduciary Issue* of £2,950 millions. The whole of this Fiduciary Issue appears as a liability of the Issue Department in the Bank Return, but a small part (£60 millions on 9 November 1966) reappears, being notes still resting in the Bank, as an asset of the Banking Department in the Bank Return. These notes 'in the Banking Department' are available for the Bank to pay out to the London clearing banks if these require more cash for public circulation or for their own tills. All the rest of the notes are 'in circulation'—that is, outside the Bank of England itself.

Against these various liabilities the Bank shows in its Bank Return an equal total of assets. These include a portfolio of government securities held 'in the Issue Department', to which we shall have to return, and a rather more varied assortment of assets 'in the Banking Department'. Of the latter, some are labelled *Government Securities*. This item consists of Treasury Bills, some other government securities such as would appear as 'Investments' in the balance-sheets of the clearing banks, and 'Ways and Means Advances' which are temporary loans, of an ordinary banking kind, to the Government. The total of government securities in the Bank can be changed at any time on the initiative of the Bank, usually by the purchase of Treasury Bills from the Exchequer or (through 'the back door') from the discount market.

The other important item on the assets side is *Other Securities*. This is subdivided into *Discounts and Advances* and *Securities*. Under Discounts and Advances there are three items, the individual magnitudes of which we do not know—one or another of them may sometimes stand at zero. First there are two items arising out of the Bank's ordinary banking business. These two items are bills of exchange discounted outright for the Bank's own customers, and advances made either by overdraft or loan to the Bank's own customers. The third item shows similar transactions with the discount houses arising not out of the Bank's ordinary banking business with ordinary customers but out of its traditional operation as lender of last resort.[1] This distinction between the Bank's ordinary customers and the members of the discount market should not be understood to imply that the members of the discount market are not in any sense 'customers' of the Bank of England. The discount houses must in fact always keep accounts open at the Bank of England, but the Bank's relations with them have a significance entirely different from that of its relations with those non-financial houses and individuals who bank with the Bank of England as though it were an ordinary bank.

The second part of the general item Other Securities is called *Securities*. It consists of non-British government bills, bonds, &c., which the Bank of England has acquired on its own initiative. Among these securities are parcels of bills bought by the Bank from discount houses, who are expected to put into such parcels a representative selection of the non-Treasury Bills handled by them.[2] There are also shares and debenture stocks bought by the Bank when, during the inter-war period, it played a prominent part in industrial development and reconstruction.

II. *The Bank of England as the Source of Cash*

The importance of the Bank of England's liabilities and assets, which we have just outlined, rests on their relevance to the cash basis of the banking system. The power of the Bank of England over the commercial banks is derived from two facts: (i) the regard paid by the commercial

[1] See pp. 101–11 below.
[2] This arrangement, of long standing, enables the Bank of England to keep some check on the *quality* of the commercial transactions covered by the activities of the Accepting Houses and other London acceptors.

banks, in the regulation of their most important operations, to their cash and other liquid assets, and (ii) the position of the Bank of England as the source of cash. The former has already been explained in Chapter 2. Before we can consider how the Bank of England regulates the supply of cash, we must explain how the Bank of England is the source of cash. In this there are four steps: first, 'cash' has to be defined and classified into Notes and Bankers' Deposits at the Bank of England; secondly, the relation between these two kinds of cash and the operation of the Bank of England as a banker (with the other banks as its depositing customers) are outlined; thirdly, we must look into the regulation of the note issue; and fourthly, the other facet of the Bank's position as bankers' bank—its operation as 'Lender of Last Resort'—must be explained. Only then shall we be in a position to understand how the Bank of England can control the supply of cash, and what power flows from this control.

What is cash? There are two forms of cash. The first is any more widely acceptable form of money into which people may wish to change their less widely acceptable bank deposits. The 'liquidity' of a bank is its ability to exchange deposits for cash of the first form when demanded by the public. The second form of cash consists of anything that a commercial bank considers as liquid as the first form. These definitions are extremely awkward; but they are, I believe, as little awkward as is consistent with true general statement of the present position. When we turn from the general definitions to apply them to English conditions our statements become more familiar. Cash of the first form consists of all legal tender money—silver and copper coin and Bank of England notes—this being the most widely acceptable form of money. Cash of the second form consists of the Bankers' Deposits at the Bank of England. In the course of decade after decade of trust in the Bank of England, because the Bank has always been able to offer its own notes in exchange for deposit claims entered in its books, there has arisen the tradition that the Bankers' Deposits are as useful to the commercial banks as are Bank of England notes.

'Cash' in England may therefore be reclassified as first, the silver and copper coin provided by the Mint at the instance of the Bank of England, and second, certain liabilities of the Bank of England—the bank notes and the Bankers' Deposits. Of these two classes of cash the first is unimportant—the amount of it varies little and, since banks and public alike endeavour to minimize their holdings of such a bulky form of money, no significant change in the total supply of money can be initiated by varying the supply of silver and copper coin. With bank notes and Bankers' Deposits the position can be quite different. If these liabilities of the Bank of England are increased there may be an important increase in the supply of money. In acquiring earning assets, and so in creating bank deposits, the commercial banks must keep an eye on their cash reserves. An increase in the notes and 'cash at the Bank of England' held by the commercial banks allows an increase in the aggregate of bank deposits, and vice versa. If it can control the notes in the commercial banks' tills *plus* the Bankers' Deposits with itself the Bank of England can control the aggregate of bank deposits in the country. (Whether it chooses to exercise this control in a positive way is another question.)

At this point we must recognize the fact that as the system works today the bank notes have become very much like silver and copper coins in that they behave as small change. The Bank of England does not ever by its own action directly add to the notes held by the commercial banks. The latter send round to the Bank of England for more or send some notes back as they choose, adding to or subtracting from their book balances at the Bank, just as members of the public draw notes from the commercial banks in exchange for bank deposits, or take notes to the bank and have their bank deposits increased. The Bank of

England allows the commercial banks to draw out or pay in notes as they choose. When the commercial banks are drawing out notes the Bank Return shows, on the liabilities side, a decrease in Bankers' Deposits and, on the assets side, a decrease in Notes, and contrariwise.

To the commercial banks, bank notes, like deposits at the Bank of England, are idle assets. They want them only to meet the demands of the public and to provide what they consider adequate till money. Accordingly they customarily restrict their holdings of notes within about 4 per cent. of their deposit liabilities to the public. If they draw more notes from the Bank of England it is either because the public are wanting more for circulation (as in the weeks before Christmas) or because their aggregate deposit liabilities have risen. Leaving aside the public demands for the moment let us remember that the deposit liabilities of the banks to the public will be increased by the action of the banks in acquiring assets. The banks will not have increased their assets, so increasing deposits, unless their cash reserves allow maintenance of the 8 per cent. ratio. As their note holdings had, as deposits increased, fallen short of the customary 4 per cent., the other part of their cash reserves—Bankers' Deposits at the Bank of England—must have increased. If the Bank of England can determine the volume of Bankers' Deposits with itself, and can supply whatever volume of notes is appropriate to that level of Bankers' Deposits, the Bank of England will be controlling the general operations of the commercial banks.

If the change in the commercial banks' cash reserves is initiated by the public the chain of events is somewhat different, but the influence is the same. Suppose, for example, that members of the public are demanding more notes for circulation. As they draw notes across the bank counters their deposits go down as their holding of notes goes up. The position of the commercial banks is simply the obverse of this: their deposit liabilities to the public are going down and their aggregate cash reserves are going down *by the same absolute amount*. The cash ratio has therefore fallen below the usual figure: the ratio of notes to deposits is very much lower and this is only partly compensated by the rise in the proportion that Bankers' Deposits bear to deposit liabilities (there being no initial change in the absolute amount of Bankers' Deposits). Then, if the Bank of England takes no action, the commercial banks will set about contracting earning assets, and so contracting deposits further, to the level appropriate to the new level of total cash. They will also draw some notes out of the Bank of England, Bankers' Deposits and Notes at the Bank of England both declining, while the composition of the commercial banks' cash reserves once more assumes its normal complexion. Let us picture this in a highly schematic arithmetical example:

POSITION I

(All figures in millions of £)

Bank of England Banking Department

Bankers' Deposits . .	240	Notes unissued . . 70
Other Liabilities . .	130	Other Assets . . 300
	370	370

Commercial Banks

Deposits . . .	6,000	Cash at Bank of England . 240
		Cash in tills . . . 240
		Earning Assets . . 5,520
	6,000	6,000

Ratio, Total cash: Deposits . . . . 8 per cent.⎫
Ratio, Cash at Bank of England: Deposits . 4 per cent. ⎬approx.
Ratio, Cash in tills: Deposits . . . 4 per cent.⎭

POSITION II

(after public has drawn £50m. notes into circulation)

Bank of England Banking Department

Bankers' Deposits . .	240	Notes unissued . . 70
Other Liabilities . .	130	Other Assets . . 300
	370	370

Commercial Banks

Deposits	. . .	5,950	Cash at Bank of England .	240
			Cash in tills . . .	190
			Earning Assets . .	5,520
		5,950		5,950

Ratio, Total cash:Deposits . . .	7 per cent.	
Ratio, Cash at Bank of England:Deposits .	4 per cent.	approx.
Ratio, Cash in tills:Deposits . . .	3 per cent.	

POSITION III

(after commercial banks have reacted to fall in cash reserves)

Bank of England Banking Department

Bankers' Deposits	.	215	Notes unissued	. .	45
Other Liabilities	. .	130	Other Assets .	. .	300
		345			345

Commercial Banks

Deposits	. . .	5,375	Cash at Bank of England .	215
			Cash in tills . . .	215
			Earning Assets . .	4,945
		5,375		5,375

Ratio, Total cash:Deposits	8 per cent.	
Ratio, Cash at Bank of England:Deposits .	4 per cent.	approx.
Ratio, Cash in tills:Deposits . . .	4 per cent.	

Position III may never be reached. For if the commercial banks feel confident that the notes will be coming back from the public directly, they will not bother to disturb their earning assets. When the public 'pay the notes into their accounts' again the banks simply revert to Position I. This is what must happen to some extent every day the banks are open. In the morning spenders of money are drawing notes out to meet the day's needs. The notes pass into the hands of tradesmen. Just before three o'clock all the tradesmen's cashiers run round to the bank and in go the notes again. More notes are paid in first thing next morning, perhaps partly through 'night safes'. The banks perhaps approximate to Position I at 10.30 a.m., move towards Position II until 2.30 p.m., then until shortly after opening time on the following morning they are moving back to Position I. The same thing happens at week-ends. On Friday afternoon the employers' cashiers go to the banks and draw out notes, these notes being paid out in wages that evening. During Saturday the workers and their wives are paying the money to tradesmen, and on Monday morning to the rent-collectors, and back come the notes into the banks. On Friday morning and again on Tuesday morning the banks are in Position I, but they had moved to Position II by Saturday morning and then back again.

It is perhaps by now apparent to the critical reader that the word 'notes' has been used throughout the last few paragraphs to mean 'Bank notes *plus* silver and copper coin'. This is true even of the simplified accounts in the example. The silver and copper coin is a small part of the total, but it behaves in precisely the same way. It is, as we shall see when discussing the regulation of the note issue, the Bank's business to see that it always has an adequate reserve of notes and coin to meet the demands of the commercial banks. But notes and coin are alike in their behaviour. Notes behave as the 'small change' to bank deposits.

In deciding whether to pass to Position III the banks have to consider whether their cash ratio is unduly low for the moment only. But there is another possibility open, which will avert the necessity of passing to Position III even when the banks feel obliged to restore the cash ratio. The drop in the cash ratio has occurred because, in the face of a public demand for more cash for circulation, the Bank of England has remained purely passive. If, however, it is within its power to force an appropriate increase in Bankers' Deposits the cash ratio will be maintained. The commercial banks will find the composition of their cash unusual, till money being short; but they can replenish it by drawing on their deposits at the Bank of England. The final position is then as overleaf.

POSITION IIIA

(after the Bank of England has provided more cash)

(£ millions)

Bank of England Banking Department

Bankers' Deposits	.	.	238	Notes unissued . .	22
Other Liabilities	.	.	130	Other Assets . .	346
			368		368

Commercial Banks

Deposits	.	.	.	5,950	Cash at Bank of England .	238
					Cash in tills . . .	238
					Earning Assets . .	5,474
				5,950		5,950

Cash ratios: as in Positions I and III

In this position the banks have not reverted entirely to Position I. The volume of deposits is smaller by the £50 millions that the public offered in exchange for the notes taken into circulation. The total supply of money of all kinds in the hands of the public will, however, be the same as in Position I—the notes in circulation being up by the same amount as deposit liabilities of the commercial banks are down. This result may be desired by the Bank of England; but it may prefer a position in which the earning assets of the commercial banks are undisturbed. In this event the Bankers' Deposits must be forced back to the original £240 millions level, and the Bank of England will lose £2 millions more of notes to the commercial banks. The latter will revert precisely to Position I; but the Bank of England's position will be somewhat different:

POSITION IIIB

(£ millions)

Bank of England Banking Department

Bankers' Deposits	.	.	240	Notes unissued . .	20
Other Liabilities	.	.	130	Other Assets . . .	350
			370		370

Commercial Banks

(as in Position I)

The reader can easily reverse the figures in order to follow the effects of the public's paying notes into the banks.

Whatever the public's action in drawing notes from or paying notes to the commercial banks, the Bank of England has control over the situation *provided that it can manipulate Bankers' Deposits at will.* Our analysis of the effects of a flow of notes from the banks to the public has been designed simply to show that, whatever the public is requiring in the way of cash, the volume of deposit liabilities of the commercial banks depends upon Bankers' Deposits at the Bank of England. How can the Bank of England control this figure?

The reader will perhaps already have noticed the clue to the answer in a certain difference between Position I and Position IIIB above. In the Position IIIB the commercial banks stand in precisely the same position as in Position I. In the Bank of England the liabilities' side is the same in the two positions; but the composition of the assets side is different. Between Position I and Position IIIB the notes resting in the Bank of England have gone down by £50 millions, this amount having passed through the commercial banks to meet the increased demands of the public. The item 'Other Assets' has increased by £50 millions. The Bank of England has increased its earning assets by £50 millions, to provide the increase in cash required for circulation. These 'Other Assets' are Government Securities and the two classes of 'Other Securities'. The Bank, that is to say, provides additional cash by buying securities. The change can occur through the commercial banks calling in money-market loans, the discount houses being forced into the Bank, and Discounts and Advances rising. But if the Bank wants deliberately to help the banking system to provide the increase in cash without disturbance, it can do so by buying Government Securities. In the latter event it is said to have engaged in 'Open Market Operations'. The term Open Market Operations also covers the converse process, when the Bank sells securities in order to reduce Bankers' Deposits. In these operations[1] the Bank takes the initiative of fixing the rate at which it will operate in Treasury Bills and then takes in or puts out the amount of securities (Treasury Bills) necessary to release or absorb the right amount of cash for preserving market rate at the chosen level.

Just as the commercial banks in fact control their deposit liabilities to the public by acquiring assets of various kinds, offering book balances in exchange, so the Bank of England controls the level of its own liabilities by controlling the volume of its assets. A change in its assets sometimes simply occurs because the Bank of England complies with the wishes of the people who come to it offering assets—e.g. bills of exchange—just as a commercial bank can change its assets by the bank manager's sitting in his office and saying that Mr. X may overdraw his account as he desires, or by the cashier's accepting notes offered over the counter. Alternatively the Bank of England can change its assets by going out into the market seeking securities or some other assets, just as the commercial bank can add to its assets by buying government bonds through the Stock Exchange, or by buying new offices from a builder.

The control of assets gives the Bank control over its total liabilities. But Bankers' Deposits, which we have seen as essential to the liquidity of the commercial banks, are not the only liabilities of the Bank of England. There remain the items Public Deposits and Other Deposits (Other Accounts). A rise in the Government's balances while the Bank of England's total assets (and therefore total liabilities) remain the same implies a fall in Bankers' Deposits. By itself every payment made to the Government has this effect and every payment made by the Government has the opposite effect. If, the Bank of England's assets remaining unchanged, payments to the

Government exceed payments by the Government, Public Deposits rise while Bankers' Deposits fall. This fall implies a decline in the cash ratio of the commercial banks. Any decided change of this kind would lead the commercial banks to make other balance-sheet adjustments and ultimately contract credit somewhat. A movement in Other Deposits (Other Accounts) would work in the same way, though such movements are rarely pronounced or prolonged. If the Bank of England, seeing the composition of its liabilities change, is unwilling to allow the disturbance to affect the operations of the commercial banks, it must manipulate its total assets (and therefore its total liabilities) in such a way as to counteract the effect on Bankers' Deposits of the change in, say, Public Deposits. If, for instance, heavy tax payments raise Public Deposits the Bank must expand its total assets, so that total liabilities are increased by the same amount as Public Deposits. Bankers' Deposits will then be unchanged and the commercial banks will be able to leave their earning assets undisturbed. As long, therefore, as the Bank of England is able to manipulate its total assets the existence of these liabilities other than Bankers' Deposits does not destroy the Bank's control over the amount of Bankers' Deposits.

We have in this section shown how the Bank of England controls the commercial banks' cash reserves in a general way only. Our answer to the question, how does the Bank of England control the amount of Bankers' Deposits? has been answered only by the general statement: By increasing and reducing its total assets. This general answer will be supplemented in Section V, but first a gap in our argument, hitherto glossed over, must be filled. The reader will have observed that to support a given volume of Bankers' Deposits the Bank of England must be able to issue over its counter as many notes as the other banks want to hold in their tills and as many notes as the public needs for circulation. In all the schematic examples given we have assumed that the Bank always has sufficient unused notes at its command, and it is high time to consider how the supply of notes is in fact regulated.

III. *The Regulation of the Note-issue*

As, on the basis of increases in the level of Bankers' Deposits, the commercial banks proceed to increase the total of their earning assets and so add to the total of bank deposits, it becomes necessary for them also to add to the notes in their tills, if they are to maintain the normal ratio of till money to total deposit liabilities. In order to secure this adjustment of till money to total deposits the banks exchange part of Bankers' Deposits for notes—or, in the contrary case of a contraction in deposits, notes for Bankers' Deposits. As the swelling deposits encourage rising prices and business activity, the change in the banks' till-money requirements is likely to be reinforced by changes, in the same direction, in the public's demand for notes for circulation. In regulating the volume of Bankers' Deposits the Bank of England has always to bear in mind the fact that changes in this volume will find a reflection in changing demands for notes for both banks and public to hold. The Bank of England's control of the volume of ordinary bank deposits is thus theoretically subject to its note-issuing powers.

What is true of the influx and efflux of notes at the Bank of England is equally true of the influx and efflux of smaller change—silver and copper coin. The Bank of England must always be prepared to exchange Bankers' Deposits for silver or copper coin on demand, in order that the commercial banks may always be prepared to exchange the deposits of the public for silver or copper coin on demand. The Bank of England must therefore always have an adequate supply, else its regulation of Bankers' Deposits might be cramped. The English system of providing subsidiary coinage (for so the silver and copper coins are described by economists) does ensure that the Bank of

England shall always have at its command an adequate supply. The coins are produced by the Royal Mint, which is a government department. The Royal Mint buys metals in the ordinary metal markets and engages labour, &c., to make the metal into coins. It makes its payments (just as does any other government department) by drawing on the Public Deposits at the Bank of England. It is always prepared to sell new coins on demand to the Bank of England. If the Bank of England finds that its reserves of silver coin are running low (because the commercial banks have been drawing silver coin from it) it buys some more from the Royal Mint. The Bank pays the Mint by adding the appropriate sum to the balance of that government department, so Public Deposits are increased. Meanwhile the Royal Mint is paying for its raw materials, labour, &c., by transferring part of its bank balance (Public Deposits) to individuals. This, like any other government disbursement, adds to Bankers' Deposits—indeed, it restores them roughly to the level at which they stood before the commercial banks drew on them to obtain the silver coin wanted by the public. There is no restriction on the supply of this money. The Bank of England, in regulating the volume of Bankers' Deposits, need never stop to think whether it will be able to supply the appropriate amount of silver (and copper) coin. The Bank has a free hand.

Curiously enough this system does not apply to the issue of that other form of small change which we call notes. The Bank of England allows the commercial banks to draw out or bring in notes, just as it allows them to draw out or bring in silver, as they please, the transaction always being one of exchanging Bankers' Deposits for notes or coin, or vice versa. But whereas when it pays out coin the Bank of England knows that there is the inexhaustible fount of the Royal Mint behind it, always ready to replenish an ebbing stock, in the case of notes there is (at least in form) no such inexhaustible fount. No Royal Mint sells notes to it on demand. Instead there is its own Issue Department which, unlike the Royal Mint, is not allowed to coin money without restriction. By the Currency and Bank Notes Act of 1954, certain restrictions are imposed on the Issue Department. The Issue Department is allowed to issue notes to the value, at the official market price, of the gold it holds; but the Bank in fact holds practically no gold, so that this provision is ineffective. The effective provision is that which allows the Bank to issue notes, 'unbacked' by gold, to the value of £1,575 millions, or whatever sum may be agreed upon by the Treasury on application by the Bank. Treasury permission to raise this Fiduciary Issue has, under present statutory regulations, to be notified to Parliament. At present (November 1966) the Fiduciary Issue is £2,950 millions. This means that the Bank Return shows in the Issue Department a total liability on Notes of £2,950 millions; of these, a small but varying part (£60m. on 9 November 1966) reappears as an asset in the Banking Department, while all the rest are 'in circulation'.

It is often said that the central bank should have a monopoly of the note-issue in the country which is its sphere of operations. The argument is based on the realization that the central bank must control the banking system by being the ultimate source of cash. If the other banks are free to provide themselves with cash by printing notes of their own, the central bank can be thwarted. This argument is perfectly sound provided that the notes of an individual bank are absolutely equivalent to other kinds of 'cash'. The less freely other cash can be replaced by commercial bank notes the less does it matter if the central bank has no monopoly.

The cash that originates in the central bank consists of its own notes and its deposit liabilities to the commercial banks (Bankers' Deposits in the Bank of England). If any commercial bank had the power to issue notes and its notes were absolutely interchangeable with the other kinds of cash, it would be free from all central-bank restraint on the expansion of its assets (and therefore its share of the total supply of bank money). Absolute interchangeability would imply readiness of the public, all over the country, to accept its notes as willingly as central-bank notes were accepted, and a willingness of other commercial banks to accept the notes of this commercial bank instead of its balances at the central bank in settlement of inter-bank indebtedness arising in the Clearing House. These are very serious qualifications. If they are not fulfilled the commercial bank that is expanding on the basis of its own note-issue will find its reserves of other cash (central-bank notes and deposits) being drained away by people and by banks who, having received payments in the commercial-bank notes, hasten to exchange them for the more widely acceptable forms of cash. A purely local bank, such as were most of the country banks of mid-nineteenth-century England, could clearly not regard its note-issue as freeing it from central-bank control. If it expanded too rapidly it would lose an essential part of its cash reserve.[1] It is not so easy to see what is to deter excessive issues by a number of commercial banks, all over the country, which keep in step with each other in their expansion, in the same way as, compelled by ebbs and flows of cash, they keep in step in any other expansion of deposits. What would then happen would be a decrease in the ratio of cash at the central bank (Bankers' Deposits) to deposit liabilities to the public all round. These reserves at the central bank are generally used for the settlement of Clearing House balances; but if the banks were equally willing to accept from each other payment in each other's notes (i.e. if commercial-bank notes were regarded by the commercial banks as precisely

---

[1] It may, however, be argued that some time may elapse between the damaging local expansion of credit and the cash drain which puts a stop to it. The question was keenly debated by many writers on English banking in the first half of the nineteenth century. A review of the controversy will be found in Viner, *Studies in the Theory of International Trade*, pp. 154–65, and in Wood, *English Theories of Central Banking Control 1819–58*; see also the examination of this question in Pressnell, *Country Banking in the Industrial Revolution*.

equivalent to deposits at the central bank) they could afford to allow their reserves at the central bank to decline relatively to their deposit liabilities. Difficulties for the central bank arising therefrom can be averted if law (or custom having almost the force of law) imposes a quite artificial distinction between deposits at the central bank and commercial-bank notes. This can be done by law or custom compelling the commercial banks to hold at the central bank balances equal to a certain percentage of their deposits plus notes. This is quite a common provision in modern banking codes, and where it exists the general argument against allowing commercial banks to issue notes breaks down.[1]

If there is any feeling that unrestricted note-issues of commercial banks undermine the authority of the central bank, the law can restrict the commercial banks' issues in such a way as to restrict to the central-bank issue all power of significant variation.[2] The commercial banks can be granted the right to issue up to certain maximum amounts —maxima which it is expected will always be approached at the seasonal peak. Then the commercial banks, though enjoying the income derived from these issues, are unable to engage in a policy contrary to the will of the central bank, for the latter, controlling the variable part of the issue, can make the *total* note-issue and total cash what it chooses. This compromise is attractive when the legislature is unwilling to transfer from the commercial banks to the central bank all the income derived from note-issues[3] but does not want to leave the central bank's powers subject to any handicap. The compromise was devised by Peel for the transitional period, following the Act of 1844,

---

[1] There remains some case against it in countries where banking is relatively undeveloped and where accordingly bank deposits are not the dominant part of the supply of money.

[2] Seasonal variations may quite harmlessly be allowed in commercial-bank issues.

[3] Notes are a possible source of income to the issuer, for he can issue them (like deposits) in exchange for earning assets.

during which the English country issues were gradually terminated, and more recently it was used in Canada. The compromise system remains the system regulating the note-issue in Scotland.

IV. *The Bank of England as Lender of Last Resort*

If the central bank is to control the monetary situation effectively, it must not only have power to issue cash in the form of notes when the public prefers this form, it must also have the unquestioned duty to create more cash when the public and the banks demand more liquidity and this demand threatens undesired disturbance of business activity. In more recognizable terms—the Bank of England must lend without stint in time of financial crisis. This duty to act as lender of last resort is highly relevant to central-banking control in that it lies at the root of the willingness of the commercial banks to work to a stable cash ratio. If the commercial banks had to provide for the extremities of panic demands for cash, they would feel it necessary to raise their cash ratios as soon as a cloud, however small, appeared on the financial horizon and, as danger became more threatening, they would attempt to raise their cash ratios further. Correspondingly, the growing confidence of quiet times would encourage them to reduce their cash ratios with benefit to their profits. If, on the other hand, they are always confident that the central bank will come to the rescue of all well-conducted institutions in time of stress, they will feel under no compulsion to raise their cash ratios when danger threatens. They will allow their cash ratios to settle down at the lowest level consistent with convenience and respectability. This level, once reached, leaves no room for squeezing under the impulses of optimisim, and the upshot is therefore a stable cash ratio adequate for the convenient transaction of business in the Clearing House and across the counter, and recognized as sufficient for public faith.

The position just described is the extreme one now reached in the English banking system, though elsewhere the cash ratio generally retains a greater or smaller degree of variability, to the embarrassment of the central bank.[1] The perfection attained in the English system is due primarily to the many decades through which the Bank of England has unreservedly accepted its obligation to lend freely in time of crisis, but it has also been helped by the unique structure of the discount market as a buffer between the central bank and the commercial banks.

Without going into the long and fascinating story of the Bank of England's evolution, we may say that the Bank came to accept its position of lender of last resort because, as a privileged corporation conducting the government's financial business, it could not stand idly by and see London's financial structure collapse in times of stress, and through bitter experience the Bank's governors learned that unstinted lending was the only remedy for such stress. The whole structure of credit depended upon the assumption that everybody entitled to cash did not demand cash at once, and the growing intricacies of London's financial structure served not to qualify this truth but only to underline it. Only by hesitant steps did the Bank recognize the implication that it must underpin the structure by acting as lender of last resort, and there were many backslidings. But a trio of severe crises in the middle of the nineteenth century saw the close of the Bank's novitiate, and after the last of them the case was put with final cogency by Walter Bagehot in his classical pamphlet, *Lombard Street*. Since Bagehot wrote, no one has ever seriously questioned the doctrine that in time of stress the Bank must lend, and lend without stint.

With the passage of time, this doctrine has become

---

[1] The embarrassment here mentioned is that referred to in the middle of the previous paragraph. Paradoxically, the extremity of the English system has led to embarrassment of a different kind. If the central bank can be relied upon to act *automatically* as lender of last resort, the limitation of cash reserves loses its effectiveness.

second nature to English bankers and its influence on their conduct, if not altogether conscious, has worked itself out to the full. But the process of refinement of central-banking tradition has been greatly helped by the position of the discount houses as intermediaries between the central bank and the commercial banks. The Bank must lend; but to whom? As the public draws cash from the ordinary banks, it is the cash reserves of the latter that call for reinforcement in times of crisis. The obvious borrowers at the central bank would therefore appear to be the commercial banks; and the laws of other countries usually provide explicitly for direct help to them. But traditionally bankers do not like borrowing from other bankers—it is thought a sign of weakness, and the grander titles given to the bankers at the central bank at first did little to modify this reluctance of commercial banks to come cap in hand to the central bank. This tradition accordingly in many countries, including the U.S.A., retarded the action of the lender of last resort and so hindered the development of satisfactory control by the central bank. London, on the other hand, has been free from this particular impediment (though its cousins have sometimes stalked round the corner). Between the Bank and the banks there has stood a small group of discount houses, holding readily negotiable assets on the basis of readily callable loans from the banks. The Bank of England could be called upon to lend to the discount houses, so enabling them to pay off the 'money at call' they ordinarily borrowed from the commercial banks. The additional cash needed by the banking system comes into existence as the Bank of England lends, and it is channelled into the reserves of the commercial banks by route of the discount houses. The commercial banks would not, in the old days, have liked to borrow at the Bank of England, but they were perfectly willing to call in money positively owed to them by the discount houses, and they could call with success because they knew that the discount houses could always get money from the Bank of England.

Reliance on the lender of last resort came more easily for being indirect; and it was London's unique institutional structure that allowed it to be indirect.

Because it is through the discount market that the Bank acts as lender of last resort to the banking system as a whole, the Bank's transactions with the discount houses are not treated as the ordinary business of its ordinary banking customers. They are governed instead by certain general rules applicable only to them and of cardinal importance to the Bank's function as a central bank. The bills brought to the Bank for rediscount or as collateral security must *either* bear two reputable British names, of which one must be the acceptor's, *or* they must be Treasury Bills. Their currency to maturity is generally limited to three months, and in ordinary circumstances the Bank takes only bills that are within a few weeks of maturity. Alternatively, the Bank of England stands ready to lend to discount houses on the security of those short bonds approved as proper for holding in the discount market.[1] As to the *rate of discount* or interest charged, there are two practices—the traditional Bank Rate practice and the simpler, less spectacular practice that has been common for some years now. The traditional system is for the discount houses to rediscount at the published Bank Rate (fixed every Thursday by the Court of Directors) or to obtain advances (ordinarily for seven days) at not less than Bank Rate.[2] This Bank Rate is normally above the discount rates ruling in the open market, so that whether the discount houses rediscount bills at the Bank or obtain

---

[1] As to which bonds are so approved, see p. 60 above. The normal practice is for the discount houses to bring Treasury Bills when they want assistance from the Bank of England, but it is essential to their business that the Bank would lend on bonds if required.

[2] Early in 1963 the Bank of England announced that it might sometimes charge for its Advances to discount houses rates in excess of Bank Rate. This device facilitates its efforts to keep Treasury Bill Rate close to Bank Rate, when the international monetary situation calls for a firm Treasury Bill Rate coincidentally with the desirability from the domestic viewpoint (as in 1963) of avoiding a rise in Bank Rate.

advances, the rate they have to pay (under this practice) is a 'penal rate' in the sense that it involves them in losses. The discount houses, being able to obtain money only at rates above those previously ruling in the market, push up the rates at which they would do new business. City commentators say that the market is 'in the Bank' (i.e. the discount houses are obtaining temporary help from the Bank) and that therefore market rates are firm. In 1965 the Bank gave 'lender of last resort' assistance in this manner on 49 days, and there was some market indebtedness, thus incurred, outstanding on 212 days.[1]

The alternative procedure may be described as that of the 'open back door'. While the practice of doing business at the front door is maintained, the Bank allows the discount houses, or the commercial banks directly,[2] temporary accommodation at the back door (i.e. through the Bank of England's own broker in the market) at a rate that does not disturb the level of market rates. This help 'at the back door' occurs on a large number of days during the year. The Bank's operator is always in touch with the market and sometimes intimates to the discount houses that they can tide over temporary stringency by bringing Treasury Bills to him. He will take the bills at the rate considered by the Bank to represent 'the market level'. When taking in bills (i.e. putting out cash) the Bank of England has special regard for dates in the early future when the Government will be releasing large sums of cash to the market, and the Bank tells the discount houses that it requires bills falling due for repayment on such a date. For example, on certain days in

---

[1] Since June 1966 the Bank, continuing to develop the flexibility of its control of the discount market, has sometimes made 'overnight loans' to the discount houses; generally these have been at Bank Rate, but occasionally somewhat lower rates have been charged.

[2] The newspaper reports of the daily conditions in the market describe direct transactions between the Bank of England and the commercial banks as '*in*direct help'. This is because the reporter is looking at the business from the point of view of the discount houses (whilst I look at it from the point of view of the cash reserves of the commercial banks).

January 1950, when the Bank had to give aid to the market, it called for bills maturing on 15 February, because on that date a large block of Exchequer Bonds fell due for repayment, and the more the authorities could (by taking in the Treasury Bills) reduce the other cash releases they would have to make on that date, the less would be the market disturbance when 15 February came round. In choosing its dates, the Bank likes to have very near dates (mostly within a month) so that the market tightness will soon recur, and the market will thus be kept 'on its toes' without further special action by the Bank of England. Now it so happens that Treasury Bills tend to be held early in their lives by the discount houses and then to be sold, as they approach maturity, to the commercial banks.[1] A large proportion of the bills near maturity is therefore generally in the hands of the commercial banks, and the dates demanded by the Bank of England when it aids the market may therefore appear only (in sufficient amount) on bills that are owned by the commercial banks. The Bank of England, hearing that the market is £2 millions short, may say, 'We will take £2 millions of Treasury Bills, maturing on 15 February' and hear that the discount houses have scarcely any such bills, having sold all of that date to the commercial banks two or three weeks earlier. In this circumstance the Bank of England buys the Treasury Bills directly from the commercial banks. The latter thereby have their cash reserves directly strengthened by £2 millions, and allow the discount houses that much more money overnight,[2] so allowing the latter to balance their books (i.e. pay off all loans called in). The discount houses, of

[1] This custom (the strict version of which is that the London clearing banks will not hold Treasury Bills in the first week of their lives) originated in the 1930's, when the banks came to a working agreement with the discount houses designed to protect the latter from being squeezed out of existence.

[2] In effect the banks, on selling bills directly to the Bank of England, cancel their 'calls' on the discount houses—the calls that occasioned the scarcity of funds now relieved by the Bank of England's purchase of bills.

course, carry no cash over, so the net effect of the operation is that the Bank of England has added £2 millions to the Bankers' Deposits in its own books—i.e. to the 'cash reserves' of the commercial banks. Owing to the Bank of England's preference for nearly mature Treasury Bills (of a convenient date) when it aids the market, the occasions when the suitable bills are in the hands of the commercial banks are very frequent, and this direct channel between the Bank of England and the cash reserves of the other banks is now very commonly used.

The Bank's operator is similarly ready to sell bills (to absorb a superabundance of cash in the market) at the ruling market rate, thus preventing temporary gluts of cash from unduly depressing market rates. The Bank, however, by choosing carefully the dates of the bills it takes in at other times, minimizes the occasions when it has to sell bills in this way. By these operations on either side of the market, the Bank can of course completely stabilize market rates if it chooses to do so. This was the position for some years before 1951, when it was as though the Bank kept at its back door an automatic machine with reversible action, from which Treasury Bills could be obtained for cash or cash for Treasury Bills at that fixed rate which the Bank wished to see prevailing in the market.

In order to illustrate the operation of the open-back-door machine, we shall consider what happens when an excess of government receipts over government disbursements causes a net transfer from the Bankers' Deposits (i.e. from the cash basis) to Public Deposits at the Bank of England. For this purpose we can ignore all other payments to and fro, which will actually be proceeding at the same time, and watch solely the effects of a net payment by members of the public to the Government. The individuals draw cheques, for say £25 millions, on their accounts with the commercial banks, the cheques being in favour of the Government. The Exchequer officials 'pay the cheques into the account' at the Bank of England. Public Deposits rise by £25 millions. The Bank of England now holds among its assets these cheques, claims against the commercial banks. It presents the cheques to them, taking at the same time £25 millions off their balances with it—Bankers' Deposits have decreased by £25 millions. The cash reserves of the commercial banks have fallen by £25 millions and their liabilities also fall by that amount, for they deduct the amounts of the various cheques from the balances (deposits) of the customers who have drawn them. At the outset suppose the position to have been:

POSITION I
(£ millions)
Bank of England Banking Department

Public Deposits	.	.	10	Government and Other		
Bankers' Deposits	.	.	240	Securities	. . .	255
Other Liabilities	.	.	55	Notes		50
			305			305

Commercial Banks

Deposits	.	. .	6,000	Cash in hand and at Bank		
				of England .	. .	480
				Earning Assets	. .	5,520
			6,000			6,000

Then, after government receipts have exceeded government disbursements by £25 millions, we have:

POSITION II
(£ millions)
Bank of England Banking Department

Public Deposits	.	.	35	Government and Other		
Bankers' Deposits	.	.	215	Securities	. . .	255
Other Liabilities	.	.	55	Notes		50
			305			305

Commercial Banks

Deposits	.	. .	5,975	Cash in hand and at Bank		
				of England .	. .	455
				Earning Assets	. .	5,520
			5,975			5,975

Notice that up to this point there has been no change at all in the assets of the Bank of England. The Bank has taken no positive action: a mere redistribution of its liabilities has occurred. As a result of this change, the commercial banks find that their cash ratio is slightly below the standard 8 per cent. and, in the absence of help from the Bank of England, they would proceed to contract their assets and a general process of monetary contraction would be set in train. As their cash is now £23 millions[1] below the level required for an 8 per cent. cash ratio, they call in the first instance for repayment by the discount houses of £23 millions of their 'Money at Call'. The discount houses, to obtain the cash wherewith to pay off the calls from the banks, sell Treasury Bills to the Bank of England. Selling the bills 'at the back door', the market gets its relief without disturbance of the prevailing level of rates. If it had been forced to 'the front door', obtaining relief there at the official Bank Rate, the dearness of accommodation would have given market rates a twist upwards.

The effect on balance-sheets is the same whether the back door or the front door is used. As the commercial banks call £23 millions from the discount houses, the latter sell Treasury Bills to the Bank of England, and we can imagine a momentary Position III in the Banking Department of the Bank of England, as follows:

(£ millions)

Public Deposits	. .	35	Government and Other		
Bankers' Deposits	. .	215	Securities .	. .	278
Other Liabilities (including			Notes .	. . .	50
Accounts of Discount					
Houses)	. . .	78			
		328			328

The Bank of England has taken £23 millions of Treasury Bills (so increasing its Government and Other Securities

---

[1] 23, not 25, because the drop of £25m. in their deposit liabilities reduces their cash requirement by 8 per cent. of £25m. (=£2m.).

from £255 to £278 millions) and has credited the discount houses with £23 millions in its books (so increasing its Other Liabilities from £55 to £78 millions). The discount houses then meet the calls of the commercial banks, by drawing on their accounts at the Bank of England cheques in favour of the commercial banks. The latter 'pay in' the cheques to the Bank of England (through the Clearing House) and the Bank credits the sums to Bankers' Deposits, debiting the Other Liabilities. We then have Position IV below.

The banks may then choose to restore their former proportion of Till Money to Cash at the Bank of England, and they can do this by paying in £1 million in Notes to the Bank of England. This refinement would leave their own balance-sheets unchanged, but would cause at the Bank of England a rise of £1 million in Bankers' Deposits and correspondingly in Notes held in the Banking Department.

POSITION IV
(£ millions)

Bank of England Banking Department

Public Deposits	35	Government and Other	
Bankers' Deposits	239	Securities	278
Other Liabilities	55	Notes	51
	329		329

Commercial Banks

Deposits	5,975	Cash in hand and at the Bank of England	478
		Earning Assets	5,497
	5,975		5,975

The action of the Bank of England in taking up Treasury Bills thus allows the commercial banks to maintain their conventional 8 per cent. cash ratio, and to distribute this cash between its two forms as they desire. And whether the Bank operates in the traditional way at Bank Rate or by the modern mechanism of the open back door, its action is entirely adequate to provide the banks with the cash necessary to support their deposit liabilities. Similarly, if the public draws out exceptionally large amounts in notes from the ordinary banks, the latter can rebuild their cash ratios to 8 per cent. by forcing the Bank of England, in its capacity as the ultimate source of cash, to take up more Treasury Bills. For any contingency this function of the Bank of England provides assurance of adequate cash for the conduct of business. The only difference (and it is an important one) between the two methods of relief (front door and back door) is that the operation of the Bank as lender of last resort causes a movement in short-interest rates, whereas the alternative method guarantees cash at the undisturbed market rate. Either way the Bank of England is the source of the cash and, by altering the rate of interest at which it operates, it can force a change in market rates if it so chooses.

v. *The Bank of England's Open-market Operations and their Effect on Bank Liquidity*

The Bank's traditional operation as lender of last resort arose out of its efforts to avert breakdown of the financial system but, as we have seen in the previous section, it was long ago extended to everyday management of the short-term rates of interest, and this management has led the Bank into continuous operation in the market for Treasury Bills. The implications of these operations for the discount market and for the short rates prevailing in that market have already been explained; we have now to turn to the further implications of these operations from the point of view of the banking system. For this purpose we have to look at *all* the open-market operations of the Bank of England, and not merely at the operations involved in daily management of the market in Treasury Bills. To understand this wider range of operations, it is necessary to look briefly at the complex of aims the Bank is pursuing. These aims are not easy to disentangle, and the priorities attached to them can change from time to time; but since the Bank explained this part of its work in considerable detail to the Radcliffe Committee, and allows some indications to emerge in its *Quarterly Bulletin*, it is possible to make the attempt.

1. The Bank seeks to protect the discount market and the banks from violent oscillation between stringency and glut of cash. This object derives from the Bank's traditional functions, but the growth in the size of movements between the public sector and the private sector have put a new complexion on it.

2. The Bank seeks a certain level of the Treasury Bill rates, primarily in the interest of influencing international short-term capital movements so as to maintain the gold and foreign exchange reserves at an adequate level.[1] The major weapon for this purpose is the fixing of Bank Rate, but market operations are necessary to keep the Treasury Bill rates in the desired relationship with Bank Rate. The relationship between Bank Rate and Treasury Bill rate is complicated by the fact that domestic considerations sometimes influence the level of Bank Rate, in a way they do not influence the desired level of the Treasury Bill rate.

3. The Bank seeks to influence the liquidity of the clearing banks. To this we shall return; for the moment, we may leave it with the general statement that the Bank, having regard to the 8 per cent. and the 28 per cent. liquidity conventions in the clearing banks, seeks to leave the banks neither under necessity to curtail lending to industry and trade with undesired abruptness (or, in some circumstances, to curtail at all) nor with such excess of liquid assets as would make future control difficult.

[1] In the 1960's the relevance of the Treasury Bill rate to the foreign exchange position has changed; this change and its implications are discussed in the Addendum to this Seventh Edition.

4. The Bank has to 'manage' the National Debt,[1] in the sense that it has to arrange issue and redemption of government securities, and the maturity distribution of the Debt, in such a way as to ensure that the Government can always meet its obligations (i.e. that there is always some 'holder', even if it is the Bank itself, for the entire Debt); to do all this, moreover, in such a way as to avoid an 'unnecessarily' high burden of interest rates and to avoid laying up extreme difficulties for the future management of the Debt.

5. The Bank encourages an upward or downward movement in long-term interest rates according to which direction it considers appropriate to the underlying investment/saving propensities in the economy. This has become an avowed objective only since 1957, and is probably still to be regarded as a subordinate aim.

It is well to emphasize the complexity of these aims, and the possibility of conflict between them. Sometimes it is said that the Bank has lost its control of the banking system because it lends in unlimited fashion to the Government, underwriting in effect unreasonably weak government financial policies. There is a grain of truth in this, in that the Bank has greater freedom to pursue other objectives (including the third, above) if its management of the Debt (the fourth aim, above) is not being complicated by additions to the total of the Debt, but even this is a simplification. It is much fairer to think of government financial policy as sometimes causing a shift in the priorities the Bank is able to attach to its various objectives. The list of objectives would obviously have a rather different complexion if Gladstonian views always ruled our Budgets;

---

[1] Throughout this Section capital letters are used for 'National Debt' (or shortly 'Debt') to denote reference to the National Debt in the legal sense. For the 'Radcliffe sense' (on which see p. 123 below) of national debt, capital letters are avoided.

it would equally have a different complexion if London ceased to be an international financial centre, or if violent fluctuations of industry and trade were tolerated, or if the National Debt were a mere trifle.

The operations in the discount market, explained in the previous section of this chapter, are governed exclusively by the first and second objectives (in effect, control of short-rates), and as nowadays conducted they deprive the 8 per cent. cash ratio of all importance as a controller of bank lending *outside the discount market*. In effect by always tending to over-issue Treasury Bills (which the discount houses undertake to buy on the understanding that the Bank of England will always help them out of difficulty) and then relieving the market stringencies at a rate of its own choice, the Bank of England lets the clearing banks have as much cash as they like (provided they can turn in Treasury Bills), and they are required by the convention to have cash equal to 8 per cent. of their deposits. The cash basis thus happens to be what it is because that is 8 per cent. of the level of deposits: deposits determine the cash basis, not vice versa. The effective restraint on the banks is in their holdings of Treasury Bills (plus discount market holdings): if their bills plus money-at-call were less than 22 per cent. of their deposits, they could not (consistently with maintenance of the 28 per cent. ratio) rebuild depleted cash to 8 per cent. by reducing their holdings of bills or their loans to the discount market. They would then be so short of liquidity that they would have to reduce their other assets (Investments and/or Advances). The effective controlling ratio is thus the 28 per cent. liquid assets ratio.

This is true only because the Bank of England chooses to keep the discount market steady at Treasury Bill rates of its own choice. If, when Treasury Bills were issued, it did not mind to what level bill rates rose, no doubt buyers could be found on a sufficient scale outside the discount market. The Bank of England (unlike the U.S.A. monetary authorities) does not believe that there is such a very elastic outside market for Treasury Bills, and it does not want the Treasury Bill rate to go sky-rocketing up and down. It wants a steady Treasury Bill rate of its own choice: and it wants this both in the interest of influencing the international demand for sterling and in the interest of its management of the markets in longer-term securities (in relation to management of the National Debt). It prefers these objects to any control of bank liquidity via control of the cash base, and is therefore driven to reliance on the liquid assets ratio of the clearing banks (the 28 per cent. ratio, as modified sometimes now by Special Deposits or other instruction from the Bank of England[1]) as the fulcrum of its influence on the general lending operations of the clearing banks.

For its third objective (liquidity of the clearing banks) the Bank is thus driven to open-market operations other than those in Treasury Bills; these other operations are in longer-dated government securities (i.e. any bonds longer than the 3-months' Treasury Bills). These operations are conducted through a different channel: whereas for the bill-market operations the Bank employs a small discount house as its agent, for all longer-term securities the Bank operates in the Stock Exchange, its operator there being the 'Government Broker'. Although a broker in the ordinary meaning of the London Stock Exchange, he naturally has a radically different position from others and his influence on the behaviour of the market is unparalleled.

When operating in these longer-term securities, the Bank has regard not only to its third objective (in the list above) but also to the fourth (management of the Debt) and the fifth (long-term interest rates). In fact, the management of the Debt is in a sense the primary objective of these operations; this is something it is forced to do by

---

[1] For Special Deposits see the concluding section of this chapter; for other modification of the 28 per cent. ratio, see p. 127 below.

the structure of the Debt and the passage of time, and it is perhaps fairer to say that the Bank is continually engaged in management of the Debt and that incidentally to this work it pays some regard to effects on the liquidity of the banks and to the bearing of long interest rates on the general economic situation. For operations for Debt management are virtually continuous and are both purchases and sales, in very large amounts, and it is only by a *net balance* of either purchases or sales that bank liquidity is affected, and rates of interest are unlikely to be affected unless the management operations are decidedly weighted one way or the other.

The Debt Management aspect arose historically from the Bank of England's responsibilities as the Government's banker. Two major wars in three decades were responsible for the issue of vast totals of government securities, some of which were for relatively short periods. To enable it to meet these Debt maturities and to provide part of the capital requirements of social services and industries brought into the public sector, the Government has to issue new bonds, on a huge scale, every year. As the Government's bank the Bank of England has to pay off the maturing bonds, and arrange the issue of new ones and receive payment for them. The sums involved are so large that effective issue and redemption on single dates, following the usual practice of the capital market, would be impossible, and both processes—of issue and redemption—have become merged into the daily market operations of the authorities. The old form of issue (with a 'prospectus') of blocks of securities, amounting to some hundreds of millions of pounds at a single date, continues; and so does the redemption of securities on a single 'maturity date' at which the Government has contracted to repay the capital sums. But both processes, of issue and redemption, have effectively become continuous operations. When a new issue of bonds is announced, only a small proportion is sold at once to ordinary investing institutions and members of the general public. All the rest goes to the Bank of England (Issue Department) which peddles the amount out gradually through the Stock Exchange, through the ensuing months and years. Similarly, when a security is approaching maturity the Bank buys the bonds gradually, through the Stock Exchange, until usually only a small proportion remains to be paid off on the formal maturity date. The government securities, both newly 'issued' and those old bonds which are nearing maturity, are held by the Bank of England, under the Bank Return heading 'Government Securities' in the Issue Department (see p. 84 above).

Because the lapse of time is always bringing maturity dates round, and is always making long-term securities rather shorter, the Government Broker is always 'buying-in' the next maturity (the bonds next due for redemption) and perhaps other near-maturity bonds as well, and is selling what he can of longer-dated bonds, including new issues, to replace them. This is a matter of 'rolling-over' the Debt, just to keep pace with time, and by itself could be entirely neutral in relation to the Bank's other objectives: the maturity-structure of an unchanged total debt could in theory be maintained absolutely unchanged. But given that there are other objectives, this is not the whole story. Even from the narrow point of view of Debt management, the Bank will want to keep gilt-edged stock in good repute as a steady investment, and will therefore want to preserve an 'orderly market', and will therefore sometimes buy more, and sometimes less, than it sells. Beyond this, it may want, either to ease Debt management in future or to facilitate the control of banking liquidity in future, to lengthen the average maturity of the debt (to replace short by long bonds); or it may want to replace Treasury Bills by medium-term or long bonds for the sake of reducing bank liquidity immediately; all these are called 'funding' operations.[1]

[1] When the Debt is being shortened—and particularly when Treasury

For any of these reasons the Government Broker may be either a net buyer of bonds or a net seller of bonds. Abstracting from the complications of an increasing *total* National Debt, the change in Private Sector holdings of bonds has to be compensated by a change in the issues of Treasury Bills: the Exchequer has to finance net purchases by the Government Broker by issuing more Treasury Bills, and in the contrary position net sales by the Government Broker allow the Exchequer to reduce the outstanding Treasury Bills. It is through these effects on the Treasury Bill issues that these longer-term market operations by the Bank of England affect the liquidity of the clearing banks. In the following schematic example, showing how this works, we shall avoid the complication of a change in the *total* of National Debt, and we shall also assume that the 'outside' demand for Treasury Bills remains constant, so that an addition to the Treasury Bills has to be absorbed by the banking system. We shall further ignore the to-ings and the fro-ings between the clearing banks and the discount houses, assuming that between them and the Bank of England there will be the necessary adjustments (on lines previously explained) to ensure that the clearing banks maintain their cash ratios at 8 per cent. We shall also assume that the Bank of England accounts for the operations in its 'Banking Department'. This is a simplification, for in fact the Bank holds its medium- and long-term securities mainly 'in the Issue Department'. A purchase of such securities 'by the Issue Department' (matching the Government Broker's sales to the public) can only be paid for by Treasury Bills being transferred from the Issue Department to the Banking Department, the latter in effect selling the Treasury Bills to the banks. We suppose that between *Position I* and *Position II* the outside public sells to the Government Broker a net balance of £100 millions of bonds, and that the Exchequer finances

Bills are increasing while long bonds are decreasing in total outstanding— the authorities are said to be 'unfunding'.

this by issuing £100 millions of additional Treasury Bills.[1]

POSITION I

(£ millions)

Bank of England Banking Department

Public Deposits	. . .	150	Government Securities		
Bankers' Deposits	. .	280	(Treasury Bills) . .	400	
Other Liabilities	. .	70	Other Securities . .	50	
			Notes	50	
		500		500	

Clearing Banks

Deposits	. . .	6,000	Cash in hand and at Bank of England 280+200 .	480	
			Bills and Money at Call .	1,200	
			Investments and Advances	4,320	
		6,000		6,000	

Liquid assets ratio: 28 per cent.

Then the public sells £100 millions of its holding of bonds to the Government Broker. The sellers receive cheques drawn on the Bank of England, and use them to add to their deposits at the banks; the banks present them to the Bank of England for payment. The cheques are met by transfer from Public Deposits at the Bank of England, to Bankers' Deposits, and so, for the moment, to the Cash Assets of the banks. So Position II is reached.

POSITION II

Bank of England Banking Department

Public Deposits	. .	50	Government Securities .	400	
Bankers' Deposits	. .	380	Other Securities . .	50	
Other Liabilities	. .	70	Notes	50	
		500		500	

---

[1] Our example is of a sale of bonds *by the public*. If the Government Broker instead buys the bonds from the clearing banks, much of the complexity of our example disappears. Bank deposits and Cash will remain unchanged, but in the clearing banks there will be a switch of £100m. from Investments to Bills, &c., implying a rise in the liquid assets ratio.

Clearing Banks

Deposits 6,000+100 = .	6,100	Cash 280+100+200 = .	580
		Bills and Money at Call .	1,200
		Investments and Advances	4,320
	6,100		6,100

The Cash ratio is now unnecessarily high, and the clearing banks will be willing (themselves or through the discount market) to take up nearly all of the £100 millions of Treasury Bills which the Exchequer proceeds to issue in order to rebuild its balance of Public Deposits at the Bank of England.[1] At first, the whole of the extra £100 millions of Treasury Bills will be taken up, in accordance with their regular undertaking, by the discount houses, but they will only be able to finance £92 millions of these by sale of the bills to, or by borrowing from, the clearing banks, because the clearing banks will require £8 millions (of the £100 millions they originally gained) in cash as the 8 per cent. against the additional £100 millions of deposits. The Bank of England will therefore, in support of the discount houses and of the 8 per cent. cash ratio, itself take £8 millions of the additional Treasury Bills. The effect is thus that, after Position II, Bankers' Deposits at the Bank of England are drawn down by £92 millions as the banks pay for additional Treasury Bills bought by themselves or the discount houses; Public Deposits rise by £100 millions, this being £92 millions transferred from Bankers' Deposits and £8 millions credited by the Bank of England in payment for the £8 millions Treasury Bills it has added to its own holding (in Government Securities on the other side of the balance sheet); the clearing banks' cash assets now are down by the £92 millions, and their bills and money-at-call are up by the £92 millions. Thus we have reached Position III:

[1] We have split the operation into two stages, for exposition; but in practice the Exchequer would not hold enough Public Deposits to allow reduction by £100m., and they would be maintained (at a very low level) by the issue of extra Treasury Bills simultaneously with our first stage.

POSITION III

Bank of England Banking Department

Public Deposits				Government Securities				
50+92+8 =	.	.	150	400+8 = .	.	.	408
Bankers' Deposits				Other Securities	.	.	50
380−92 =	.	.	288	Notes .	.	.	.	50
Other Liabilities	.	.	70				
			508				508

Clearing Banks

Deposits	.	.	.	6,100	Cash 288+200 = .	.	488
					Bills and Money at Call		
					1,200+92 = .	.	1,292
					Investments and Advances		4,320
				6,100			6,100

The cash ratio has now reverted to 8 per cent.[1] The big difference between Position I and Position III, apart from the £100 millions the public has added to bank deposits, is that the *Liquid assets ratio* of the clearing banks has gone up from the bare 28 per cent. of Position I to over 29 per cent. in Position III. Even this change, if it came in the February–March 'revenue season', would relieve the banks from the feeling that they had got to watch the Advances position very closely. If it came in the autumn, when they reckoned to have more like 31 or 32 per cent., a change from an actual 28 per cent. to over 29 per cent. would allow them to modify the very substantial measures (selling Investments and/or reducing Advances) they would be having to take.

Correspondingly, larger purchases of bonds by the Government Broker would add still more to the liquidity of the clearing banks; and by the opposite process, sales of bonds by the Government Broker, allowing the Exchequer to reduce its issues of Treasury Bills, would

---

[1] If the banks wish to hold more notes, now that they have more cash in total and more deposits, they will surrender, say, £4m. of Bankers' Deposits at the Bank of England for £4m. of the £50m. notes held by the Banking Department.

reduce the liquid assets ratio of the clearing banks. Further schematic illustration of the balance-sheet effects of these open-market operations is given in Appendix 2, in the context of the support given by such operations to a certain policy on long-term interest rates.

It may be supposed, from this analysis, that the Bank of England's power over the liquidity of the clearing banks is absolute: the Bank has only to instruct the Government Broker to operate on the necessary scale. This, however, is to ignore the constraints implicit in the other objectives of open-market operations. Most important of all, though it may be true that *at sufficiently attractive prices* there will always be buyers of bonds, the prices may be a long way down, implying such high levels of interest rates as are altogether inconsistent with the Government's other aims. Short of such extreme movements, it may not be possible to make any net sales, and the Government Broker often has, in the interest of (for example) orderly markets, to make net purchases even at a time when the authorities would have wished to reduce the liquidity of the banks. There is a close parallel here between the Bank's operations in the discount market and its operations in the bond market: in both markets, it cannot dictate *both* the amount of securities it can sell *and* the rate of interest (the price at which it sells). In the discount market, the Bank's stress on the desirability of steadiness in the Treasury Bill rate compromises its control over the cash base; in the bond market, the more it cares about the prices of bonds, the less control it has over the liquid assets basis of the clearing banks. Conflicts of this kind greatly embarrassed the authorities in the 1950's, and this was one element leading to unusual stress on quite different measures, as we shall see in the next section.

Because open-market operations have inevitably been greatly extended in the middle decades of this century, and because they are being used for such complex purposes, it is now widely appreciated that the management of the National Debt is an important function which must be completely integrated with other monetary measures. This is, however, more true than is often supposed, for in the contemporary English system almost everything the central bank does is management of the national debt, if we mean by 'national debt' all financial obligations of the State, held in the Private Sector. (This is the way the term is defined and used in the Radcliffe Report; hence references to 'national debt in the Radcliffe sense'.) Bankers' Deposits, Bank of England notes, Treasury Bills, and government bonds held outside the Government are all 'national debt' in this sense, and when the Bank of England trades in these, or fixes prices at which it is willing to trade, it is engaged in management of the national debt. This applies to operations in the discount market, the fixing of Bank Rate, operations in the bond market, and even some operations in the foreign-exchange markets. Hence the Radcliffe Committee's statement: 'It is not merely that monetary action and debt management interact so that they ought to be under one control: they are one and indivisible; debt management lies at the heart of monetary control. . . .' This is not a statement of universal validity, but it is certainly true of the contemporary English system.

VI. *Special Deposits and the Development of Moral Suasion*

The late 1950's and early 1960's saw some development of the Bank of England's methods of control. These developments arose from dissatisfaction with the operation of monetary policy during the fifties. From 1951 onwards there had been a new readiness to employ monetary weapons for contesting the inflationary elements in the British economy; in this changed atmosphere the authorities gradually became more venturesome, especially from 1955 onwards. The boom of 1955-7, the inflation scare of

1957 and the international short-term capital crisis of sterling in the summer of that year eventually drove the Bank of England to a severe 'credit squeeze' (instruction to the banks to reduce lending) and to unusually high short interest rates. Dissatisfaction with this experience, and particularly the desire to avoid over-working for comparatively long periods the weapon of moral suasion (on which the credit squeeze rested) led the Bank of England at last to modify its unwillingness to adopt the method of variation of reserve ratios. This, in the form of a power to call for 'Special Deposits' from the commercial banks, was announced in 1958 and the power was exercised for the first time in 1960.

The new system is based on the existence of the conventionally required ratios of a fixed 8 per cent. cash and a minimum of 28 per cent. liquid assets including cash. The essence of the plan is that, in addition to the 28 per cent. of liquid assets, the banks may be called upon to hold additional balances (the Special Deposits) at the Bank of England, beyond the Bankers' Deposits required to make the 8 per cent. The Special Deposits called for are announced, like an ordinary change in Bank Rate, after the Court of Directors has held its Thursday meeting. The announcement is of a percentage requirement, this being a percentage of the gross deposits of the banks concerned. Having announced the percentage, and the date when it is to become operative (for an increase in the percentage, a little notice is given), the Bank of England notifies each bank of the precise amount it has to deposit; this is taken from the Wednesday figures of the banks, and is adjusted monthly to allow for gains and losses of deposits by individual banks.

The banks concerned have been the eleven London Clearing banks and the five Scottish banks. The inclusion of the Scottish banks is anomalous, in that they are not bound by the liquidity rules which the Bank of England requires the clearing banks to observe. They were, however,

included in the credit squeezes of the fifties, and it therefore seemed equitable to include them in a plan that
was in a sense designed to replace credit squeezes, or at
any rate to avoid squeezes of such severity and prolonga-
tion. However, the Scottish banks have not suffered the
full rigour of the Special Deposits system, for the percentage calls on them have been only half the percentages
applied to the English banks. This difference has not been
explained; possibly it is based on recognition of the fact
that the Scottish banks have rather more of the element
of savings bank business, and have held rather higher
proportions of government bonds.

The banks receive interest on Special Deposits at the
multiple of 1/16 per cent. nearest to the average Treasury
Bill rate at the weekly tender of the preceding week. In
effect, therefore, the Special Deposit is an additional non-
negotiable Treasury Bill, and a call for Special Deposits,
just like an issue of Treasury Bills or the proceeds of
taxation, is used for financing the Government. When
Special Deposits are repaid, the Government has to sell
more Treasury Bills outside the Bank of England.

The range of Special Deposits in the period 1960–66 has
been from 1 to 3 per cent. and down to zero, for the English banks. These are small figures when seen in relation
to the investments ratios, which were running between
11 and 20 per cent. in the same period. The investments
are now, it will be recalled, the effective cushion protecting
the advances from any pressure resulting from closeness
of the liquid assets to the required minimum. It was therefore possible, when the Special Deposits were called, for
the banks simply to hold less government bonds (under
'Investments'), avoiding any reduction of bank advances.
Whether the penalty suffered by selling government bonds
was serious, having regard to the high yield of bank advances, depended upon the extent to which the authorities
were prepared to let the gilt-edged market fall. The new
weapon was thus in itself meaningless, but it could be

made an important deterrent to lending by the banks if the authorities were prepared to allow a steep rise in interest rates or to call for altogether higher percentages of Special Deposits. In 1960, when the weapon was first used, neither of these conditions was met, and the operation could be regarded as no more than a warning of what could be done.

When further calls were made in 1961, the banks had somewhat smaller cushions of investments (14 per cent. against 20 on the earlier occasion) but they were still substantial. On this occasion the authorities forced interest rates up a little more than on the earlier occasion, but not much. By itself once more the new weapon would have meant little, but on this second occasion the banks were told by the Bank of England that the adjustment in their assets was to be made by reducing advances rather than investments, and they were told the broad lines on which they were to curtail lending to customers. The operative factor on this occasion was thus not the Special Deposits call, but the direct instruction to the banks. The weapon, that is to say, was the moral suasion on which the Bank of England had relied so heavily ever since 1945. The Special Deposits system, as so far exercised, remains like the power of statutory Direction under the 1946 Act: it is a threatening gesture whereby the Bank of England can ensure that the commercial banks take notice of the 'requests' made to them.

This regard for the Special Deposits system as a signal, rather than in itself an effective weapon, was underlined by the strange way in which the Bank of England handled the situation early in 1961. As a result of various circumstances, including successful funding operations, the liquid assets of the clearing banks were unusually close to the required minimum. The authorities did not at that moment want to force the banks either to restrict advances or to unload bonds. They could have met the situation by repaying Special Deposits, but this would have needed a public announcement, which could have been interpreted as an encouragement to an expansion such as was not then desired by the authorities. They were able to avoid this by taking advantage of the initiation of the export credits refinancing scheme (see p. 194) to widen the definition of liquid assets allowed to count towards the 30 per cent. then required. Thus pressure on the banks was avoided, and so also was the parade of a change in Special Deposits. Clearly it is for announcement effect rather than for effects on the balance-sheets of the commercial banks that the authorities choose to use the Special Deposits plan.

Similarly announcements of reductions in Special Deposits were used early in 1963 to encourage the general public and the business world to expand commitments, in order to counter the deflationary tendencies then evident. There was also at that time, however, some evidence of real concern on the part of the authorities lest the banks should feel short of liquid assets, for they openly acquiesced in falls of liquid assets ratios below the 30 per cent. level. It has certainly begun to look as though the Bank of England is moving towards a more flexible system of liquidity controls.

Major reliance continues, however, to be placed on the weapon of moral suasion: what really matters, at each critical juncture, is what the Bank of England tells the financial institutions to do, and what is announced to the public. In some ways the British authorities seem to be relying on this weapon more than ever before. Particularly it has been noticeable that at each new step, in the struggle against inflation and against crises in the balance of payments, the Bank of England has extended more widely the circle of financial intermediaries to which instructions ('requests') are issued. Insurance companies, merchant bankers, 'industrial bankers', and hire-purchase finance companies are all nowadays regarded as proper recipients of 'requests'. The Radcliffe Committee assumed that such requests would sooner or later have to be underpinned by statutory powers, and was fearful of the difficulties of any statutory regulation. The authorities have not lost much time in showing that in this the Radcliffe Committee was too timid: the British financial intermediaries, over a wide range, can in fact be given instructions by the Bank of England, and these instructions can continue for considerable periods without any statutory basis.[1]

The post-war period has seen a great extension of use of moral suasion in other countries as well as Britain. The more extreme cases have always been in the small countries—Switzerland and Norway are the clearest examples —and this for the good reason that the dominant financial institutions in these countries can be fairly easily brought together. This holds true of Britain too, in contrast to the United States (see Chapter 11). Where—as most obviously in the City of London—all the important people in the world of finance work and live in close proximity to each other, the views of the monetary authorities are likely to find sympathetic response among the people who run the banks and other financial businesses. In such circumstances there is great advantage in the weapon of moral suasion: it can even be called a 'gentlemen's agreement'. In many ways action can be more flexible: the institutions involved can be called in without being legally defined, the administrative limits to a control can be dictated by convenience instead of statutory specification, and the control can more easily be switched on and off as required, instead of awaiting some legislative process. Especially, as the Bank of England has demonstrated, the authorities can change their minds about who must be brought in, without having to seek a change in statutory powers.

This flexibility of moral suasion particularly suits the kind of monetary policy pursued by Britain in the early sixties. Given the view—shared by the bankers and their

---

[1] For important developments in control by the Bank of England in 1963–66, see the Addendum to this Seventh Edition.

customers—that the bank advance is not merely the most flexible financial instrument but also that the good customer is almost as entitled to overdraw as he is to draw down a credit balance and, given the political commitment to full employment, the authorities have to avoid monetary controls that might be very abrupt and sharp in their action. Flexible controls that can be bent in one direction rather than another are much more in keeping with general ideas about economic policy. So moral suasion is in fashion. But it is a weapon that draws much of its substance from the knowledge that other and sharper weapons exist, and these other weapons can still be useful for their announcement effects.

6

EXTERNAL TRANSACTIONS AND THE BANKING SYSTEM

1. *External Payments and Receipts*

DURING the last four chapters we have largely ignored the outside world and have tacitly assumed that banking transactions are confined to one country. We have assumed that bank deposits are transferred from one person to another, in final settlement of debts, and that the recipients are content to hold the transferred deposits, unless for convenience in making small payments they choose to have 'cash', into which the deposits are readily exchangeable. All this is valid enough if the recipients and the payers are people living and transacting their business all within the confines of one country. In fact many transactions fall beyond these limits. Goods are 'imported' and 'exported'. Travellers move from one country to another, both on business and on holiday, and they find it necessary to make payments in moneys that are 'foreign' to their own—payments that cannot be made by the simple process of drawing on one's bank balance. Shipping overseas brings receipts to the great maritime nations, and occasions payment by others—receipts and payments not in a single currency equally acceptable to debtor and creditor. Other services rendered by the nationals of one country to those of another also occasion external payments—as those made in the shape of film royalties on American films shown to British audiences. Emigrants often want to transfer their personal savings— amounts in one currency—to the currency of the country to which they are going; then in later years they sometimes send financial help back to elderly or youthful relatives left in the home country. International capital movements form another very large group of these 'external transactions': an American firm constructing a pipe-line in the Middle East, for example, has to incur a large expenditure in the Middle Eastern country. An intergovernmental loan, unless required expressly for buying goods in the lending country, also involves ultimate payment to the borrower of money different from that which circulates in the lender's country. Interest charges on and repayment of former foreign loans, and dividends to foreign shareholders in a company, all involve payments to people who will not readily accept either the bank deposits or the cash that circulates in the payer's own country.

The purpose of this chapter is to consider how these 'external transactions' are accommodated by the banking system and how the banking position in a country is affected by them. The very important questions relating to the volume and composition of these transactions, and to their variation from time to time, lie beyond the scope of this book: they may be studied in works devoted to this part of economics, which is called 'the theory of international trade'. Here we simply take it for granted that such transactions are continually arising and that payments have to be made in settlement of them; and we have to consider just how the banking system accommodates these payments. The word 'accommodates' is particularly appropriate, for it is by an extension, a stretching, of the ordinary banking facilities available for internal payments, that a very large proportion of these transactions are conveniently settled. It is possible to imagine two countries with simple metallic monetary systems, between which all trading is settled by payment in a monetary metal (e.g. gold) which could be made up by local mints into the money of the one or the other. Again it is possible to imagine two countries with banking systems entirely independent of each other (i.e. not accepting credits with each other), and here also all external transactions would have to be settled by payment in some such medium as gold which could, according to the monetary laws of the two countries, be manufactured into local 'cash'. In either of these cases, there being no 'accommodation' by the banking system, a description of the banking system would not need to take special account of external transactions, since these could affect the banking system only via their effects on the cash position.

The extent to which banking systems accommodate external transactions varies from country to country, according to the strength and diffusion of the overseas ties of its banking system. The overseas ties of the English banking system are stronger and more widely spread than those of any other; the complexity of the methods of settling its external transactions is therefore extreme. It is this most complex case of the English system that will be outlined here—not described in its full complexity but in its main elements. The reader who has mastered the general principles of the complex English case will have no difficulty in understanding for himself the simpler states of affairs that exist elsewhere.

When an English debtor has to make a payment to an external[1] creditor, he will be required to pay either in sterling (English money) or in foreign money (e.g. by credit in some foreign bank). If payment is made in sterling, the foreign creditor will ordinarily not want to hold the English money (a balance in an ordinary English bank) since his own liabilities are in the main in terms of his own money. The foreign creditor will therefore, in general, *sell* his sterling to his own bank in his own country—this local bank will give him, in exchange for his claim on a London bank, a balance at his home town branch. The Bank of Western Barataria, instead of Mr. English Debtor, will

---

[1] I use at this point the word 'external' to include both overseas British countries and those ordinarily called 'foreign'. In general it is convenient to use the word 'foreign' in the connotation it has in the term 'foreign trade'—i.e. to *in*clude overseas British (Dominion, colonial, &c.) territories; and this practice is followed in the remainder of the chapter.

then have a balance of $£x$ with the Midland Bank in London; and against this increase in its assets, the Bank of Western Barataria will have a new liability, equivalent to $£x$, in the shape of Mr. Foreign Creditor's deposit balance in Jumbly-Crumbly, a provincial city in the west of Barataria. All that has happened in the English banking system will be that in the Midland Bank $£x$ of deposits are due to the Western Bank of Barataria instead of being due to Mr. English Debtor. The total purchasing power at the disposal of Englishmen is down by $£x$; but the total deposit liabilities of the English banks, their cash position, and the position of the Bank of England are all unchanged. If the Bank of Western Barataria has its own office in London, or prefers to bank with some bank other than the Midland, the Midland will lose $£x$ in cash and $£x$ in deposits to that other bank; the Bank of England will owe $£x$ less (in Bankers' Deposits) to the Midland and $£x$ more to the other bank.

Further developments depend upon whether Barataria is inside or outside the *Sterling Area*. If Barataria is inside the Sterling Area, the British authorities will not have bothered to inquire into the transaction; but if it is outside, the whole transaction will have been subject to the Foreign Exchange Control whose permission will have been required for the original transaction and who will be very particular as to the precise manner in which payment is made. The difference between the two classes of transactions—those within the Sterling Area and those going outside it—is so great that many people will think only of the latter as 'foreign exchange transactions'. There is, indeed, some sense in this way of looking at it, for the essence of the Sterling Area is that London acts as banker for the whole of it and English money ('sterling') is freely used for payments from one part of the Area to another (though not for all payments throughout the Area). The closeness of the connexion between the monetary systems of the various parts of the Sterling Area—the banker-and-customer relationship—lies at the root of the Foreign Exchange Control's lack of concern about transactions within the Area; and, if we are to understand the banking situation that makes this possible, we must give the nature of the Sterling Area and its foundation some particular attention.

II. *The Sterling Area*

The Sterling Area is a collection of countries associated not by any formal arrangements nor as the result of any conscious design: it 'just growed'. It is not confined to the British Commonwealth and it has varied in extent. Just now it happens to be almost limited to Commonwealth countries (Canada is outside) though in the past it has quite clearly included other countries such as Argentina and Denmark. It comprises all those countries *between* which payments are freely made in sterling and which therefore look to London as their banker. The payments are all those passing between the countries—those made by traders and tourists, by bankers themselves (in settlement, for instance, of capital transactions) and occasionally by governments.

Inside a country the usefulness of bank deposits for making payments from one individual to another and the loan facilities offered by bankers cause the development of the banking habit. As the banking habit develops, people get into the way of holding bank balances. In precisely the same way the usefulness of sterling for making international payments causes countries outside Britain to hold London balances—money in London to be used as a working balance. When I say 'countries . . . hold London balances' I mean not necessarily that governments hold London balances (this is exceptional) but that banks (especially central banks), whose main business is elsewhere, keep balances in London. Among the banks operating in this manner are many established as English companies and having their Head Offices in London. These are the 'British overseas banks' whose formation became rapid from the eighteen-sixties onwards. They have most, if not all, of their branches overseas, and their principal business is centred in their overseas branches and particularly between their overseas branches and London. While their most profitable assets are their loans and advances to overseas customers, they hold their main reserves of cash and other liquid assets in London.

Some other 'overseas banks' have their Head Offices as well as most of their branches overseas, but have branches in London. Some of the Australian banks, for example, are organized in this way while others have their Head Offices in London. Although sometimes the London office is only a branch, it is a very important branch, playing a vital part in facilitating the international transactions of its customers, and holding cash and other liquid assets in London. These London assets are vital to the financing of their international transactions.

Almost all of the other countries of the Sterling Area (i.e. countries other than England—the area that official circles have come to label 'R.S.A.'—Rest of the Sterling Area) have their own central banks. These central banks generally, for purposes of control in their own countries, take over from the commercial banks the 'variable' part of the London liquid assets. Working balances in London are held by the overseas commercial banks; but the London 'reserves' are held by the central banks.

These London balances of the other Sterling Area countries are the international reserves of these countries —their reserves against excesses of external spending over external receipts, just as an individual's bank balance is his reserve against a temporary excess of spending over receipts. For reasons that will emerge later the 'R.S.A. countries' do not usually hold any other international reserves. The 'London balances' consist of cash (mainly deposits at the Bank of England, and a small amount of notes, &c., as till money), short loans to discount houses, Treasury Bills, and sometimes other bills that can be readily discounted in the London market.[1] A country with large London balances ordinarily has these balances largely concentrated in the ownership of its own central bank, only relatively small 'working balances' being left in the ownership of those commercial banks which have offices or agents in London. Much the greatest part of the central bank's balance is (it is understood) held in the form of Treasury Bills,[2] the remainder being held in the form of an ordinary deposit balance at the Bank of England. The immediate impact of a payment made in London by another country of the Sterling Area is therefore a transfer of cash (balance at the Bank of England) from a commercial bank or central bank of that country to some other bank's account at the Bank of England, but a substantial and continuing net payment to be made in London will occasion a running-down of the amount of U.K. Treasury Bills held by the central bank of the country concerned.

The essence of the Sterling Area is thus that London is banker to a large number of other countries. Payments between one part of the Area and another are made by transferring claims in London (just as an ordinary private debt is settled by a cheque which transfers a claim against a bank). And, for the sake of convenience in meeting variations of payments and receipts, the countries in the Sterling Area hold their working balances in London, just as you and I hold working balances in ordinary bank deposits. Every other feature of the Sterling Area derives from this

---

[1] Some countries' banks or other monetary authorities hold, in addition to the liquid sterling assets of the classes mentioned, some highly marketable British Government securities. They do not ordinarily reckon to use these for meeting variations in the balance of payments, but hold them in reserve. Reserves exist, however, to be used, and from London's point of view these securities have to be regarded as part of the liabilities which London may be called upon to meet.

[2] Each week the Bank of England, on behalf of these other central banks of the Sterling Area, takes up new Treasury Bills to replace those maturing.

fundamental point that London is banker to the whole Area.

The foundations upon which this extraordinary phenomenon rests are worth some attention, if we are to understand readily the functions of London as banker to the whole Sterling Area.[1] London's financial position had its roots in London's position as the leading centre of world trade during the nineteenth century, and in London's position as a great and successful international lender. London became an international financial centre because *sterling was always useful* and *sterling was always obtainable*. An ordinary banking account is something that everybody wants because it is always useful and always obtainable. People use banks because they find that cheques on their banks are acceptable to their creditors and because they can always get bank balances by selling goods or services to other people or even by borrowing from the bank. And so it has been historically with sterling as an international currency. In the nineteenth century sterling was always useful—it could be used for buying goods in England, which was the world's greatest market; it could be used for paying interest on English loans; and it could be used for the employment of English ships to carry goods anywhere in the world. Secondly, sterling was always obtainable: it could be obtained by selling goods in England— the English market had a great appetite for the food and raw materials that other countries were producing for export. Also, sterling could be obtained by borrowing in London: a country that wanted more sterling to spend could almost always obtain long-term capital in the London market and, even when long-term loans were temporarily unobtainable, the crisis could be tided over by getting short-term accommodation in London. As the Bank of England came, by fits and starts, to recognize its position

[1] The following passage owes much to the stimulating discussion of 'Sterling as an International Currency' by Professor B. Tew in the *Economic Record*, June 1948.

as lender of last resort, it became true that money could always be borrowed in London at a price. This price might occasionally be very high, but at some price sterling was always obtainable, and an expensive short-term loan could be replaced by a cheaper long-term loan as soon as London money-market conditions eased.

London could not have gone on lending to other countries year after year and decade after decade if her position as leader in the Industrial Revolution, followed by the development of cheap food production in the outside world, had not given her an inherently strong balance of payments throughout the period of London's rise as an international financial centre. The hold of sterling as an international currency tightened partly because in those days London could afford to lend abroad.

But it was not merely a matter of being able to lend abroad. There were attractive opportunities in the opening-up (especially by railway and harbour construction) of the great new food and raw material lands of the world. And London went on lending because the borrowers on the whole met their obligations—as they could afford to while England provided such a good market for their produce. As, with the aid of English capital, their production of food and raw materials expanded, their sales in the English and other markets expanded and enabled them to pay their debts.

It is important to realize how well England's potentialities as an exporter of capital fitted in with the fundamental trading position of the nineteenth-century world. England could produce the goods and the finance that other countries wanted, and England wanted the food and other goods that other countries were being developed to produce. This was the peculiar combination of basic facts that gave strength to London as an international financial centre. At the right time her own monetary institutions were being shaped in a helpful way. Adherence to the gold standard was an important secondary point; but the really fundamental conditions were that, due to the trading and lending position, *sterling was always useful and sterling was always available*.

In the light of these historical foundations, we can now go a little farther into the geographical shaping of the Area and the services that the countries in the Area came to expect London as their banker to provide. The extent of the Sterling Area was determined simply by the dictates of convenience. Sterling had become an international currency, used not only for transactions between England and overseas but also for transactions that never touched England (or even English traders) at all. But although everybody was apt to use sterling, no one was under compulsion to do so—there were no international agreements regulating its use. Consequently, some people used it more than others. Those who used it most were, naturally, those who had the closest business relations with England— those most dependent on England as a source of goods, those most dependent on the English market as an outlet for exports, and especially those wanting to borrow in London and those having sterling obligations to meet as the result of former borrowing. Such were the traders, the bankers, and the governments of the British colonies and Dominions, South America, and to a less extent many other countries. The variation in the closeness of economic relations with England was reflected in a variation in the extent to which they used sterling and held their international reserves in sterling. One circumstance making for wide extension of the Sterling Area was the fact that throughout the formative period sterling was interchangeable with gold at a fixed rate (i.e. sterling was on a gold standard)—making sterling even more useful, and as sterling balances could earn interest while gold was 'barren', the commercial bankers who were (more often than not) responsible for arranging these matters had an inducement to hold sterling rather than gold for reserve purposes.

Gold was useful because in the last resort it could be

used for settling debts outside the Sterling Area. However, it was not only gold that could be obtained in London, but also (and much more usefully) the money of any country in the world. London had the greatest foreign exchange market in the world—any currency could always be bought or sold at the keenest price in London. Consequently, anyone in the Sterling Area having to make a payment to someone outside the Area—to an American exporter, for example—could use a London balance for purchasing in London the foreign currency which the American exporter required. The debtor might be an English importer, who would buy U.S. dollars through his own London bank. Or he might be an Australian importer, who would ask his bank in Australia to obtain dollars: the Australian bank would then use some of its London balance to buy U.S. dollars in London. Thus the London Foreign Exchange Market came to cope with the foreign-exchange requirements not only of England but also of all other countries in the Sterling Area.

Correspondingly, a payment received in U.S. dollars (say from an American importer) would be settled in London, no matter where in the Sterling Area the receiver lived. The dollars would be sold in London by the receiver's bank, whether this were an English or an Australian bank, the Bank of Iceland, or any other bank in the Sterling Area. Thus all the foreign-exchange receipts of the Sterling Area came to flow naturally into London, and all foreign-exchange requirements of the Sterling Area would fall on London and be bought by the use of the London balances of the Sterling Area countries. It follows that what matters most directly to those responsible for London's foreign-exchange reserves is the balance of payments not of England alone but of the Sterling Area as a whole. England may be earning more 'foreign exchange' than she is spending, and yet be losing 'foreign-exchange reserves' because the rest of the Sterling Area has a heavily adverse balance with the outside world. When this is happening, the Sterling Area countries will be drawing heavily on their London balances—the total of English Treasury Bills they own will be falling sharply. Alternatively, English reserves of foreign exchange may be untouched while she has a heavily adverse balance of payments, for the Sterling Area as a whole may be earning as much as it is spending in the outside world. England will then be paying for its adverse balance by adding to its debts to the other Sterling Area countries; the latter will find that their London balances are rising.

The hypothetical case just stated in fact roughly describes what was happening during part of the Second World War. The net needs of the Sterling Area as a whole, for the currencies of outside countries (largely U.S. and Canadian dollars), were being taken care of broadly by the American and Canadian aid programmes and by British sales of securities in the United States, so that the relatively meagre reserves of gold and dollars held by the British authorities were not falling. But the other Sterling Area countries had huge surpluses of earnings and thus accumulated large London balances. These altogether abnormal London balances, which the owning countries wanted to turn into useful goods (often American goods) as rapidly as possible, were a source of strain in the Sterling Area in the early years after the war. Their abnormality originated in the abnormal war-time balances of international payments, but the mode of accumulation was perfectly normal: the 'sterling balances' grew through the normal functioning of the banking mechanism of the Sterling Area.

The fact that all the external transactions of Sterling Area countries (including their transactions with each other inside the Area, as well as those with countries outside it) are performed through London gives importance to the question of rates of exchange between the various currencies (Indian rupees, Australian pounds, &c.) and the London pound ('the pound sterling'). The Sterling

Area grew up in a world in which there was considerable stability in these rates of exchange, and it is sometimes suggested that there is a necessary fixity in these exchange rates. This is not the case; but there are strong forces making for such rigidity. The closeness of trading relations implies that import and export prices are, to the denizens of the importing and exporting country, likely to have most stability if there is also stability in the exchange rate between England (the principal market) and that country. Similarly with capital transactions: a country with interest and repayment obligations fixed in sterling will be making difficulties for itself if it drops the rate at which its own currency exchanges for sterling. Again, as for convenience the reserves are in London funds (sterling claims), the reserves maintain fixed values in local currencies only if the exchange rate on London is fixed. So, though there is no absolute fixity, there is a good deal of stability in exchange rates between the various currencies within the Sterling Area, and this has held good even at times such as the early nineteen-twenties and the early nineteen-thirties when there was great instability outside the Area.

As for the exchange rates between the Sterling Area countries and the outside world, this is (given the general stability within the Area) essentially a question of the rates between sterling itself and the outside currencies. If the sterling–dollar rate moves, it takes all or most of the Sterling Area currencies with it, because their convenience lies in stability in terms of sterling rather than stability in terms of dollars or other outside currencies.[1] Variations of this kind—variations of the 'master-rate' linking all sterling

[1] In September 1949, for example, all moved together except the Pakistan rupee, which retained its lonely eminence largely because the circumstances of her international trading position at the moment made stability of her prices in terms of U.S. dollars peculiarly attractive. But the consequent rupture of her exchange rate with her immediate Sterling Area neighbour (India) posed some awkward problems for Pakistan, and it was not very long before the Pakistan rupee was devalued.

currencies with those of the outside world—were considerable in the early nineteen-twenties and again in the early
nineteen-thirties, and experience then showed that these
variations are compatible with the continued existence of
the Sterling Area. But such variation does make sterling
rather less usable, and this is especially important to countries that also have big transactions with another currency.
The outstanding example of the latter countries is Canada,
whose close trading and financial connexions with the
U.S.A. led her to wobble away from the Sterling Area in
the period of sterling instability in the early nineteen-
twenties, and to leave the Area completely in the nineteen-
thirties. Variation of sterling rates in important outside
currencies is damaging to the 'fringe' countries of the Sterling Area, and therefore tends to narrow its boundaries.

Similarly, restrictions on the convertibility of sterling
tended, in the years between 1939 and 1959 when these
restrictions were severe, to drive out fringe countries,
because it reduced the usefulness of sterling. The clearest
case of this is provided by the behaviour of the Argentine
in the twenty years after 1930. Through the nineteen-
thirties, although the Argentine had growing trade and
financial relations with the U.S.A. and although the
sterling–dollar rate varied, the Argentine remained more
or less within the Sterling Area. But during the nineteen-
forties sterling became convertible into dollars only by
special arrangements that had to be negotiated between
governments, and it became less useful for buying goods
from Britain. When the Argentine found that she could
use her sterling neither for buying British locomotives nor
for buying dollars that could be spent on American locomotives, she decided not to take sterling with her old
readiness—that is to say, she left the Sterling Area.

The foreign-exchange troubles of the last fifty years
have thus tended to narrow the Sterling Area. Just as its
early strength was derived from Britain's strong balance
of trade and her position as a lender to countries whom

she helped to develop into good payers, so the chronic weakness of the balance of trade in the decades after 1925 undermined the foundations of the Sterling Area. First the variability of the exchange rates between sterling and the outside world and then the restriction of sterling's convertibility encouraged the 'fringe' countries to break away, so that the Area now consists of less than the Commonwealth. But it remains the largest area in the world free from internal payment restrictions. The outliers of London banking bring to the London money-market the net adjustments of all the external transactions of the countries within the Area; and no account of English banking can be complete without some reference to the impact on London of these transactions.

III. *Transactions outside the Sterling Area: the Exchange Equalization Account*

Transactions between people in the United Kingdom and people in countries outside the Sterling Area can be settled only through the mechanism of the foreign exchange market. This is obvious enough when English goods are sold for, say, French francs: the English supplier does not want the francs, but sterling, and he will ask his bank to sell the francs. But it is equally true if goods exported from England are invoiced in sterling (as they often are), for in this case the French importer will sell francs in order to get the sterling with which he can settle the account. Similarly, French exports to England give rise to a demand for francs: either the goods are invoiced in francs, and the English importer has to buy francs in order to make the payment, or, if the invoice is in sterling, the French exporter wants francs in exchange for the sterling with which he is paid. All these transactions in 'foreign currencies' are subject to the Foreign Exchange Control, a statutory control exercised by the Bank of England in conjunction with the Treasury. This control restricts the purposes for which foreign currencies may be bought by United Kingdom residents, and restricts disposal of the foreign currencies which come into the possession of residents (e.g. as a result of the export of goods).

The Exchange Control does not itself supply the foreign currencies demanded, or buy the currencies which come into the hands of U.K. residents. To obtain foreign currency, or to dispose of it, the resident has to go to an 'authorized dealer'—a bank authorized by the Control. These authorized dealers are able to cover the great bulk of their customers' requirements by 'marrying' the demands of customers wanting foreign currencies with the supplies of foreign currencies offered by other customers who are wanting sterling. But there is no automatic balance between these demands and supplies: sometimes the daily transactions show an excess of foreign currencies on offer, while on other days the authorized dealers may find that demands for these currencies exceed the amounts coming in. To absorb these excesses, sometimes on one side and sometimes on the other, the *Exchange Equalization Account* stands behind the authorized dealers. This Account is an official reservoir of gold and foreign currencies, managed by the Bank of England. Gold is held by the Account because it can readily be sold, at fixed prices, to the monetary authorities of other countries, for the currencies (e.g. U.S. dollars) which the Exchange Equalization Account requires at any time. Being willing to absorb excess demand for an excess supply of foreign currencies, the Exchange Equalization Account is able to hold the rates of exchange between sterling and other currencies within the narrow limits imposed by Britain's international obligations as a member of the International Monetary Fund.

All transactions involving the exchange of sterling for other currencies lean upon the willingness of the Exchange Equalization Account to 'clear the market'; this is true not only of transactions to which U.K. residents are parties but also those which originate in other parts of the Sterling Area. If an Australian wool exporter sells francs to his own

Australian bank, the francs will be offered for sterling in London by the Australian bank; and a demand for U.S. dollars, e.g. to pay for machinery shipped from America to Australia, is satisfied by the use by an Australian bank of some of Australia's 'sterling balance' to buy U.S. dollars in London. Thus the British Exchange Equalization Account operates as the reserve of gold and foreign currency not merely for the United Kingdom but for the entire Sterling Area. And in every operation what the Account does is to sell foreign currency *for sterling* or *sell sterling* in exchange for foreign currency offered to it. As a matter of practice, it turns practically all its sterling bank balances into Treasury Bills, and its foreign currencies into gold or balances with foreign central banks. When the balance of international payments is flowing in favour of the Sterling Area as a whole, the Account's gold and foreign balances will be running up and its Treasury Bills will be running down; and vice versa. The impact of the Account's transactions on the English financial system can best be seen as that of an exchange of foreign balances for U.K. Treasury Bills; its foreign balances can be converted into gold, or its gold into foreign balances, without disturbance of its holding of Treasury Bills.

The object of continual exchange of sterling and foreign assets, in the Exchange Equalization Account, is to hold the foreign exchange value of sterling within narrow limits. But the operations have effects also on the internal financial system, and it is these effects we have next to investigate. We begin by assuming that English people have an excess of payments to make to countries that claim dollars or gold. Then they through their banks and the latter through the Bank of England buy dollars from the Account. The Account receives English bank deposits in the shape of a transfer from Bankers' Deposits to Public Deposits at the Bank of England. The Account proceeds to use its balance at the Bank of England to buy Treasury Bills in the market, and this gives the English banks the chance to rebuild their cash ratios at the expense of their Money Market Assets. Putting these steps into our usual schematic form we have:

POSITION I
(£ millions)
Bank of England

Bankers' Deposits + Note Liabilities to Commercial Banks	80	Government Securities (Treasury Bills) . .	180
Public Deposits . .	100		
	180		180

Commercial Banks

Deposits	1,000	Cash in hand and at the Bank of England . . .	80
		Money Market Assets. .	200
		Other Assets . . .	720
	1,000		1,000

Cash ratio 8 per cent. Money Market Assets ratio 20 per cent.

POSITION II
(After the public has paid 40 for the required dollars, and the Bank of England has charged their cheques to Bankers' Deposits and credited the proceeds to the Exchange Equalization Account under 'Public Deposits'.)

Bank of England

Bankers' Deposits + Note Liabilities to Commercial Banks	40	Government Securities .	180
Public Deposits (incl. 40 for E.E. Account) . .	140		
	180		180

Commercial Banks

Deposits . . .	960	Cash in hand and at the Bank of England . . .	40
		Money Market Assets. .	200
		Other Assets . . .	720
	960		960

Cash ratio 4 per cent. (approx.).
Money Market Assets ratio 21 per cent. (approx.).

POSITION III

(After the commercial banks have rebuilt their cash ratio to 8 per cent., by unloading Money Market Assets on to the Bank of England, but before the Exchange Equalization Account has used its balance.)

Bank of England

Bankers' Deposits + Note Liabilities to Commercial Banks	. . . 177	Government Securities (180 + 37 taken from market through the back door)	. 217
Public Deposits .	. . 40		
	217		217

Commercial Banks

Deposits .	. . . 960	Cash	. 77
		Money Market Assets.	. 163
		Other Assets . .	. 720
	960		960

Cash ratio 8 per cent.
Money Market Assets ratio about 17 per cent.

Then the Exchange Equalization Account proceeds to use its balance to buy Treasury Bills in the market. The discount houses and the banks together have no desire to sell Treasury Bills—in fact the banks have rather less Money Market Assets than they would like to have if their cash position were a little easier. Then to prevent the competition for Treasury Bills from forcing the discount rate below the level it thinks right, the Treasury Bills are made available in effect by the Bank of England. The latter reduces its holding of Treasury Bills, charging the unloaded bills against Public Deposits. So we have:

POSITION IV

Bank of England

Bankers' Deposits, &c.	. 77	Government Securities	. 177
Public Deposits	. 100		
	177		177

Commercial Banks as in Position III

The transition from Position III to Position IV is likely to be made quite unobtrusively, without any intermediary strain on the discount market, by an increase of 'tap' issues of Treasury Bills to the Exchange Account countered by an equal decrease in tap issues to the Bank of England—or even by direct transfer of bills from the Bank to the Exchange Account.

Position IV is, we should emphasize, the position reached when the Bank of England operates readily 'at the back door' without allowing any disturbance of market rates. Given the Exchange Equalization Account's habit of using the proceeds of foreign currency sales to buy Treasury Bills, the commercial banks can maintain their cash ratio without forcing any further contraction of the supply of money. But in Position IV there remain two significant differences from Position I : the public's deposits at the commercial banks are down by 40, and the commercial banks' Money Market Assets ratio is down from 20 to 17 per cent. The public and the commercial banks will therefore both be a little less liquid than before, and if these changes are at all pronounced there will be a tendency for interest rates to rise. If it wishes to prevent this rise, the Bank of England will have to buy securities, so adding to the cash reserves of the commercial banks and inducing them to expand their earning assets and their deposit liabilities to the public.

As in the case discussed in the previous section, this deflationary effect of an adverse balance can be offset by a simultaneous inflationary factor such as a government deficit. Again, if the excess demand for foreign currency originates not in England's balance of payments but in that of the Rest of the Sterling Area, the banks of the R.S.A. will find the 'cash at the Bank of England' for paying for the foreign currency by selling Treasury Bills, and these Treasury Bills will be taken up by the Exchange Equalization Account. There will in this case be no strain at all on the English banking system and no residual deflationary effect in England (though there will be in the R.S.A.).

In the reverse case—an excess supply of foreign currency in English hands—the English people sell the foreign currency through their banks to the Exchange Equalization Account, which obtains the English cash required in exchange by selling Treasury Bills. Taking as the starting-point Position I as on p. 147 above, and supposing the excess supply of foreign currency to be absorbed by the Exchange Account as 40, we shall have corresponding to Position IV in the opposite case:

POSITION IVa
(£ millions)

Bank of England

Bankers' Deposits, &c.	83	Government Securities	183
Public Deposits	100		
	183		183

Commercial Banks

Deposits	1,040	Cash	83
		Money Market Assets	237
		Other Assets	720
	1,040		1,040

Cash ratio 8 per cent.
Money Market Assets ratio 23 per cent.

In this Position IVa, the banks have got their cash ratio right, but they will feel that their Money Market Assets ratio is rather high. They will be inclined to unload some Treasury Bills on to the Bank of England, using the proceeds for buying more remunerative though longer-term securities. Similarly, the public, with the supply of bank deposits up from 1,000 to 1,040, will feel unnecessarily well supplied with money balances and will tend to demand more securities. Thus the pressure of excess liquidity both in the banks and among the public will tend to drive down the rate of interest. No automatic action of the authorities will prevent this inflationary factor from appearing, though simultaneous deflationary factors (a government surplus, or an excess of private saving over private investment) will neutralize it if they happen to be present.

Our analysis has thus led us to the general conclusion that an adverse balance of English payments will set up slightly deflationary forces, and correspondingly a favourable balance will set up slightly inflationary forces. These deflationary or inflationary forces are part of the situation on which the Bank of England has to operate; the authorities will do exceedingly well if they always diagnose the current situation correctly.[1] It is for the authorities to consider, in the light of other circumstances, whether they want these deflationary or inflationary forces to work unimpeded or whether they ought by deliberate action to neutralize them. Why the authorities should bother their heads about the disturbance of the interest-rate structure, why, indeed, we say they are 'inflationary' or 'deflationary', are questions we must seek to answer in Chapter 9.

[1] It is important to remember that for purposes of practical policy the diagnosis has to be made while a change is proceeding, and cannot wait upon the appearance of a comprehensive statistical record.

7

OTHER FINANCIAL INTERMEDIARIES

IN Chapters 2-6 the financial institutions described have been the commercial banks, the discount houses, the accepting houses, and the central bank: all of them traditionally regarded as parts of 'the banking system'. A major purpose of this book, however, is to show how the operations of the banking system, in this narrow sense, affect the more basic business of economic life—the production and distribution of goods and services. From this point of view we can no longer ignore the many other financial intermediaries who win their way in the world by methods not unlike those of banks, and whose operations have at least some of the effects theorists have associated with banks ever since bank deposits were recognized as money. Money serves as a store of value as well as a medium of final payment, and in an advanced financial system many firms, whose business is the borrowing and lending of money, can affect the supply of the store of value, with repercussions on the need for the medium of payment. The relevance of these non-bank financial intermediaries will become clearer as we describe the main classes of them in the present chapter, and we shall return to the theme in Chapter 10.

The financial intermediaries described in the present chapter are those existing in Britain in the early 1960's. Many of them have close parallels in other countries, particularly in the United States; but it is exclusively in British terms that we shall review the field in this chapter, and the inferences we shall draw, as to their monetary significance, must be taken as valid only for current British conditions, which are in many respects unique. Most

sections of the chapter draw heavily on Chapter 4 of the
Radcliffe Report and on the Memoranda and Minutes of
Evidence of that Committee; in these documents the
reader can find much fuller information. The account
given of financial institutions in Chapter 4 of the Report
is based very closely (occasionally a little too closely) on
evidence collected in 1958, and in bringing the material
up to date (mid-1966) use has been made of the statistics
(and some descriptive matter) published by the Bank of
England in recent issues of its Quarterly Bulletin. This
Bulletin has become an important source of information
on these financial intermediaries, and the reader can keep
himself up to date by using it in continuation of the
description given in this chapter.

1. *The Savings Banks*

The Post Office Savings Banks and the Trustee Savings
Banks operate under legislation having its origin in
nineteenth-century attempts to tackle the problem of
poverty by encouraging thrift among the poorer classes of
the community. The Post Office Savings Bank (P.O.S.B.)
has the advantage of operating at most of the post offices
throughout the country and this, together with its more
direct government guarantee for depositors, allowed it to
displace some of the earlier Trustee Savings Banks,
especially in the south of England. The latter banks, some
eighty in number, are however particularly strong in
Scotland and the north of England, and have been gaining
ground since the war, especially in the London area.

The P.O.S.B. gives direct State guarantee to its depositors. It allows withdrawals of up to £10 on demand at the
great majority of post offices, which are open for much
longer hours than are the offices of the clearing banks;
larger amounts are withdrawable at (in practice) about
four days' notice. The deposits are thus highly liquid,

although a considerable proportion is firmly held and appears insensitive to the appeal of higher rates of interest offered elsewhere. The competition of the Building Societies and hire-purchase finance companies has, however, been important since 1950, and in 1966 the P.O.S.B. offered a competitive rate on 'investment accounts'. An important indication of the ordinary business of the P.O.S.B. is in the timing of withdrawals: short-term saving for spending on summer holidays and on Christmas festivities evidently plays a large part. Other important withdrawals are known to be for the purpose of house-purchase.

Apart from several millions of dormant accounts (nearly all with balances under £1), there are 22½ million active accounts, the balances adding up to some £1,800 millions. Half the depositors have less than £10 each, but the other half account for 99 per cent. of the total deposits; 21 per cent., each with over £100, have 86 per cent. of the total deposits. Thus some five million people have at their disposal—almost on demand—some £1,500 mn. Although much of this is in fact tightly held, it is quite clear that a very large amount of individual spending on house-purchase, on summer holidays, and on Christmas is well cushioned against any restrictive monetary or fiscal measures.

An important development, in the middle decades of this century, has been in the use of P.O.S.B. accounts as *current* accounts of the ordinary banking type. This has been encouraged by the payments facilities offered by the P.O.S.B. for the purpose of attracting deposits; like other such encouragements, the result has been a growth in the liquidity structure of the economy. The arrangements for making periodic payments on depositors' behalf resulted in 1956 in 920,000 payments totalling £3½ millions; three-quarters of these payments were to insurance companies, and most of the remainder to building societies or hire-purchase companies, so that it is 'saving' rather than 'spending' that is affected by these facilities. More significantly, some 460,000 depositors were clearly using their P.O.S.B. accounts as current accounts, passing through them 80 and even more transactions a year, much to the embarrassment of those who have to watch the expenses of administration of the P.O.S.B. Such figures as these, large as they look in absolute terms, are of course small beer in relation to the national expenditure on consumption, and there are no business accounts that might have some relevance to business investment. But the facts do serve to emphasize how blurred are the lines of distinction that separate money as the means of payments from other financial assets, and the rapidity with which the situation has developed shows how dated are the habits that underlie all such distinctions. At present, however, the more important aspect of the Post Office Savings Bank is in the liquid 'stores of value' represented by the great bulk of its deposits, stores that may give a certain freedom to the turnover of other financial assets more recognizable as 'money'.

The Post Office Savings Bank is a part of the governmental machine and a payment into it is clearly a payment by the private sector to a government account, with all the consequences discussed in Chapter 5 above; there may be some elaborate ballet-dancing between the P.O.S.B., the National Debt Commissioners, and Her Majesty's Exchequer, but the basic position is that the P.O.S.B. is a government account. The position regarding the Trustee Savings Banks is not quite so simple, although they also have their powers narrowly circumscribed by statute and are substantially within the public sector. There are some 80 of these banks, with 1,300 offices. They are identified with particular localities, particularly Scottish and north of England towns, and each bank is administered by trustees (usually local solicitors, accountants, and other professional men) and by a manager appointed by the Trustees. Overlapping of accounts makes numbering uncertain, but there are probably about nine million depositors

and their total funds (including reserved profits) amount
to about £2,000 millions. A recent analysis showed that
nearly half of the *new* depositors are manual workers.

The Trustee Savings Banks have three main departments: the Ordinary, the Special Investment, and the
Stock Departments. The last is purely a broker for the
sale of government securities, and is irrelevant to our
immediate purpose. The Ordinary Department runs on
lines similar to the P.O.S.B., paying a fixed $2\frac{1}{2}$ per cent.
rate and its expenses, out of interest allowed by the
National Debt Office with which all Ordinary Department
funds are placed. The Government guarantees repayment
of all these funds, to the Trustees. Any depositor having
at least £50 in the Ordinary Department may also make
deposits in the Special Investment Department of the
same bank. This Department is allowed to invest its funds
in a certain range of government securities, including local
authority 'mortgages', subject to detailed approval by the
National Debt Office; this employment of their funds
allows payment of appreciably higher rates of interest on
deposits in this Department. There is no uniformity in
the administration of the Special Investment Departments
of different Trustee Savings Banks, nor is there uniformity
in the costs of administration of their Ordinary Departments. For these reasons the experience of societies in
paying their way varies; these variations are to some extent
reflected in variations in rates paid on deposits in the
Special Investment Departments, and for the rest they
are substantially evened out by pooling arrangements
between the banks. When an individual bank has been
persistently in difficulty, a solution has been found in its
absorption in a neighbouring and stronger Trustee Savings Bank. The upshot of these practices is that deposits
in the Trustee Savings Banks are as safe and as liquid as
those in the P.O.S.B., though there is not the same convenience of repayment at any place in the kingdom. It is
not surprising, in these circumstances, that the higher rates

of interest paid by their Special Investment Departments since the middle 1950's have attracted a great increase of deposits. The position now is that in Scotland 2 people in every 5 have accounts with them, in northern England 1 in 5, and in London and the Home Counties the much lower proportion (perhaps 1 in 20) is increasing quickly.

In these banks, as in the P.O.S.B., the tendency is for increasing use of accounts as ordinary current accounts. There are no business accounts, but the turnover of individual accounts has been greatly encouraged by arrangements whereby employers pay wages and salaries by direct credit to accounts, and by the 'Direct Transfer' schemes allowing payments to third parties. In 1965 an ordinary cheque scheme was established by these banks, and they have also shown themselves more willing than the clearing banks to adapt their hours of business to the needs of customers. Altogether, they are becoming near-banks and their liabilities are undoubtedly a part of the structure of liquid assets in the economy. The facts that (1) their funds are closely controlled and are all channelled into the government sector, and (2) they do not include business firms among their depositors, prevent their being a serious embarrassment to the authorities in the implementation of monetary policy. Nevertheless, habits are changing, the Trustee Savings Banks have shown themselves alive to possibilities of development, and the movement may come to occupy a much more important place in the country's monetary system.

11. *The Building Societies*

Building Societies are non-profit-making associations, whose primary objects are to encourage both thrift and home-ownership by marrying the accumulation of small savings with the needs of house purchasers for loans that can be steadily repaid out of income. The societies were originally highly localized in their areas of operation,

though this has ceased to be characteristic of the larger
societies which now dominate the 'movement'. The word
'movement' remains appropriate, for even the largest
societies retain something of the broad social aims that
were the inspiration of founders of the little local societies
during the last century. But nowadays the importance of
the building societies goes far beyond what they can do to
encourage the virtues of thrift and home-ownership. The
movement, says the Radcliffe Report, 'has come to hold
a large place in the total credit structure of the economy,
with potentially quick liabilities amounting to some £2,400
millions at the end of 1958, and [it] provides finance for
about two-thirds of private house-building, a large and
sensitive part of total net investment'. Since that date they
have continued to win for themselves an ever-larger place
among the country's financial institutions, new branch
offices of the larger societies appearing right across the
country, echoing the spreading tentacles of the branch
banks a few decades earlier.

The societies gain their resources from, and therefore
have liabilities to, 'shareholders', and 'depositors'. The
words 'shareholder' and 'share' are used, however, quite
differently from their ordinary usage in the context of
joint-stock company organization: a building society share
is effectively a deposit the withdrawal terms of which are
slightly stiffer than those for deposit liabilities that are
actually called 'deposits', and the share carries slightly
higher interest than the deposit. Notice of withdrawal—
commonly one month—is formally required, but in their
competition for deposits the societies have gradually
broken down the original rigidity of this requirement,
and in practice the shareholders—who provide 90 per
cent. of the total funds—know that they can get much of
their money very quickly indeed. This is the way things
normally go when financial institutions compete at all
closely with each other. The prestige attached to quick
repayment is one of the most powerful magnets, and

institutions that so arrange their business that they can always provide this service are those most successful at attracting resources most of which they can proceed to lock up in remunerative employment.

Large investors in the building societies are relatively few, and most of the money comes from a very large number (the total runs to millions) of small accounts, the average holding being well under £1,000. The small accounts are those the societies most like: they remember their social purpose in encouraging regular savings in small amounts, and their experience has been that these small amounts are much less liable to withdrawal than are the large amounts sometimes placed on deposit by corporations or wealthy people. For historical reasons connected with their original social purposes, the building societies have special arrangements with the taxation authorities, enabling them to advertise tax-free rates of interest.

On the other side of the balance-sheet, their principal assets are mortgages, particularly those covering their loans to home-owners who borrow a large part of the cost of the house and repay steadily over periods of years. Some societies lend to builders while the houses are being built; a few lend appreciable sums for other classes of real property. In addition to the mortgages, the societies hold a margin—in effect a liquidity reserve—of their resources in the form of government securities (with a wide range of maturities) and bank balances. Taking all the societies together, these liquidity reserves amount to about 15 per cent. of total assets; the ratio is not subject to any statutory control or official suasion, but the Association to which a large proportion of the societies belong requires its members to maintain not less than 7½ per cent.

The societies have to cover, and no more than cover, the interest they pay on shares and deposits, their tax liabilities and their running expenses, out of the interest earned on mortgages and securities. Because of the general terms

on which they lend, it is awkward for them to alter the
rates of interest at which they lend; their tradition is,
moreover, in favour of stable rates. And, since they must
make neither profit nor loss, stickiness in lending rates
makes also for stickiness in the rates they can offer on
shares and deposits. But the societies are competing with
other classes of financial intermediaries, and with the
opportunities savers have for investing in various kinds of
government security. So, when interest rates generally are
rising, but the building societies try to hold theirs unchanged, the societies find that they have much less money
coming in than house-purchasers are seeking to borrow
from them and, if the movement in rates persists, the
building societies sooner or later have to raise their rates.
Similarly, when rates are falling, the building societies
find themselves glutted with funds (as people see that they
can get better terms from the building societies than elsewhere) and would-be borrowers seem scarcer than usual
(because some are finding that they can get the money on
easier terms elsewhere). In these circumstances the building societies sooner or later follow suit. There is always,
however, when interest rates are moving substantially, a
period when the societies are lagging behind the general
movement and the flows of funds in the capital market
become abnormal in one direction or the other.

The occurrence of these disturbances, incidental to a
broad movement of interest rates, is one reason for taking
notice of the building societies when we are investigating
the relevance of banking operations to the total pressure of
demand for goods and services. A rather different reason
is the place that has come to be taken by the liabilities of
building societies (the 'shares' and deposits) in the structure of liquid financial assets held in the community. The
evolution of the societies has tended to make people think
of these shares and deposits as liquid assets: assets that
have become more and more like money. The more of such
assets people hold, the less will they worry themselves

about depletion of the real value of their bank deposits and other money balances, for their claims against the building societies come to be regarded as a contingency reserve, replacing the more tightly-held bank deposits in this function. It must be emphasized that this imputation of a monetary quality to building-society liabilities is not dependent on the addition of any new services (such as facility of transfer to third parties) by the societies. The trend—the nearer-money trend—is however hastened by the addition of services, and as one sees branch offices of building societies jostling the branches of the clearing banks here, there, and nearly everywhere, and the building societies offer increasing facility of withdrawal and transfer, it is impossible to resist an expectation that these could become as nearly banks as are their continental counterparts such as the cantonal banks of Switzerland.

III. *Hire-Purchase Finance Companies*

From financial intermediaries that had their origin largely in Victorian stress on the social importance of private thrift, we turn to a group of intermediaries, a century younger, that have come into existence in response to opportunities of private profit opened by the desire of twentieth-century consumers to equip themselves out of anticipated income. The contrast can be overdrawn: a large part of the population used to buy clothes on instalment credit provided by the retailers, and the building societies, after all, depended almost entirely on the use of instalment credit for house-purchase; but at least the comparison reminds us that private profit is still a mainspring of innovation and that other motives could be important in moulding economic institutions in the Victorian era. The opportunity for profit that called the new 'finance companies' into existence did arise, however, from the appearance of new durable goods, mainly but not exclusively for 'consumption' purposes. Most important of these was the motor-car, but radio and TV sets, and kitchen items such as washing-machines, cooking-stoves, and refrigerators are all large items in occasioning the use of instalment credit.

Excluding (for traditional rather than logical reasons) the instalment credit used for house-purchase, the amount of instalment credit outstanding in the U.K. was in 1966 over £1,300 millions. Of this total, about £500 millions is owed directly to retailers, who no doubt finance themselves partly out of bank credit and partly out of their 'own resources'. The remainder (a little under £860 millions) is owed to about 1,500 firms who describe themselves variously as hire-purchase finance companies, industrial bankers, or simply finance companies. They are usually referred to collectively as the hire-purchase finance companies, although they have a small amount of other lending as well as the £860 millions of hire-purchase credit outstanding. Of the 1,500 companies, thirteen have assets exceeding £10 millions each, and these thirteen account for two-thirds of the resources of the whole 1,500. At least ten among the largest companies are wholly or partly owned by London clearing banks and/or Scottish banks.

Of the total of £1,300 millions outstanding, about half relates to motor vehicles (commercial as well as private), 10 per cent. to industrial plant and equipment, and the remainder to household equipment. Some of the loans are repayable over six months, but most cover longer periods —up to three years for cars, and five years or more for industrial equipment; quite a large proportion of the contracts are, however, terminated by repayment of the balance before the final date. On the average, the amount outstanding turns over about once a year. The rates charged are a long way above those charged on bank overdrafts. Most rates are fixed for the period of the contract, but rates on new contracts tend to change in reflection of any persistent movement of Bank Rate, and a few of the larger contracts now have a Bank Rate clause providing for variation within the contractual period.

Apart from their own capital funds (about one-fifth of their total resources) the hire-purchase finance companies have three classes of liabilities. Much the largest consists of deposits, in 1962 half of the total resources (including capital); one-tenth was owed to the banks on overdrafts, and another tenth to the banks and discount houses on bills discounted. The share of deposits in the total has greatly increased as the companies have grown; particularly the larger companies have been able to attract large individual amounts by offering rates 2 or 3 per cent. above the clearing banks' Time Deposit rate. These rates are paid for fixed-term deposits (three or six months) and, with the largest customers, are settled by negotiation; for deposits subject to three or six months' notice, rates are similar but are, in the more important cases, tied to Bank Rate movements. It is notable that rates not so tied do move a little up and down in relation to a given Bank Rate: the market price is still a competitive one, and does not fit perfectly into the automatic gearing of the banking system.

Both in borrowing directly from the banks and in arranging acceptance credits under which they may draw bills, the finance companies habitually try to keep a margin in hand: they try, that is to say, to arrange borrowing limits well above what they normally expect to require, so that they may shift the weight of their borrowing from one source (deposits, bank overdrafts, bills discounted) to another according to their relative cheapness from time to time. Such arrangements have the further advantage of allowing the finance companies to call more on one source (e.g. the banks) when another source (e.g. deposits) shows signs of drying-up, thus avoiding the necessity of curtailing the lending side of their business. This element of 'give' in the liabilities-structure of the finance houses—an unusually clear example of the way in which any financial intermediary is always trying to conduct its business—was an embarrassment to the monetary authorities in their efforts to impose a credit squeeze in the middle 1950's. Though by no means the most important case, in that period, of the kind of embarrassment to which a restrictive monetary policy is subject in a highly developed financial system, it was a peculiarly obvious example, and received much attention. Notably the authorities themselves attended to it, by calling upon the banks to restrict their lending to the finance companies, and finally in 1961 by asking the finance companies (through the two associations that cover the bulk of the field) not to seek to replace bank advances by other borrowing except to the extent necessary to carry existing commitments. The extension of the ancient central bank weapon of moral suasion into this field is a sign of the times; the confidence with which it has been applied and its efficacy have perhaps had some connexion with the linking of several of the large companies with London clearing banks.

This close association between banks and hire-purchase finance companies—which developed rapidly in 1958—has already had other effects, and there may be more to come. The connexion has inevitably raised public opinion of the security of the companies, and their competition for deposits has therefore become much more relevant to the situation of the banks themselves. The finance companies in general bid only for longer-term deposits, and the clearing banks stick to their seven-days' notice, but the finance companies' terms are interesting to many who hold money on deposit account, now that the finance companies begin to look almost as safe as the banks. On the other side of the balance-sheet, the finance companies are also competing: in 1966 they had over £120 millions outstanding in 'Other Advances and Loans', including loans to finance stocks of goods, 'bridging finance' for new investments, and for house-purchase. The gradual spread of their branch offices is making the companies more convenient to deal with, and this again—as the banks themselves have found throughout their history—is an important aspect of the competitive effort to swell balance-sheet totals.

How far the banks who own, or part-own, the finance companies will wish this competition from their own sub-sidiaries to develop, is uncertain. Hitherto they have tended to keep the management of their own hire-purchase connexions at arm's length, and have left them more or less free to develop their competition. They carried this policy, at first, even to the length of not infusing the finance companies with anything of the banks' traditional ways of safeguarding themselves against over-commit-ment to individual borrowers, and the sudden flood of credit in 1958–9 inevitably led to some burning of fingers, among companies that are associated with the banks as well as among the independent companies. But all this may be changing: future development may see the com-panies growing much more like banks (on both sides of the balance-sheet) and growing relatively to the clearing banks, or it may see the banks themselves responding by preventing these finance companies from being anything more than convenient side-doors at which they can do business of kinds they do not want to do in their ordinary offices.

IV. *Insurance Companies, Pension Funds, and Investment Trusts*

The financial intermediaries discussed in the first three sections of this chapter have clear relevance to the mone-tary situation both because their liabilities are readily exchangeable for cash at fixed rates and because they are important lenders. We now turn to three rather different groups, in which the liabilities side of the balance sheet has relatively little monetary significance, though as lenders (or investors) these groups are of great weight. The differ-ence is partly one of practice, and partly one of attitude;

it is not immutable, and it is important to remember that the position described here refers to the early 1960's. (A generation earlier, it would have been appropriate to include the building societies with these groups.)

There are some four hundred insurance companies operating in Britain, undertaking business they classify into 'life' and 'general', the latter including fire, accident, and marine insurance. Their 'general' business need not concern us; it is their life business, which has given rise to the total of £4,000 millions of assets, that has monetary importance. It includes a variety of life insurance business (technically referred to as 'assurance') including the provision of pensions: people insure on a huge scale both against the risk of living too long and against the risk of not living long enough. The companies receive premium payments, largely as annual payments fixed for long periods of years. They invest the sums received, and hold the resulting assets against their liabilities to pay, under the terms of contracts called 'policies', either to the heirs of people who have not lived long enough or to the contractors themselves if they have lived too long. For various reasons, their funds are growing; that is to say, their receipts in premiums paid by policy-holders exceed the payments falling due *to* policy-holders and their heirs; this excess of receipts has recently been running well above £300 millions a year, a sum sufficient to finance nearly one-fifth of all net fixed capital formation (both public and private) in Britain. The liabilities to the public, created in this way, are not themselves regarded by the public as liquid assets: the additions made year by year are almost entirely regulated by long-standing contracts, and are not subject to rapid increase or reduction in response to relative changes of interest rates or the varying attractions of spending on real resources. The policy-holder can, it is true, use his policy as security when he seeks a loan from a bank, and he can, if hard-pressed, 'surrender' his policy in exchange for bank deposits; but in general people regard their policies as a hard core of savings, the existence of which has little bearing on the flow of spending.

The activities of the insurance companies are of greater significance, from the viewpoint of monetary policy, on the other side of their balance-sheets: the disposition of their assets, the use they make of 'their funds'. They lend on mortgage of houses and shops and, in a small way, on agricultural property. The sums outstanding are of the order of £500 millions. This is not large by comparison with the total of bank advances, and the turnover of the insurance companies' loans is certainly much lower, but this is a source from which millions of private individuals and small firms can borrow when other channels are obstructed.

In terms of figures—and perhaps of disturbance to the country's financial structure during the 1950's—the insurance companies' operations in securities are much the most important aspect of their activities. Well over £3,000 millions are invested in securities nearly all of which are readily marketable on the Stock Exchange. Normal practice is to invest mainly in long-term securities including government stocks, ordinary shares, and other industrial and commercial securities. The preference is for long-term investment, reflecting the long-term nature of their liabilities, and with this goes some presumption in favour of holding any security, once acquired, for a very long time. This means—fortunately for the monetary authorities— that the companies are not looking for new outlets every year for the whole of their funds: in the main, it is the accretion to their funds they seek to invest each year, though in 1957, for example, their total of investments was £470 millions, of which no more than £307 millions represented 'new funds'. During the 1950's the companies were changing investments to a degree that may perhaps be regarded as abnormal, in that they were trying to restore in their portfolios a balance between government and other securities after the extraordinary war-time concentration on government securities. But even the 'new funds'—the £307 millions the disposition of which cannot be evaded—give room for large swings that can make a big difference to the facility with which industry can finance spending on new capital equipment. If the companies swing heavily towards industrial investment, this means a big flow of money into the market for industrial securities and therefore ease in the raising of money for industrial expansion; contrariwise, if the insurance companies swing their 'new money' heavily to the purchase of government securities, the monetary authorities have a much easier task in holding industrial expansion in check—but a much more difficult situation if they are wanting the industrialists to spend more.

The importance of the insurance companies in these ways has been recognized, and in later phases of 'credit squeeze' the authorities have requested the insurance companies to restrain their lending operations on lines similar to the restraints required in the banks. But on the distribution of their portfolio investments the insurance companies have escaped this kind of moral suasion; only in the extremity of war were they brought into line with the regimentation of the banking system in support of government finance.

The *Pension Funds* are really the extreme species of the insurance company genus. Indeed, many are administered by insurance companies, and the funds involved are included in those referred to in the above paragraphs. Others are 'self-administered', and these have assets totalling over £3,000 millions, growing by some £300 millions a year. The liabilities of these Funds are to the prospective pensioners; as these cannot borrow from the Funds or exchange their rights for immediate payment, the Funds' liabilities form no part of the liquid assets of the public. But their control of these huge resources, their necessity to invest them, means that their activities are potentially of great importance to the distribution of immediate purchasing power and therefore to the functioning of the economic system. In fact they do relatively little shifting of investments, but this still leaves them with some £300 millions a year to place. Their investment policies in recent years have been much coloured by their fear of continuing inflation, which implies pressure from pensioners—and prospective pensioners—to invest more of the funds in equities that are expected to provide bigger yields as inflation proceeds and the pensioners' cost of living rises. This has meant a tendency for the Funds to make the financing of industrial development easier, and has been among the underlying sources of weakness in control of the financial structure. The behaviour of the Funds has not, however, been erratic, and partly for this reason they have not been regarded as requiring regulation for the general purposes of economic policy.

The *Investment Trusts* are still further from the banking system, and require only brief reference here. Unlike other financial intermediaries, they are not primarily concerned with borrowing and lending. They do, it is true, borrow some of their funds, by the issue of debentures, and they do lend in so far as they hold government bonds and industrial debentures. But more characteristically they *own* and *are owned*; that is to say, they are effectively co-operative societies for the indirect ownership of equity claims on the profits of commercial and industrial companies. Their advantage lies in the risk-spreading that can be reconciled with comparatively small holdings: £100 invested in an investment trust may effectively represent investments of a few shillings in each of a large number of companies, often with a leavening of government bonds.

In Britain about 300 joint-stock companies are investment trusts in this sense, and their total assets are well over £2,000 millions. In addition there are about fifty *unit trusts*, providing much the same kind of service for small investors, and having total assets over £200 millions. In spite of the ease with which shares and debentures issued by investment trusts can be sold on the Stock Exchange, and the 'units' in a unit trust can be sold to its managers, people do not ordinarily regard their holdings as part of their liquid assets. Rather they are held as 'long-term investments', and their fluctuations in market value (despite the risk-spreading) are so considerable that there is little risk that assets of this kind will acquire the characteristics of money.

v. *Some Recent Developments in Financial Intermediaries* (*1955–66*)

Financial intermediaries have been described in this chapter as they appeared to be operating in the late 1950's and early 1960's, and it is necessary to emphasize once more that financial institutions—especially the newer ones—can change rapidly, and that new intermediaries are springing up all the time. An example of how new business can develop, giving new scope for established firms and opportunities for new comers, and amounting to the growth of a new financial market, is afforded by what has been happening in these years in relation to the short-term debt of local government authorities. Early in the 1950's the central government, which had through the war and early post-war years provided the capital requirements of the local authorities, adopted a policy of forcing the local authorities to borrow independently. The local authorities were not, however, given freedom to make public issues of bonds whenever they liked, nor, as interest rates tended to rise, did they always wish to meet their requirements by long-term issues. The result was that they borrowed—and continue to borrow—heavily on very short paper, considerable amounts being on terms as short as seven days.

The sums involved have been very large. In 1962 total local authority debt stood as £7,653 millions; of this £3,111 millions had been provided by the central govern-

ment, and £432 millions was from the local authorities themselves and related sources, leaving rather more than £4,000
millions as the 'privately held' debt, no small addition to the
central government's debt. Of this £4,000 millions, about
two-thirds had been added during the seven years 1955–62,
and out of this new debt the amount falling due within
one year increased by £1,500 millions in the seven years.
Although some of this huge amount has been raised by
each authority in its own locality, the great bulk has had
to be obtained by the offer of terms (of interest and repayment) that would appeal to comparatively large lenders
over an altogether wider area. These lenders have been
banks, merchant banks, discount houses, trustee savings
banks, insurance companies, industrial and commercial
companies, charitable and similar corporations and, on an
appreciable scale, overseas financial concerns. There are
nearly 2,000 borrowing local authorities; the bulk of the
borrowing outside their own localities is however that of
the largest 200 among them, but even this is such a number
that their varying needs and the continual turnover of very
short-term debt make for a huge number of operations.
The lenders being even more numerous and varied, there
are obvious opportunities for intermediaries who can
bring borrowers and lenders together day by day, and
there are in fact four or five firms who make this their
main business. They are brokers—they do not operate on
their own account—and their brokerage on turnover is
generally at the rate of one-sixteenth of one per cent.

The repayment of the sums borrowed is absolutely certain but, mainly because the borrowers are so fragmented
and look different from the central government, the rates
of interest paid are a little higher—sometimes appreciably
higher—than those available on Treasury Bills and other
obligations of the central government. In fact, it is only
by offering rather higher rates and a variety of maturities
that the local authorities have been able to attract the huge
sums they have required. The security and the shortness

of this paper makes it a very liquid asset, though it is not allowed to count for the 28 per cent. of liquid assets required to be held by the clearing banks. For all other holders, however, the attractions are obvious, and the bulk of the amount must have been attracted from firms that would otherwise have held Treasury Bills or time deposits. In so far as this local authority paper has in the portfolios of lenders displaced Treasury Bills, the forcing of the local authorities on to this method of direct borrowing has of course forced the central government to borrow more on Treasury Bills from the banking system; that is to say, the effect on the liquidity base of the banking system has been no different from what would have resulted from centralization of local government borrowing in the pre-1952 fashion, though the interest paid has been higher. In part, however, the authorities have been able, by the payment (again at the expense of the local ratepayers) of higher interest, to attract funds that would *not* otherwise have gone into either Treasury Bills or other government paper, and to this extent they have forced a relative contraction of the clearing banks, as well as providing a good living for the brokers.[1]

Another example of the rapid development of financial institutions has been seen in the appearance of a practice, to which the old word 'factoring' has been applied, in the handling of trade credit. This is not entirely new but is rather to be regarded as the development into a regular business, with its own specialist firms, of a practice that sometimes appears wherever trade credit is important. In the post-war period, with its relatively slight depressions of trade and the consequently increased dependability of

---

[1] This short-term borrowing by local authorities has been increasingly important in the 1960's, and the reader will find further reference to it in the Addendum to this Seventh Edition.

trade debtors, trade credit seems to have greatly increased —such figures as there are suggest that it is of much greater significance than bank lending—and it is not surprising that regular business by new intermediaries in this field should develop. The general principle of the business is simple enough: the 'factor' takes over, from a firm selling goods on credit, the claims against the firm's customers. It makes to the creditor firm immediate payment of the outstanding sums less its percentage (to cover interest plus remuneration for the trouble, and allowance for bad debts). Sometimes the entire work of collection is taken over by the factor; in other cases the factor may employ the creditor firm (especially if the firm has a strong sales organization in touch with the customers) as its agent for the actual collection.

The advantage to the creditor firm, even if it still undertakes the actual collection, is that it gets cash down and avoids the risk of bad debts (or part of this risk, depending on the terms of the agency for actual work of collection). The factor earns a good percentage on the amount he lends, a percentage that will be higher the more efficient he is in selecting the firms with which he operates and in assessing the credit-worthiness of its customers. He is, in fact, like any other financial intermediary, in that he makes a living by the pooling of risks and the bearing of risks that would not be as cheaply borne by the people from whom he draws his funds. The service offered to firms that can press their sales by offering credit to customers allows these firms to extend such sales: the development of factoring, that is to say, encourages further growth of trade credit, just as trade credit was encouraged by the appearance, long ago, of banks that would lend to manufacturers and shopkeepers. How greatly factoring will develop depends partly on whether they appear to run their businesses efficiently enough to make them trusted by bankers and others who can lend them money to enable them to extend their operations. In the United States, at least, some of the factors have made a considerable impression, and are supported by banks which regard the factors not as competitors but as useful intermediaries undertaking a specialist business they themselves would not wish to undertake.

These two examples show how the structure of financial claims can grow, independently of the growth of the economy, and how this growth can be outside the banks. Some of this growth, which is always going on in a developing financial system, can represent a clear addition to the structure of assets and liabilities: the liquidity structure of the economy will then be different from what it was before, with the banks playing a relatively smaller part than before, though still in their very important central position. In other cases the development of new forms of financial claims and of new financial intermediaries may imply an absolute reduction in the resources of the banks: bank deposits may become smaller than before, although national income continues to grow. The more ready the banks are to adjust themselves to the changing requirements of lenders and borrowers, the less risk do they run of thus losing ground to new intermediaries. There is no fixed barrier between what is and what is not banking business, and how important the banks are, and how important are other financial intermediaries, depends upon the extent to which the innovation of financial devices is shared by the banks or is left to the ingenuity of financiers outside the banks. When it comes to government policy, the use of monetary measures to influence economic activity has to take account of the entire structure of financial institutions and their business practices; in this structure, the banks may play a more important or less important part, according to how they have been faring in an essentially competitive struggle to suit the changing needs of borrowers and lenders.

8

COMMERCIAL BANK LIQUIDITY AND LENDING POLICY

1. *A Recapitulation of the Nature of Banking*

COMMERCIAL banks exist, in most countries, to make a profit for their shareholders. Their practices have become so firmly moulded by the impact of experience in the context of competitive enterprise that even in countries, such as France and Italy, where the principal commercial banks are owned by the State, the general nature of their business and the attitudes of the people who run them have continued to be those of the profit-seeking bankers of England and most other countries. Like other financial intermediaries, their business is in financial claims: the banks borrow from some customers (the depositors) and they lend to others (those who have overdrafts, or are debtors on bills of exchange, and the governmental bodies that issue bonds). Like other financial intermediaries, they seek to make themselves so attractive as debtors and so efficient as creditors that they can earn a substantial gross income from the difference between the interest they charge as creditors and the interest they pay as debtors. Unlike other financial intermediaries, to a degree amounting to a difference in kind, they make themselves appear so very attractive as debtors that they can get a large part of their resources (the balances on current accounts) without paying any interest at all; they can even charge their creditors commissions for some of the services they provide in connexion with these accounts.

From this it follows that success in their business depends

partly on the efficiency with which they can provide services for their creditors and partly on their efficiency in
attracting good borrowers and serving them so well that
they will not be driven to other lenders. It will depend—
and in this they are in the same position as other financial
intermediaries—on their acknowledging that good service
to borrowers implies the taking of some risk, however
small, of occasional losses, and on their cushioning their
creditors against these losses. As a matter of history, they
have beyond all this attracted creditors (depositors) by
committing themselves to repayment on demand; in this
respect they are distinguished from other financial intermediaries. As other financial intermediaries have become
bigger, more specialized, and more efficient, their nature
has approached that of banks in this feature, and the distinction between banks and others has now come to rest
not so much on confidence that the banks will repay on
demand as on the extreme convenience with which banks
do repay on demand. The modern distinguishing feature
of the banks is due primarily to the efficiency of the clearing system they have developed, but it has its roots deeply
in the command they have achieved over public confidence.

The banks won this high place in public confidence by
adapting their lending policies to the implications of their
obligations to the depositors. It is true that the position
reached is that their ability to meet their obligations to
depositors now depends, in an important sense, more on
the attitude of the central bank than on the nature of their
lending. But this is not the whole truth, and the attitudes
of central bankers have themselves been partly shaped by
their regard for the historical rules of successful commercial banking. Therefore, in looking for the basis of modern
ideas about how a commercial bank should run the lending
side of its business, we shall have to consider how earlier
conditions, somewhat different from those of today,
shaped the ideas of the bankers. Our aim will be to show
how these historical forces, modified by some reaction to

changing circumstances, have shaped the lending practices of commercial bankers. Throughout this chapter we shall be thinking of the reactions and the practices of *commercial* men, seeking to enlarge the profits and to ensure the continuance of the banks they control. The shape of banking as we find it emerging under these forces has its relevance not only for the commercial aims of the bankers but also for the broader working of the economic system and particularly for the implementation of monetary policy; but these wider aspects will be left aside for the moment.

II. *The 'Liquidity' of Bankers' Assets*

The profit which, as we have seen, is the ultimate object of a commercial bank, is derived from the income attached to the assets it is enabled to hold by the public's being willing to hold the bank's debts (deposits) as money balances. The profits are greater the higher the yields of the assets it holds. They can quickly be turned into losses if the capital value of the assets falls; but such a fall may be relatively harmless if continuing public confidence allows the bank to continue holding the asset until its value recovers. The possibility of earning profits at all depends absolutely on the public's acceptance of the bank's debts. There must be 'confidence' in the bank. The public accepts the bank deposit as being 'as good as cash'. Public confidence in the bank depends therefore on the belief that the bank will always be able to exchange deposits for cash on demand. Power to offer cash in exchange for deposits is therefore a prerequisite of the profits which a commercial bank is seeking.

'Liquidity' is the word that the banker uses to describe his ability to satisfy demands for cash in exchange for deposits. To earn profits at all the banker must maintain confidence. To maintain confidence he must maintain an adequate degree of liquidity in his assets. The perfectly liquid asset is cash itself, since payment of the cash to the depositor would fully satisfy the depositor's claim. The more cash a banker holds the more obviously can he, without any difficulty of any kind, offer cash in exchange for deposits. But cash is an 'idle asset'—it earns no income at all. To make a profit the banker must hold some assets which are imperfectly liquid.[1] What should be the nature (other than income-earning) of the imperfectly liquid assets of a bank? The answers that bankers have given to this question have generally left an ambiguity about the word 'liquidity', an ambiguity that has its root in the banking conditions of earlier days. To satisfy depositors' claims a bank must be able to convert its assets into cash *quickly*. But that is not all. If the depositors' claims are to be fully satisfied the bankers' assets must be convertible into cash *without loss*. When bankers have said that they aim at liquidity they have generally included *both* these attributes.

The ambiguity is realized at once when we ask whether long-term British Government securities are highly liquid or relatively illiquid assets. The uncertainty of bankers' treatments of this question has its origin in the ambiguity of their use of the term 'liquidity'. The securities can be turned into cash very quickly, for there is an excellent market for them on the London Stock Exchange. That is to say, these particular assets are readily shiftable on to other banks or institutions or persons willing to supply cash. But the amount of cash that can be so obtained depends upon the market price at the moment—it may be more or less than the price at which the bank acquired the asset. Only by waiting until the distant maturity date can the face value certainly be obtained. This asset is attractive to the banker in that it is shiftable and, if he can

[1] There is the possibility that a State institution can perform the business of creating a readily transferable asset for public use in settling debts, meeting the cost by charging individuals a commission on the amount they draw; it is difficult to imagine how a private enterprise could make its liabilities sufficiently attractive to enable it to run on the same basis.

wait until the maturity date, devoid of risk of loss. But
it is unattractive in that earlier realization may involve
the banker in a capital loss. It is almost perfectly 'shiftable',
but despite the absence of any risk of the British Government's not meeting its obligations the security has not all
the qualities the banker includes in perfect liquidity.

The distinction between shiftability and the second
attribute of liquidity may be further illustrated by reference to the ordinary shares of an outstanding industrial
company—say Imperial Chemical Industries. A bank holding such shares could turn them into cash very quickly by
selling them through the Stock Exchange where these
shares enjoy a wide market. But there would be all sorts
of risk of loss attached to these securities and, despite their
very high degree of shiftability, the banker would probably
describe them as illiquid. Contrast the example of a bank
(or individual) lending to a traveller going to Tibet or to
explore the Desert of Gobi. The lender may well know the
traveller to be an honest man who will make a point of
paying his debts when he returns. The debt may be well
covered by assurance of the traveller's life, the policy being
held by the creditor. There may thus be practically no risk
of loss attached to the loan, yet a bank may well hesitate
to offer a bank deposit in exchange for the traveller's
promise to repay. For it would be very difficult to arrange
for some other institution to take over, in exchange for
cash, the bank's claims against the traveller while the
latter was in the middle of the Desert of Gobi. The asset
would be shiftable only with great difficulty, and, despite
the virtual absence of risk, the banker would describe the
asset (the traveller's promise to repay) as illiquid. Many
bank loans to business men are probably more or less like
this: the bank managers know that the firm's assets amply
cover the amount of the loan, and that the firm is an
honest one, but the informality with which the loan has
been arranged between banker and customer makes it
shiftable only at considerable inconvenience. To many

other business loans serious risks of loss are also attached. The banker rightly ranks his loans on overdraft arrangements among his least liquid assets.

The astute reader will have noticed, particularly in the discussion of the example of British Government securities, that shiftability and low risk of loss as the two elements that constitute the banker's liquidity are not completely disentangled. *If the banker can wait until maturity* there is no risk attached to a redeemable British Government bond. If, therefore, the banker has a fair proportion against deposits of assets that have high shiftability and low immediate risk (cash being the extreme case), he can feel reasonably secure in holding some assets that are highly shiftable but only riskless if not shifted. Similarly, if he has a fair proportion of the most liquid assets, he can afford to hold some assets that have a low risk degree but also low shiftability. Assets that are both unshiftable and risky will be viewed with much more disfavour. The banker must, that is to say, pay regard to both aspects of liquidity at once. He should always have some assets that have both attributes clearly. In addition he should have some assets with a high degree of shiftability that involve no risk of loss if shifting can be avoided. His remaining (less shiftable) assets should at least not involve him in losses. These are among the fundamental rules of sound commercial banking.

We must now look more closely into this matter of 'shiftability'. One particular commercial bank can look upon some of its assets as readily shiftable on to other banks or non-bankers willing to diminish their balances. For the purpose of meeting temporary adverse Clearing House balances or for meeting a run that is, for domestic reasons, restricted to one bank this shiftability is adequate. But a much more dangerous situation may arise. The demand for cash in exchange for bank deposits may not be confined to one bank. Indeed, if a crisis arises it is unlikely that a run will be restricted to a single bank. The more consolidated the commercial banking structure the more likely is the demand for cash to be generalized. In America the correspondent connexion between unit banks is apt to be a channel through which shocks to one bank can pass to many other banks. In a country where the business is all in the hands of a few great banks serious disturbance of one of those banks is bound to cause such a disturbance of the entire economy as to spread the difficulties to other banks. Such considerations as these make it imperative to think of shiftability very much in terms of shiftability on to the central bank—the lender of last resort, the ultimate source of cash. In judging the shiftability of any asset regard must be had primarily to shiftability (either direct or indirect) on to the central bank. The eligibility rules (the rules by which the acceptability of assets is determined) of the central bank are therefore of vital importance to the liquidity of the commercial banking system.

Maximum shiftability is attained by assets that can be most readily shifted on to the central bank. This depends entirely on the eligibility rules of the central bank. Generally speaking central banks will give cash on demand for Treasury Bills and bills of exchange fulfilling certain conditions. Why these happen to be the typical eligibility rules of central banks we shall discuss in the next section. We may simply add here that since the implications of central banking have been fully understood there has been a disposition to extend eligibility to other classes of assets. Any such extensions are subject, however, to obstacles not placed in the way of the rediscounting method of obtaining cash. Treasury Bills and bills of exchange that meet central bank requirements are therefore *generally* the most 'liquid' earning assets; but not in London. The rediscountability of a bill makes it very attractive for its shiftability; but the length of its life—typically three months—implies risk of a small loss. For if the bill is rediscounted at a higher rate of interest (discount) than that at which the commercial bank took it, there may be a capital loss.[1] The shorter the life of the bill the smaller is the loss that may be involved in rediscounting. Hence the preference of banks for short-dated bills. The 'eligible' bill is a highly shiftable asset, and becomes less risky as it approaches maturity. London, with its highly developed discount market and its system of indirect contact between the central bank and the commercial banks, has been able to provide the banker with an even more liquid asset. The call loans to the discount houses have the shiftability advantages of bills of exchange because the Bank of England is always ready to give the discount houses cash in exchange for the eligible bills which the commercial banks expect to be deposited as collateral security for their loans to the discount houses. But if the banks want to obtain cash they can call in these loans and secure *the full sum originally lent*, with interest at the prearranged rate. There is no risk of loss. In London, therefore, the Money at Call, in so far as it is covered by eligible paper deposited by the discount houses, stands next to cash in order of liquidity. After that, and immediately after cash in other banking systems, come Treasury Bills and bills of exchange in order of their nearness to maturity. The very slight risk there is of wholesale default by all the other names on an eligible bill of exchange is the only reason for placing Treasury Bills before ordinary bills of the same maturity. No other assets are so shiftable. Wherever there is a well-developed central-banking system banks are apt to consider their proportion to deposits of these highly liquid assets as almost as important as their cash ratios and their readiness to expand on the basis of increased cash may be checked by a scarcity of these assets.

III. *The Attractions of Self-liquidating Paper*

But so far we have, in a sense, evaded the issue. We have said, in effect, that commercial banks have a certain prefer-

[1] For the discountable value of a bill, see pp. 47–48 above.

ence for those assets which the central bank prefers. To understand the problem thoroughly we must ask why the central bank has historically preferred assets of certain types, and the superficial answer unfortunately seems to take us round the circle again. Whether we look at the United States, which to some extent viewed the problem independently, or at England, or at the many countries which have simply followed American or English practice, the ultimate answer to our historical question is that central banks have, in order to protect themselves against loss and to discourage bad banking, preferred 'sound banking assets'. The ultimate reason for bills of exchange (and derivatively loans to reputable houses collaterally secured by bills) being considered 'sound banking assets' still eludes us.

We have only to glance at the literature of banking to find the banker's own explanation of the bill of exchange constituting 'a sound banking asset'. The bill of exchange, says the banker, is the ideal *self-liquidating paper*. The kind of bill a banker likes has its origin in an actual commercial transaction—say the export of Australian wheat to England—which will bring money into the hands of the debtor automatically at the end of a very short period of, say, three months. The banker simply has to sit back in his parlour for that very short time while the wheat is coming across to England, and the debtor will meet his bill without the slightest difficulty, provided, of course, that the debtor is an honest man—and the banker looks for reputable names on the bill to guarantee that he will receive in due course *the money that is bound to emanate from the conclusion of the transaction*. The banker has his theory of self-liquidating paper in mind not only when he is taking bills of exchange but also when he is making advances to business men—a loan for the purchase of raw materials needed to meet an order for the business man's product is normally more attractive to the banker than is a loan to an undergraduate to enable the latter to complete his university course. The great difference between the bill of exchange and the informal commercial loan is that in the former case there is, and in the latter case there is not, a negotiable legal instrument that greatly facilitates the shifting of the loan. And if we want to know why the bill method is used in one case more than in another the answer is that bankers have devised the negotiable legal instrument to increase the marketability of those assets which, by reason of bankers' taste for their 'self-liquidating' nature, already have most chance of finding a market. The existence of a legal instrument called a bill of exchange is not the hall-mark of the self-liquidating asset.

A self-liquidating loan is thus one the debtor is thought sure to be able to repay, because there is evidence (often in the shape of shipping documents or warehouse receipts held by one of the parties) that he is engaged in a genuine commercial operation, closure of which will provide him with the wherewithal for repayment. But, to revert to our example of the Australian wheat exporter, will the closure of the transaction—the sale of the wheat in England—necessarily enable the debtor to repay? That depends on the price the wheat realizes. The loan arrangement will generally, by keeping the amount of the bill below the expected sale value of the wheat, allow some margin to cover a slight unforeseen fall in wheat prices. If, however, there is a catastrophic fall in wheat prices before the cargo of Australian wheat comes on the market, the transaction itself provides no guarantee of the debtor's ability to meet the bill on maturity.[1] And what generally prevents such a catastrophic fall of prices? The maintenance of the total volume of lending by the banks. If bankers, in a misguided attempt to 'liquidate' their assets, refuse to take up any new bills and do simply sit back in their parlours and wait for the maturities of the bills in

---

[1] I ignore, for the sake of simplicity, the complicating fact that the merchant will probably have 'hedged'. Readers familiar with the process will realize that my conclusion is unaffected if the appropriate complications are introduced.

their portfolios, there is a catastrophic fall in the supply of purchasing-power and the catastrophic fall in prices which makes it impossible for debtors to meet bills out of the proceeds of their operations. Only by maintaining their assets can banks maintain the 'self-liquidating' character of a substantial class of them. The banks are for the most part important direct lenders in the short-term capital market, and the availability of means to pay off maturing short-term debts depends essentially on the banks' readiness to make new short-term loans. The certainty there appears to be that holding a bill will not involve a bank in loss if only the bill is held to maturity depends on the assumption that the banking system as a whole will not be contracting credit. Hence the widespread ruin of even the 'soundest' of institutions if a crisis is allowed to go unchecked. On the other hand, it is within the power of the banks themselves to ensure that bills will be met at maturity (always provided the various signatories are honest).

It might at first glance be supposed that the same argument should be applied to the market for long-term securities and that these could, by the action of the banks themselves in always supporting the market, be made equally attractive as liquid assets. Against this there are two substantial objections. First, the central bank may want interest rates to rise, and in pursuit of this aim the central bank will have to keep the cash basis small enough to deter the commercial banks from supporting the gilt-edged market. A rise in the long-term rate of interest implies a much greater fall in the market prices of securities than a rise in short rates causes in the capital value of short-term bills. Consequently, the banks have always to face the possibility that their balance-sheet position will be vulnerable if they hold a large proportion of long-term securities, no matter how 'safe' these securities are in the sense of certainty of full repayment at maturity.[1]

---

[1] If the central bank appears, over a sufficiently long period, to be

Secondly, even if there were assurance of stability in long-term interest rates, there would remain an objection to long-term financing of industrial and commercial activity. Traditionally bankers, as providers of short-term capital for traders, have been accustomed to consider primarily a borrower's honesty and good faith *and his balance-sheet position.* If the honest borrower has a reasonably liquid position—if he has stocks of marketable raw material and finished products, and goods in process that will emerge as marketable finished products fairly soon—he can be counted upon to repay a temporary advance. A provider of long-term capital, on the other hand, is concerned not so much with the balance-sheet position as with the *long-term earning capacity* of the borrower. Assessment of earning capacity is a task very different from assessment of the current balance-sheet position. It calls for a long view of markets, both for raw materials and for products, of technical possibilities, of labour supplies, and of the likelihood that the firm will maintain an adequate level of managerial competence. Assessment of all these factors can be reasonably undertaken only by large groups of specialists, each one specializing in one or a few industries. The traditional bank manager is not qualified for such 'industrial consultant' work. Ability and training of one kind are required to judge whether A, B, C, &c., will be solvent in three months' time: quite other abilities and experience are required before a man can judge whether A (let alone B, C, &c.) will be solvent in twenty years' time. It is this distinction that lies behind the traditional view that a banker should make only 'self-liquidating' loans, and the discredit into which the naïve theory of self-liquidating loans has rightly fallen does not justify forgetfulness of the

firmly attached to a policy of stable interest rates, the force of this objection is weakened and bankers become willing to enlarge their proportion of long-term securities. This was at least beginning to happen in the U.S.A. in the period 1945–51, when in deference to Treasury ideas the Federal Reserve System itself supported the long-term securities market at fixed prices.

important truths that lie behind it. Now that full understanding of central banking has made all assets ultimately
shiftable on to the central bank, bankers must not imagine
that all assets are 'liquid'. The loss-avoiding aspect has
to be remembered, as well as the shiftability aspect of
liquidity. If losses are to be avoided, the risks taken should
not fall outside the practicable range of the bank manager's
judgement.

IV. *Changing Practices in Lending by Banks*

Ideas about what constitutes 'sound' banking—the
ideas analysed in the last few pages—developed most
notably in England in the nineteenth and early twentieth
centuries, but the basic principles are to be found all over
the world. Everywhere, bankers look in their assets for
a nice combination of profit and liquidity, and this common approach leads to a considerable degree of similarity
in balance-sheet structures. The similarity cannot amount
to uniformity, because there is not uniform *availability* of
assets for bankers in different countries. To make an
extreme example, Money at Call in England consists
largely of loans to the discount houses: highly liquid loans,
almost as good as cash. But in many countries there is no
discount market at all, so that this most attractive type of
banking asset is simply unobtainable. Again, in many of
the less developed countries, local law and custom do not
give the banker any reasonable chance of covering a loan
with useful collateral security, and in such countries the
commercial banks have tended to confine their operations
to the great trading ports and their assets have been
heavily weighted with the finance of overseas trading and
with short-term loans made in the London money market.

The shape of the assets structure can sometimes be explained only by reference to historical circumstances that
have passed away. The most extreme examples of this are

the result of wars: in modern wars, governments use the banking systems as engines for raising funds for paying the cost of war, and commercial banks as well as central banks emerge into the post-war period with portfolios overweighted with government securities which have never had any connexion with 'sound commercial business'. This was true of the English banking system for at least thirteen years after 1945, and some continental banks —the Belgian for example—still carry this legacy of war finance. A quite different mark of history is to be found in some continental banking systems where the preference for short-term lending is carried to the point of legislative insistence, in reaction against the much broader practices of an earlier phase. In the early years of this century, many continental banks were deeply involved in long-term finance of industrial development, a kind of business English banks by this time had come to abhor. The contrast was not the result of different banking theories but of the different order of events in economic history on the two sides of the Channel. Industrial development on the Continent was often much more rapid; the use of the large firm, coming after English industry had shown the way to large-scale production, was often too rapid for its capital needs to be met in the piecemeal way in which English industry had obtained its long-term capital. In these circumstances banks were sometimes established to mobilize the savings of a country for the benefit of the new industries, and it became common practice for industrialists to look to the banks not only for working capital but also for fixed capital. Bankers thus became deeply involved in the fortunes of particular large industrial firms, and they paid the penalty in times of slump, most of all in the great slump of 1929 and the early 1930's. There would have been banking losses anyway, but the authorities in several countries rightly took the view that the involvement of ordinary deposit banks in the 'permanent' capital structure of industrial firms (the practice of 'mixed banking', as it was called) had much increased the severity of the banking crises that punctuated these years. In the passion of reform thus provoked, many countries enacted laws enforcing separation of business as deposit banks from business as industrial investment trusts; deposit banks were in effect prohibited from 'long' lending to industry. The success of British banks in withstanding the crisis naturally encouraged this process of 'purifying' deposit banking elsewhere and, even where the new laws did not push the banks to extremes, the tendency throughout western Europe was for commercial banks to confine themselves strictly to short-term lending. In 1966 memories of 1930–3 are still fresh enough to keep commercial bankers in some continental countries within limits that have meanwhile been breaking down in England.

In England since 1930, at any rate if we except the war and early post-war period, the tendency has been rather to broaden concepts of the proper lending range of the banks. One result of the great amalgamation movement (1890–1918) had been to make lending practices more uniform, narrower, perhaps more rigid. Partly because of this, but partly also because of other developments in English business life (industrial integration, and the spread of cash payment in retail trade), the importance of bank lending relatively to national income was already tending to shrink before 1930. Then the great slump and the economic stagnation of the early 1930's knocked down the opportunities for profitable lending along traditional lines, and the English banks found themselves, even when trade had revived substantially in 1934/7, lending a great deal less than they wanted to lend: the advances/deposits ratio seemed to stick well below 50 per cent., against the 60 per cent. ratio they had always thought perfectly safe. The processes of war finance and the informal control of bank advances, which continued through the early post-war years in the interest of the anti-inflation policy, aggravated this position, and the banks found their advances ratios doing no better than creeping up from 18 to 30 or thereabouts.

This 'underlent' position, persisting over many years, had its effects on the organization of the English banks. The selection of branch managers, the discretion given to them, the relation between branch manager and head office, the extent of reference by general managers to directors, were all substantially influenced by the fact that, while the making of an advance was an action to be carefully weighed by a sensible and experienced man, the refusal of an advance had become a very serious step indeed, to be taken only with the support of quite high authority within the bank. This attitude, cultivated through twenty years of easy-money conditions, has bitten deeply into the habits of the English banks and has had many incidental effects: among these, not the least was the difficulty of changing course when a general curtailment of advances eventually become necessary.

Another effect of the chronic shortage of opportunities for lending by the banks was a tendency to take a more generous view of what was proper lending business. When bankers are eager to lend, the 'unsatisfied fringe' of borrowers tends to disappear, and the banker shows no hesitation over the kind of proposition upon which he would previously have frowned. Most of all, his range tends to broaden where the limits had been set by inherited doctrine rather than direct experience; if a lending opportunity looks reasonably safe and his resources are abundant, the banker tends to allow traditional doctrine to retreat to the back of his mind.

This trend was perhaps imperceptible to most of those operating in the field, but over the years it had before 1959 already gone quite a long way. There was still no general disposition to involve a bank in the permanent financing of the fixed capital of industry, but bankers had become willing to make temporary loans for such purposes and for the anticipation of individual incomes if first-rate collateral security could be deposited. Mortgages on real property or life assurance policies were (and are) commonly regarded as such security. Banks might even, for customers whose professional, industrial, or trading position was known to the bank and whose credit-worthiness was beyond suspicion, make loans for any purpose without requiring any collateral security. No doubt all these things were done in the nineteenth century; but whereas in those days the speeches and books of bankers frowned upon such transactions as rather shady banking, the speeches and books of today discuss them as perfectly respectable transactions.

A notable direction in which bankers have become more ready to lend is the hire-purchase field; especially their attitude has changed towards instalment credit for consumer-durables. For many years after 1945 English banks were restrained from any open movement into this field, in furtherance of the Government's anti-inflation policy of restricting the total pressure of demand for goods and services. Through these years many English bankers were quite content with this restraint, because they regarded such business as not proper to banks, and they were quite happy to see new specialist financial intermediaries springing up to deal with such business. Others watched with increasing envy the successful ventures of American banks, and regretted that another opportunity for developing banking business seemed to be passing them by. In 1958 the Government gave the banks a free hand, and their hesitations and their restrictive doctrines seemed to vanish overnight; perhaps some of their reasonable caution went as well. At any rate, several of the banks plunged at once into part-ownership of hire-purchase finance companies, so that in their subsidiaries they became large-scale lenders for hire-purchase. The strange thing is that they, pursuing a policy of keeping these subsidiaries at arm's length, did not infuse them with any of the spirit that has enabled English banks to combine the flexibility the borrowing customer likes with the safety that minimizes calls on the

Bad Debts Account. As one of the bank chairmen has recently said (repeating many generations of his fore-runners), the banker's experience has taught him 'to make loans to people rather than upon the security of things'. The hire-purchase finance companies, on the other hand, have emphasized 'the security of things'; the banks, on taking over the companies, left this emphasis unchanged, and there appears to have been some gross over-lending in particular cases in the boom of 1959, with a conse-quential trail of bad losses in the subsequent years. At this same time, however, the banks began to make loans directly for their usual customers for precisely similar purposes, and with agreed repayment by instalments, and in this direct consumer credit business the banks have certainly applied their normal criteria of personal solvency and character. This has been equally true of their lending for house-purchase; this is business they have always been willing to do in a quiet way, especially where the customer has been able to repay in a fairly short period of years, but since 1958 they have greatly extended this side of their business and have more openly claimed it as a business in which banks may properly engage.

Another development, and one of great importance to the British economy, has been in the field of export finance. Agitations for special provision for the financing of export business are nothing new in British economic history, but since 1944 the problem has become altogether more important. There are four main reasons for this new emphasis. First, export business has grown relatively to the total business of the country: roughly a quarter of the nation's product is for export. Secondly, because of the chronic weakness of the balance of payments, this growth of exports has never been big enough: in order to maintain the volume of imports desired by the fully employed British people, public policy has been directed to stimu-lation of exports, especially by ensuring that British exporters enjoyed facilities as good as those of their competitors in other countries. Thirdly, there has been a big change in the character of British exports, the emphasis being increasingly on capital goods which last a long time and often present great credit problems to their purchasers. Fourthly, partly because of the balance of payments difficulties, countries purchasing large amounts of capital goods have not been able, as they had been before 1930, to finance their capital development by raising long-term loans on the British market. For these reasons, there has been a large and growing demand for loans to finance, often over periods of years, the purchase of British exports. To a large extent, the problem has been one of arranging some insurance to cover the lender against the more important risks of loss; this has been provided by the work of the Export Credit Guarantee Department (E.C.G.D.), which has gradually extended the insurance cover allowed. Once covered (or largely covered) by E.C.G.D. arrangements, any reasonably short business would readily be financed by the banks. But, with increasing emphasis on capital goods and great works of capital construction, an important part of the business tended to require loan periods of five years or even longer. As long as they were obviously 'underlent' (their Advances/ Deposits ratios being much lower than they liked) the banks were ready to do such business, especially as the authorities were continually asking the banks to facilitate export business. They became somewhat uncomfortable as the proportion of fairly 'long' business rose, and special arrangements were made to share out certain very large transactions.

The position became rather different from about the beginning of 1960, when the burst of bank-lending in 1958 and 1959, coupled with the success of the authorities in keeping down the supply of liquid assets for the banks, found the latter no longer in such an obviously 'underlent' position. It was not that they were unable to make advances to exporters forthwith, but that many of these transactions involved commitments to lend for two or three years ahead, before the goods could be shipped and the instalments of repayment would begin. The banks were thus faced with demands they could meet only at the risk of being unable to meet the normal—and important—demands of other customers two or three years ahead. The emergence of this difficulty caused the Bank of England, in furtherance of government policy on export questions, to seek some means of assuring the banks of adequate liquidity to support further extensions of medium-term export credit without compromising the Bank of England's control (through the control of liquid assets) of the more general supply of bank credit. The solution adopted, and announced on 6 February 1961, was for the Bank of England to stand ready to re-finance (i.e. lend *to* the banks) part of what had been, or would be, lent *by* the banks in respect of certain defined export business. The export credit transactions eligible under this scheme are of course carefully defined; they all require E.C.G.D. cover of one kind or another. The part refinanceable by the Bank of England consists of instalments repayable by the buyer within eighteen months: thus, if the total lent is £10,000 and it is repayable in equal quarterly instalments over the next five years, £3,000 is at any time refinanceable by the Bank of England. Moreover, for the purposes of the 28 per cent. minimum liquid assets rule (p. 38 above) all refinanceable export credits (including those arranged before announcement of the scheme) count as 'liquid assets'. The Bank of England thus, when it initiated the scheme, by a stroke of the pen added some millions to the liquid assets of the banks, at a time when these were rather low and the Bank did not wish to make a more ostentatious relaxation of credit. Also—and more importantly—its action encouraged the banks to engage in fresh export credit business by giving them the assurance that a proportion (commonly as much as 30 per cent.) of any such advances would at once count as an increase in their *liquid* assets. The banks were thus free to add to their export credits without seriously compromising their future capacity to take care of the normal business requirements of their other customers.

A complaint of exporters, unsatisfied by this innovation, has been the absence of any protection against rising interest rates. In granting advances for export business, the banks continued, after the 1961 changes, their long-standing practice of charging interest geared to Bank Rate, the formula commonly being 'one per cent. above Bank Rate, minimum 5 per cent.' However long the credit ran, interest charged was always liable to fluctuation under this clause, sometimes to the borrower's disadvantage. Exporters were particularly vociferous in their complaints of their exposure to such unforeseeable increases in the cost of finance after Bank Rate was raised to 7 per cent. in 1961, this being the second such occasion in five years. Following this, the London clearing banks and the Scottish banks agreed to supply medium-term finance for the export of heavy capital equipment at a *fixed* rate which, for an initial period of five years, was set at $5\frac{1}{2}$ per cent. Under this new arrangement (credits under which are eligible for the Bank of England's 'refinancing' scheme) the borrowing exporters sometimes pay less (as in early 1962) and sometimes pay more (as in early 1963), *but they know from the outset what their financing costs are to be*, a state of certainty preferred by many exporters when tendering in close competition against firms in other countries.

The development of medium-term export finance by the banks thus began as a response to a growing need, a response the banks could easily make if they were prepared to qualify the more rigorous doctrines of confinement to short-term business. But it has continued, and gone much further after the bankers themselves became uncomfortable on account of their declining liquidity, because the authorities were anxious that inferior credit facilities should not impede the growth of British exports.

It must not be supposed that these official blessings have in some way exempted increased bank lending for exports from the general rule that increased bank lending to producers stimulates aggregate demand for goods and services and so adds to inflationary pressures. Increased export credits are inflationary; but so is almost anything that successfully stimulates the growth of exports. The trouble is that the development of exports has been so vitally and so urgently important that the Government has had to regard it as an aim of policy in favour of which even the containment of inflation must give way.

These developments in the English banks will serve to show how in their lending policies the clearing banks do respond to pressures of various kinds in the economy, modifying without abandoning the rules of good banking inherited from earlier generations. Inhibitions on the lending side tend to give way when the banks find themselves chronically underlent; correspondingly, habits that restrain the eagerness with which deposits are invited tend to give way when the banks year after year find themselves unable to satisfy the 'reasonable' demands of their established customers. Which of these two is the prevailing atmosphere is determined by a host of circumstances in the country's economic structure: the payments habits of firms and individuals, 'finance-consciousness', the development of other financial institutions, savings habits, and many others. Through most of the post-war period, and for some time before, the position was that the banks were 'underlent', and the characteristic attitude was a willingness to extend the range of lending. Since 1960 government policy has checked further extension of lending, but the banks are at least showing a new anxiety to attract deposits in support of more active lending policies as soon as their freedom is restored.

9

THE EFFECTS OF BANKING POLICY ON
ECONOMIC ACTIVITY

1. *Short-term Rates of Interest and the Holding of Goods*

BANKERS sometimes allege that they are power-
less to influence the volume of economic activity,
and that they merely sit in their offices and welcome
the opportunity to provide temporary financial help for
any sound business that comes along. At the other extreme have been monetary cranks who sometimes, and
especially at times of trade depression, gain the public ear
by imputing to the operations of bankers most of the ills
of our economic society. Between these two extremes lie
the opinions of most economists and quite a large number
of bankers; some are nearer to the passive view, while
others are nearer (at least in their conclusions) to the
monetary cranks. In this chapter and the next, we shall
consider what reasons there are for supposing that the
operations of the banks influence the tempo of economic
activity: we shall be examining, that is to say, the rationale
of monetary policy, for all monetary policy in a modern
community is based on the belief that in greater or less
degree the operations of the banks are relevant to the
tempo of economic activity. In the present chapter we
shall be concentrating on the effects of changes in the rates
of interest ruling in the banking system; then in the next
chapter we shall look in rather more detail at the inter-
action of banking operations and the functioning of the
wider network of financial intermediaries that has become
characteristic of the highly developed capitalist or mixed
economies outside the Iron and Bamboo Curtains.

The tempo of economic activity depends upon the readiness and ability of the business men to employ real resources in the processes of production, and it is through their influence upon both the business man's readiness and his ability to set resources to work that the banks can influence the level of activity. It is important to remember throughout these two chapters that the business man is influenced by many factors not in the least under the banker's control, and we shall have to consider how the banking factors compare with others in weight. The banking factors may be divided into three: (1) the short-term rates of interest, which have their most direct impact on the cost of holding goods temporarily; (2) the long-term rates of interest, which have their impact more upon the demand for fixed capital equipment; and (3) the availability (as distinct from the cost) of bank loans, which can have direct impact on the business man's capacity to purchase any real resources, including finished goods as well as labour, capital equipment, and goods in course of production.

We have seen, in Chapter 8, how the banker always has a strong preference for short-term lending. In the main, he lends to cover 'temporary' outgoings, and this means that, of all business transactions, it is the ownership of stocks of finished goods or marketable raw materials that he most likes to finance. The liquidity of the traders' balance-sheet position, if substantial marketable stocks are held, provides the banker with some assurance that the borrower will, by the sale of the goods, be able to repay the loan, and in these circumstances it is not necessary for the banker to consider at all closely the longer-term earning capacity of the borrower. The price of these short-term loans to business is (in English terms) the overdraft rate which is fixed by the banks on the basis of the officially fixed Bank Rate. By raising overdraft rates the banks can, it is argued, stimulate business men to reduce the stocks of goods they are holding with the help of overdrafts, and

this will check the tempo of economic activity; and similarly, a fall in overdraft rates will encourage stock-piling
and so raise the tempo.

The mechanism by which the bankers' charges for overdraft are linked with the demand for stocks of goods
requires a little more attention. The argument runs thus:
operators in most lines of business hold stocks, in one
shape or another, in order to meet variations in customers'
demands and in order to avoid the consequences of inter-
ruptions in the supply of materials, &c. The convenience
of holding stocks has thus a clear money value to the
trader, and although this cannot, from the nature of the
case, be a sharply determined value, it is real enough to
be balanced against the costs of holding stocks. Among
the costs of holding stocks is the interest that has to be
paid on the money that has to be borrowed to enable the
trader to pay for and to hold the goods. Consequently a rise
in the rate of interest charged on bank advances constitutes an increase in the cost of holding stocks and will provide an incentive to traders to reduce stocks. This they
can only do by buying less rapidly than they are selling.
In effect, they exchange part of their stocks of goods for
money, which they use to pay off their debts to the banks.
Producers of the goods being 'destocked' would find their
sales falling off, and they would tend to reduce output and
perhaps cut their prices. The deterrent to stock-holding,
if pressed far, would thus be followed by the typically
deflationary symptoms of falling prices and shrinking output. Contrariwise, if the banks reduced their overdraft
rates, the cost of holding stocks would fall and traders
would be encouraged to increase their stocks, and this
they could do only by buying more rapidly than they were
selling. Orders to producers would rise—output expand—
employment increase—money incomes rise—and so on.
Inflationary conditions would, in short, be promoted by
a reduction in bank interest charges.

The importance of this argument depends upon just

how much weight is attached by business men to changes in the interest charge when they are reviewing the level of their stocks. There are many other costs of holding stocks: warehousing, insurance, allowance for perishing, and, above all, the risk that the price of the commodity will fall while it is being held. These various charges differ widely for difference commodities, but in most cases they are sufficient to swamp any but the most extreme changes in interest rates. The supposition that changes in rates of interest do not have substantial effects on 'buying for stock' was confirmed by the evidence collected by the Radcliffe Committee. This evidence, which referred only to Britain and mainly to the middle 1950's, has sometimes been misinterpreted because individual answers sometimes indicated an important effect; but most such answers referred, the Committee found, to a peculiar conjunction of circumstances and were no basis for judging more normal reactions.[1] National statistics for inventories all pointed the other way, and the Committee was therefore inclined to pay more attention to the business men who alleged that interest rates were almost irrelevant to their policy on inventories. The relevant circumstances may, of course, have been different at some times in the past (possibly in England in the first half of the nineteenth century) and there may be in some other trading communities today conditions in which the inventory positions of business firms are highly sensitive to the rate of interest; but in general, in speaking of most modern economies, we can say that the bankers cannot substantially influence economic activity through this particular channel.

It should not be supposed that the level of stocks is therefore insensitive to anything that bankers can do. The

---

[1] The early post-war habit of scrambling for stocks had outlived the circumstances that bred it. Consequently many firms found themselves with stocks much in excess of any reasonable requirements, and, when interest rates emerged from their long period of insignificance, firms were shocked into measures of stock-control the introduction of which had a once-for-all effect in stimulating reduction.

availability of credit is likely to be highly relevant. If, as is normally the case, rising interest rates are associated with lowered willingness to lend (and therefore greater difficulty in borrowing), the business man often finds a running-down of stocks the easiest way of adjusting his financial position. But it is *tight credit* rather than *dear credit* that produces this reaction.

11. *The Connexion between Short-term and Long-term Interest Rates*

In the main the interest rates directly determined by banking policy are rates for short-term financing. The influence of the bankers' decisions, however, penetrates far beyond the temporary business operations they themselves prefer, because there are substantial connexions between short-term rates and long-term rates of interest. Any persistent and appreciable change in short-term rates is always associated with some change in long-term rates; and banking policy is thereby enabled to influence those business decisions which turn on the level of long-term interest rates, as well as on those rather rarer cases in which short rates are of direct importance. If we are to understand how banking policy affects economic activity, we must not be content with observing that changes in long-term rates are generally associated with changes in short-term rates: we must attempt to explain *why* a decided movement in short-term rates is bound to be followed by a movement, in the same direction, in long-term rates.

In the first place it is important to remember that a rate of interest is a *price*—the price of money now in exchange for money at some later date. Every price has its own market. To find the connexion between two prices we must look for some connexion between the short-term capital market—the market dominated by the relations between banks and their customers—and the markets in which money is invested for longer periods, a field in which the banks play only a minor part. What connexions are there between the various parts of the capital market?

The answer is to be found in the facts that people prefer cheap borrowing to dear borrowing, and lending for high rates rather than low rates, and that they are not absolutely rigid in their ideas about the periods for which they borrow or lend. The *time-structures* or *maturity-structures* of their investment portfolios, and of their commitments as borrowers, are not rigid; people are ready to alter the time-structure in order to take advantage of a relative cheapening of shorter- or longer-term loans. This applies to individuals and to industrial and commercial firms, but most of all it applies to financial intermediaries (sometimes including the banks themselves). The business of these financial intermediaries is mainly that of lending and borrowing, and it is natural that they should be quick to take advantage of relative changes in the terms of lending and borrowing for different periods. A drop in short-term interest rates (which can be brought about directly by the monetary authorities) makes the financial intermediaries anxious to lend rather less at short-term and rather more at long-term, and to avoid borrowing at the relatively high long-term rates. Thus the pressure of lending is increased, and the pressure of borrowing reduced, in long-term markets, and this change in the relationship of supply and demand makes long-term loans cheaper—i.e. tends to pull down long-term rates of interest. The weight of the financial institutions is great, because of the huge funds under their control, and their action alone would be sufficient to ensure that a reduction in short-term rates would tend to drag down long-term rates; but they are not alone in reacting in this manner. Every company finance director who has funds available for investment will feel the same pull, and so will treasurers of charities and trusts, and rich individuals too. The banks' Time Deposit rate, which varies automatically with Bank Rate and so is under clear official control, is of particular importance in encouraging reaction in other parts of the capital market, because the Time Deposit is the easiest and most obvious employment for idle funds: if the yield obtained on Time Deposit drops, people are more ready 'to put their money into' government securities. Similarly, since purchase of Treasury Bills became an important short-term use of funds by large companies, the Treasury Bill rate (under almost as close official control) has become very important as a drag (in one direction or the other) on the interest rates that can be obtained on short- and even medium-term government securities. Again, the rates charged on bank overdrafts have some influence, for people or companies finding that overdraft charges have gone up will be more ready to sell any securities they have and pay off the relatively expensive overdraft: and their selling tends to depress the prices (and so raise the yields) of securities.

The men whose business it is to put purchases and sales of securities together—the jobbers in the Stock Exchange, particularly in the gilt-edged section—know that this is how people react. To protect themselves against a flood of sales, and insufficient buying orders, when short-term interest rates rise, they put down ('mark down') the prices of gilt-edged securities at once; particularly they will mark down the prices at the shorter end of the market. Similarly, when short rates go down, the jobbers mark up gilt-edged prices, without waiting for a flood of buying orders. The market, that is to say, *anticipates* the change in the supply-and-demand situation, and the appropriate reaction in the yields of securities comes at once.

In order that a change in short rates should react in this way on longer-term rates of interest, it is not necessary to imagine that any lenders, or any borrowers, are prompted by the change in short-rates to switch their operations right across from, say, three-months' Treasury Bills to a forty-years' government bond. All that is necessary is that some people should be prepared to switch to *rather longer* (or rather shorter) securities, while others switch from the rather longer (to which the first people switch) to longer still, nobody moving very far along the time-scale but many moving short 'distances' that overlap. Thus a *chain effect* is produced, the net effect of which may be just as powerful in linking the shortest and the longest rates, as if a few large operators had been ready to switch from one end to the other end of the time-scale. No one is likely to alter the maturity-structure of his portfolio radically, but if the maturity-structures overlap, and many investors with varied maturity-structures react at all to relative changes in the interest rates that directly affect them, a change in short-rates will tend to drag all the longer-term rates in the same direction.

The strength of this repercussion, and the smoothness with which it comes about, will, it must be emphasized, depend on the overlapping nature of investors' portfolios (particularly those of the financial intermediaries) and the ease with which each can shift *just a little*, so as to get an advantage without running up against the general principles on which each regulates the balance of his investments and commitments. The more varied, and the more nicely graduated, are the securities available in markets, the more effectively will the repercussions sweep through the whole structure of interest rates. From this point of view the very elaborate structure of the U.K. National Debt is of great importance: there is a great variety of British government securities, with a wide and full range of maturities. The development of financial intermediaries, with their great variety of portfolios and of investment principles, operates in the same way, to strengthen the links between the shorter and the longer-term rates of interest. In other countries there is no precise parallel to the elaboration of the U.K. National Debt, and in many of them there is no such proliferation of financial inter-mediaries. Even in some of the economically advanced countries there is little in the way of safe medium-term

securities and the operator with funds to invest has either
to put them to very short-term use or to commit them to
the long-term market. In such circumstances it is natural
that people should think in terms of two quite different
markets, sometimes referred to as the 'credit market' or
'money market' on the one hand and the 'capital market'
on the other. This terminology, though reflecting a reality
of the business circumstances in those countries, can only
confuse when applied to a country such as Britain where
there are infinitely varied opportunities for exchanging
money available at one date against money available at
some later date.

The upshot of our argument thus far is that, even if the
direct operation of the monetary authorities is confined
to short-term rates of interest, the long-term rates will be
driven in the same direction by market forces whose
existence depends on the 'spilling over' of capital supply
and demand from one part of the market to another. This
conclusion is not, however, sufficient for purposes of
policy. We must face the further question, how much?
The shift of demand and supply from one part of a market
to another merely points to the conclusion that, to the
extent that prices move, they will move in one direction
and not in the other, and we cannot tell whether the price
change in the long-term part of the market will be appreciable without knowing more about the forms of the
demand and supply functions.

The short answer to our question is that the extent to
which the 'spilling-over' will cause the long-term rate to
reflect a movement of short rates will depend very much
on the state of market expectations. Public opinion about
the future course of interest rates is a very powerful factor
in determining the prices (and so the yields) of long-term
securities, and a mere reduction of short-term rates may
not by itself do much to modify that opinion. And unless
opinion is modified, the shifts in investment portfolios
provoked by the movement in short-term rates may not

do much to modify that opinion. Even if the shifts in port-folios are reinforced by official operations in the security markets, so that the market has to absorb less short and more long securities (if we are to think of rising interest rates), the disturbances of the supply-and-demand situation may be absorbed with comparatively small movements in the prices of long-term securities.

This conclusion, which is of critical importance to an economic policy depending upon encouragement or discouragement of private capital spending, has been thrust somewhat abruptly on the reader and an example may help. We shall, to simplify the arithmetic, use some extreme and rounded figures, but the reader should remember that normal course of economic life shows gentler movements and more awkward arithmetic. We shall also simplify the example by directing our attention to an investor who is willing, on a suitable incentive appearing, to switch from some very short-term use for his funds (such as holding a bank deposit, or three-months' Treasury Bills) to the 'infinitely' long-term security, the $2\frac{1}{2}$ per cent. Consols that are in practice irredeemable.

We take as our starting-point the supposition that the price of Consols has lately been fluctuating around 50, which gives a running yield of 5 per cent. ($\pounds 2\frac{1}{2}$ is paid on $\pounds 100$ stock, and this can be bought for $\pounds 50$). We shall suppose further that there is a general expectation that for at least the next year or two the long-term rate will remain at about 5 per cent. Applying to this particular case the conclusion we have reached above, we have to show that, no matter how far short-term rates are now reduced, the long-term rate will not fall much below 5 per cent. (i.e. the price of Consols will not rise much above 50).

Anyone who pays *now* a price much above 50 will have to meet severe capital depreciation in the next year or two. It will be better to hold off the market, holding a bank balance although the latter yields no interest, rather than incur a capital depreciation that would swamp any yield obtained from interest payments on the Consols. A man would do better for himself by holding a bank balance or lending his money out in the short money-market at a very low rate of interest than by buying Consols immediately at 62. A man with £620 to invest in Year 1 could, by buying Consols at once, secure a perpetual income of £25 per annum; but by waiting until Year 3 he could use his £620 to buy Consols yielding £31 per annum; alternatively, he could use £500 to secure the income of £25 per annum, and have £120 'profit' to set against the low interest he has had to take on his £620 during the two years through which he waited for the price of Consols to fall. If everybody expects the market to move in this way no one will buy in Year 1 at 62, and all holders will wish to sell—the pressure of sales unmatched by demand would send the price down, and (on our assumptions) it would in fact fall almost to 50—perhaps to 52, the exact figure depending on the precise level of short-term rates. Thus the effect of a change in short-term rates upon the long-term market is narrowly limited by what people expect the long-term rate to be in the near future; and unless the change in short rates of itself causes a decided change in expectations about the long rates, even a very great change in the short rates will cause only a very small change in long rates.

This importance of the market's expectations about long rates has been abundantly illustrated in the experience of London markets in the last few decades. The failure of the 'Dalton drive' for ultra-cheap money in 1946–7 showed how a sceptical public can resist falling rates by throwing their securities on the market. After the successful cheap-money policy of the nineteen-thirties, a 3 per cent. rate of interest was comfortably held throughout the war of 1939–45. Then in 1946–7 the authorities, by their open-market operations and by propaganda in which the then Chancellor of the Exchequer (Hugh Dalton) played a prominent part, forced the long-term rate down momentarily to about $2\frac{1}{2}$ per cent. But the market took the view that, in the light of the basic economic forces of high demand for capital investment and scarcity of resources, $2\frac{1}{2}$ per cent. was an unnaturally low rate—a rate that could not be held. Believing that $2\frac{1}{2}$ per cent. could not be held meant believing that security prices must fall below the current level (the level that gave $2\frac{1}{2}$ per cent. yields). For this and other reasons the private sector of the market was therefore pressing sales of government securities, and was not willing to buy. The 'unnaturally' high prices of securities—the prices that represented the $2\frac{1}{2}$ per cent. yield—could be held only by continued official buying of the long-term securities. As more and more holders of government securities came to believe that this was a mere juggling operation and that prices must fall, more and more unloaded their holdings and the official support began to involve an enormous pumping of money into the market.[1] In the months of disillusion that began in February 1947, the authorities took fright at the length to which they were having to go in support of the $2\frac{1}{2}$ per cent. line, and they withdrew their support. Gilt-edged prices promptly fell away, and the long-term rate was soon fractionally above 3 per cent., a level thereafter held for some considerable time by a free market, because people thought this a level that, given the various government controls, could reasonably be held.

In the Dalton episode the influence of market expectations was a factor forcing the rate of interest up. In the middle fifties, on the other hand, the state of market expectations for a long time acted as a drag on the upward movement of the long-term rate. Especially this was seen in the period 1953–5, when a purely temporary easing of the balance of payments problem allowed the authorities

---

[1] In some earlier editions of this book, the mechanism of these official operations and their impact on the banks were explained in some detail. This detailed analysis can now be found in Appendix 2 (pp. 309–18 below).

to drop short rates and this was interpreted by the market as a sign that the danger of a spell of altogether higher rates of interest had diminished. Long-term rates therefore ceased to rise, and actually fell, although the conditions that had underlain the rise of 1949–52 had not changed. For a time this drag on long-term rates was welcome to the authorities, but from about 1957 onwards they came to regard a higher level of long-term rates as appropriate, so that when certain developments in 1957 shocked the market into a drastic revision of ideas about the future of the rate of interest, the authorities actually encouraged the new view. Thereupon long-term rates rose to levels that were extraordinarily high by any historical standards, and in 1958–62 remained in that high range although short-term rates were little different from what they had been in earlier years.

III. *Long-term Rates of Interest, the Availability of Capital Funds, and Investments in Fixed Capital*

The moral of all this is that, in an economic system such as that of Britain in the nineteen-sixties, a movement of short-term rates, such as can be brought about by the monetary authorities, will tend to push long-term rates in the same direction, but that this reaction will be only very slight unless public expectations are changed. A large and persistent movement of short rates will, however, itself have some effect in modifying expectations. The publicly expressed views of the authorities may encourage the change in expectations, especially if the official pronouncements are attuned to the investing public's ear. But, when all allowance has been made for the power of official propaganda, the monetary authorities remain peculiarly at the mercy of public opinion when they seek to operate on the long-term rate of interest. In so far, therefore, as monetary policy hangs upon the effect of changes in the rate of interest, it hangs upon a slender thread. Things are, however, a little brighter than that. Rising prices for long-term government bonds—a fall in the 'pure' long-term rate of interest—are logically associated with rising prices for securities generally (including those of public utilities and industrial companies), a greater willingness of the 'investing public' to take up new securities, and a readier flow generally of capital funds into the hands of business men who are ready to spend them on the construction of fixed capital equipment.

In the previous section we were discussing only the prices and yields of government long-term bonds. There are, of course, quite other classes of securities of far more direct interest to the industrial borrower. Besides the government (gilt-edged) securities, there are bonds issued by public utilities; debentures, preference shares, and ordinary shares of all sorts and sizes of industrial and commercial undertakings; and all these classes of securities are subdivisible into very many grades. At any given moment, however, there will be a certain relationship between the prices of securities of various grades, a relationship reflecting the investing public's preference for one grade as compared with others. *Given* these preferences, a rise in the price of one large class (e.g. government bonds), resulting from monetary operations that have depressed short-term interest rates, must be followed by a rise in the prices (a fall in the yields) of all other grades. Provided the public has a definite preference for one particular distribution between the various classes of its assets, a shift in the price of one must be followed by a general shift in the whole range of prices. It is true that the effects of a fall in the prices of government bonds on, say, ordinary share prices may be entirely obscured by a simultaneous shift in the public's preferences in favour of ordinary shares—an actual rise in the prices of the latter following the fall in the gilt-edged market. But the ordinary shares will tend to stand lower *than they would otherwise have done*. The general position in the capital market will, that is to say, have been made, by the movement of government bond prices, less favourable than it otherwise would have been to new seekers of money to spend on capital development.

A fall in the interest rates at which money can be obtained for new capital development will automatically increase the attraction of such development. When a firm is thinking of embarking on some capital extension—whether it be the purchase of a new machine, the doubling of a railway track, the addition of another runway to an airfield, or the sinking of another shaft at a mine—its decision will depend on a number of factors, some purely technical, others economic. The technical factors will include such points as the difference the investment will make to the physical output of the firm, the rapidity with which the new equipment will wear out, and the ease with which the extension can be fitted into the general framework of the firm's activities. The strictly economic questions will be, what will be the price of the additional product, and at what rate of interest can the purchase money for the new equipment be raised? Given all the technical factors, and given the firm's estimate of the receipts that will be realized from the use of the machine, whether or not the capital extension is embarked upon will depend upon the rate of interest at which money for such purposes can be raised. The lower the rate of interest, the more likely is the firm to decide that the capital extension is worth undertaking. On the other hand, the higher the rate of interest the less attractive is any form of capital extension.

Two examples may help to make this clear. Suppose a printing-works to be contemplating the purchase of another machine of some kind. The machine is, we will suppose, priced by the machine-makers at £1,000. Then the firm calculates that the machine would last twenty years, and that after making allowances for repairs, depreciation, adjustment of labour costs, &c., but not allowing for the interest charges, the use of the machine would make a difference of £50 a year to the gross profits of the firm. Then, as long as the rate of interest, at which the firm can obtain £1,000 for twenty years, is below 5 per cent., a net profit is to be gained from the introduction of the machine (for 5 per cent. on £1,000 = £50). When the effective rate of interest is 5 per cent. the venture is only just worth while —the machine is then a 'marginal' investment. When the effective rate of interest is above 5 per cent., the firm would incur a loss if it acquired the machine in question. It should be noticed that the relevant receipts are the *extra* receipts that would result from the introduction of the machine —whether the firm is incurring a loss or a profit on its previously invested capital is irrelevant (though it may affect the rate of interest at which the firm can obtain the capital sum required). Or suppose that a railway is contemplating electrification of part or all of its system. The managers have to make a number of estimates of the results of electrification—changes in the volume of traffic, in labour costs, in the costs of electricity, &c. Suppose that their guess is that an electrification plan, which would involve a capital expenditure of £20 millions, would increase the gross profits (or diminish the gross losses) of the company by a million pounds a year. Then, whether the railway was previously paying its way or not, the electrification scheme would appear worth adopting as long as the rate of interest at which the railway could obtain £20 millions was not above 5 per cent. Once the rate rises above 5 per cent., the venture becomes completely unattractive, unless anything happens to make the authorities revise their estimates of the results of electrification, or the costs of the electrification process itself fall.

Not only will these decisions have to be made about *new* capital development: precisely the same considerations must determine whether or not a firm should replace some plant which is wearing out. Reinvestment is only worth while if the firm could not do better for itself by investing the depreciation fund elsewhere.[1] As steam presses wear out, the company can always choose between replacing them and not replacing them, just as it can choose between erecting and not erecting an additional factory.

These examples have been highly simplified in order to enforce the main point—that the effective rate of interest will be one of the crucial factors in coming to the decision whether or not to embark on capital development. But, lest we should overrate the efficacy of an interest-rate policy, it is important to emphasize the extent to which the entrepreneur's estimates are likely to be guess-work. In the railway electrification example given above, it was assumed that gross profits would, as a result of cheaper running, larger traffic, &c., immediately rise to a new level and stay there. In fact this is most unlikely to be the case. The growth in traffic is likely to be a gradual process, and whether the enterprise is or is not worth while will depend to an important extent on how rapidly the growth of traffic occurs. If the growth is very slow, that is equivalent, from the company's point of view, to extra capital outlay, even if the growth does eventually attain the expected maximum. The rapidity of growth is, of course, very much a matter for conjecture. The responsible people will have various earlier experiences to work on; but to some extent every new enterprise is unique, and this is especially true of such big capital innovations as these. Moreover, labour costs and price levels over a period of twenty years or more will be extremely conjectural. As compensation for all these uncertainties, which are involved in the decision to invest, the entrepreneurs will look for some chance of profit, and their stress on this profit margin will vary very much from time to time, according to whether they are inclined to look through rose-coloured spectacles or to take gloomy views of the future.

[1] In extreme cases the relevant rate of interest may be quite different. For the alternative to replacement of, say, a flour-mill, may be holding gilt-edged securities, while extending an established flour-mill may mean issuing new debenture stock for which the public has little taste.

The uncertainties that obscure the business outlook are thus of great practical relevance to the question of the effect of interest changes. Many of the estimates business men make are necessarily highly conjectural, and against the wide margin of error a fractional change in the rate of interest may appear to make no difference worth bothering about. Far more important is likely to be the business man's general frame of mind about the future. In a depression things look so gloomy that no conceivable drop in the rate of interest is likely to induce him to embark upon any but the most blatantly desirable ventures. In a boom, on the other hand, things look so rosy that a fractional rise in the rate of interest, to be paid on the capital sum required, is unlikely to deter him from some investment, failure of which appears unthinkable. Even public investments— those made directly by central and local government bodies —are susceptible to similar influences that very easily outweigh the influence of the rate of interest. A town council considering the construction of public baths, for example, will find that the higher the rate of interest, the higher the 'rate' in the pound which is necessary for financing the service of the debt incurred for the purpose. But experience, decade after decade, has shown that public authorities are less influenced by a slight difference in the rate poundage produced by a change in the rate of interest than by whether or not they feel that the town is prosperous and 'can afford' the public works.

The reservations that we must therefore have in mind, when we are considering the stimulus given by a fall in interest rates to the demand for capital goods, of course apply with varying force in varying circumstances. In most branches of manufacturing industry, for example, a continuous (but not constant) stream of inventions occasions high obsolescence allowances that completely swamp the interest charges on a new machine. On the other hand, much capital outlay by the great public utilities is on construction of earthworks, permanent way, and other items that have very long lives and will not easily be replaced by alternative equipment. For such things as these the depreciation and obsolescence allowances are quite small, and the interest charge is correspondingly more important, and more *visibly* important to the firm or public body that will have to pay the piper. Dwelling-houses are undoubtedly among these items that are relatively 'interest-sensitive'— the interest on the original capital outlay is a very large part of the annual rent charge. More generally, we can say that the more durable is a capital good, and the less uncertain is its productivity, the more sensitive will be the demand for it to changes in the rate of interest. During the last twenty years, an increasing proportion of investment in long-lived capital goods (e.g. houses and railways) has come under direct governmental control; in these circumstances investment decisions have come to depend more on broader questions of public policy and less immediately on movements in interest rates.

When the effectiveness of the rate of interest as a stimulant of demand is hedged about in this way, the influence of monetary factors in determining the volume of economic activity seems to be slight indeed. Changes in the rate of interest often, however, receive some reinforcement from the changes in the practical *availability* of capital funds that accompany changes in interest rates when these are engineered by the monetary authorities. A cheap-money policy implies a sufficient pressure of money supplies to satisfy all the people and institutions who think that the rate of interest will go up presently and who therefore prefer to hold money rather than government bonds at present prices. Insurance companies, building societies, and ordinary business firms will all be tending to hold rather more money than they would normally expect to hold. It is in fact by this glutting of markets with money that we have supposed the authorities to be enforcing their low interest rates. Now when financial institutions and business firms hold unusually large balances, and are loth to 'invest' them in government bonds, other ideas in course of time enter their minds. They decide perhaps that although government bonds are not worth buying because their prices are high and yields low, it would be worth engaging in some quite speculative proposition that would give an altogether higher yield, in preference to 'holding all that money idle'. At any rate, they may be venturesome with *some* of the money. For business firms especially, the unusually high liquidity of their balance-sheets will tell in course of time—the power of the cautious directors to resist the cajolings of their more venturesome colleague, who wants to set up a branch factory or install a new kind of machine, will be worn down more easily when there is money in the kitty—or money to be borrowed unusually easily from an insurance company or finance house—than when the money could be had only by going to the bank and mortgaging the firm's assets up to the hilt. Similarly in the building world: when Building Societies find rates low and their liquid funds are mounting, they will find other ways, as well as cutting mortgage interest rates, for expanding their loan business. They will reduce the first 'down payments' on a house from 20 to 10 or even to 5 per cent., and they will extend the maximum repayment period from 15 to 20 or even 25 years, so as to inveigle poorer and poorer people into buying houses.[1] In a variety of ways the sluices of the capital market will be opened, so that it is not just a matter of loans being cheaper, but of all kinds of enterprisers, who previously could not get hold of money at all, or could not get it on any tolerable terms, now being able to get it to spend on capital development.

How strongly a change in rates of interest will stimulate

---

[1] Building Societies did in fact operate just in this way under the pressure of 'cheap money' in the 1930's in Britain; and their activities played an important part in encouraging the housing boom that helped to pull Britain out of depression. Correspondingly, rising interest rates in 1955–7 were associated with sharp tightening of the general terms on which Building Societies would lend.

the demand for capital goods is a matter of some doubt. Certainly the reinforcement of the rate changes themselves, by their consequences on the availability of funds through various channels, is an important part of the story. As far as the rates of interest themselves are concerned, the evidence heard by the Radcliffe Committee in 1958 indicated that the reaction of firms may be very slow, and will not come at all if the movement in rates is soon reversed. Those who plan a great part of the spending on capital works and equipment in the private sector of the British economy appear to base their calculations on conventional rates of interest, whatever the rate ruling in the market at the moment. These conventional rates do, however, respond eventually to a change in market rates that is persistent and is a move big enough to represent 'a change of gear'. The implication is that the rate of interest itself is not a particularly effective weapon if the authorities want to produce a quick change in the tempo of economic activity, but that it may still have an important part to play in a longer range policy designed to secure full employment of the country's resources consistently with avoidance of such excessive pressure of demand as would encourage an undesirable inflation of prices and other strains disturbing the steady growth of the economy.

10

THE PROCESSES OF CREATION OF CREDIT
AND FINANCIAL INTERMEDIATION

1. *The Nature of Credit and of Financial Assets, and their Relation to Saving*

IN the wealth owned by persons and corporations, some assets (especially physical assets) are scarcely relevant at all to the pace of spending on goods and services. Others are, in varying degree, highly relevant. The actual means of payment (money) is most obviously relevant. Some other assets are so readily exchangeable into money with little or no loss that they are almost equally relevant; these assets we say are more or less highly 'liquid'. The principal characteristic common to banks and all other financial intermediaries is that, while by their operations they do not add directly to the total of wealth, they add to the liquidity of the economy in that they put into the hands of potential spenders assets (liabilities of the financial intermediaries) that are more liquid than the assets (including promises to repay) that they take in exchange. This is what is meant when it is said that financial intermediaries (including banks) 'create credit'. Equally, this is what people mean when they say that banks and other financial intermediaries perform the useful service of 'mobilizing savings', making these savings available to those who will use them for adding to the real capital equipment of the economy.

This second notion, of intermediation between the supply of and the demand for savings, is responsible for the term 'financial intermediaries' that has now become common as a label for firms whose principal business is in financial claims rather than in goods. Yet they are clearly not mere intermediaries in the sense in which brokers in a commodity market or a Stock Exchange are pure intermediaries. The financial intermediaries accept various claims on other people, and in exchange offer their own liabilities: claims against themselves. They operate, that is to say, as principals, dealing separately on their own account with lenders (e.g. 'depositors') on the one side and with borrowers on the other side. Customers do business with the intermediaries because the liabilities of the intermediaries are more useful, for market purposes, than are the liabilities of the customers themselves. This is true of non-bank intermediaries, as it is of the banks themselves; the one difference (how crucial a difference is another question) is that the liabilities of the banks are *more* useful for market purposes than are the liabilities of other intermediaries. For all alike, the operations are exchanges of claims. The addition to the market effectiveness, by reason of the regard in which the banks or other financial intermediaries are held, is the essential nature of the 'creation of credit'. It is because financial intermediaries 'create credit', in this sense of exchanging a more marketable for a less marketable claim, that we ascribe to them some influence on the total pressure of demand for goods and services and on the working of the economic system generally. But this process of credit creation is quite different from the processes of saving and investment, with which the activities of financial intermediaries are also associated. The primary purpose of this chapter is to show just how the activities of the financial intermediaries are related to the processes of saving and investment and thus to show the nature of the connexion between these processes and the creation of credit.

In our first steps we shall omit the possibility of transactions with the Government, or, what comes to the same thing, assume that the Government is no different from any private firm in its market operations and their consequences. We shall also at first group the banks with others in the comprehensive term 'financial intermediaries'; later we shall try to distinguish between them, if only to show that in some respects they can *not* be distinguished.

The first step is to remember that in every transaction of a financial intermediary there is, in addition to the intermediary, a second party: the customer who is the lender or borrower.[1] This may seem a trite enough observation, but it is one whose implications have often been overlooked. It is important to remember that the financial intermediary cannot offer to borrowers the facilities they want unless it can find some other customers who are content to hold claims against the intermediary, and who are prepared initially to sacrifice some other asset in order to get the claim against the intermediary. The banker's way of making this point is to say that 'a bank cannot lend more than is deposited with it'; when economists take exception to this way of putting it, they should admit the slightly different fact that a bank's outstanding loans cannot exceed the deposits standing in its books (except by its 'Liabilities' to its own shareholders), an amount which, in its turn, is limited to the amount the bank can persuade customers to hold. The same is true of every other financial intermediary and of financial intermediaries in total.

In this first step we have been remarking on the transactions between financial intermediaries and their customers as essentially exchanges of claims outstanding at a moment of time: as instantaneous changes, that is to say, in balance sheets. Our second step is to investigate *the connexion between these balance-sheet changes and the flows* that are of direct significance in the processes of production and distribution of the goods and services on which we live. Every economic unit aims at maximizing the net

[1] In some intermediaries the transaction takes the form not of borrowing or lending but the outright sale or purchase of a security. For our immediate purpose this is the same thing; in fact, there is much to be said for thinking of all borrowing as the sale of a 'bond' and of all lendings as the purchase of a bond.

flow (properly discounted) of income over all future time. Production, investment, income and saving are all flows over time. Capital is a stock of assets from which an income is expected to be derived. In other words we can consider the economy either dynamically with its flows through time or statically, taking an instantaneous snapshot of the system, in which future flows of revenue and expenditure appear as capitalized values at a moment of time. Balance sheets are static statements showing both stocks of 'real capital assets' and financial claims in both directions. The real capital assets (land, buildings, machines, goods in process, &c.) are entered in the balance sheet at the present (discounted) value of the future flow of income expected from them. The financial claims (both assets and liabilities) are entered at the present (discounted) value of payments due to be made in the future.[1]

The assets of a financial intermediary are claims against governmental bodies, against producers (corporate or personal), and against consumers (mostly personal). In a rough way it may be said that the claims against governments have a present value because the Government will receive a flow of tax and other revenue; the claims against producers have a present value because the producer owns 'capital goods' and a productive organization from which a future flow of income (profits) is expected; and claims against a consumer have value because (a) he is expected to have a future flow of money income and (b) he owns certain durable goods. Claims of all these kinds may be held as assets by financial intermediaries. Claims *against* the financial intermediaries—the liabilities of the intermediaries—have a *derived* value, a present value to the creditors (e.g. bank depositors, building society shareholders, &c.), based on the creditors' belief that the intermediaries hold claims against debtors who as producers or consumers have prospective income flows.

[1] For example, a government bond has a current market price, which is the present discounted value of (a) the future stream of dividends plus (b) the final redemption payment of the 'nominal value' of the bond.

Thus a balance sheet always *looks forward*. It is based on expectations, whether reliable or not; the past enters only as a guide to these expectations of future economic flows. The importance of the operations of financial intermediaries, in their business of dealing in financial claims, lies partly in their relation to future flows: for acts of spending on consumption or on capital goods ('investment')—the acts that determine the employment of real resources—depend upon disposal of financial claims (most directly, bank deposits or cash). That the economic unit is concerned to maximize his net discounted *future* income does not alter the fact that this future prospect itself results in part from what has happened in the past—from economic flows in the past—and it is in this way that savings are relevant to the activities of financial intermediaries.

Our approach must be from the point of view of the customer, using this word to indicate any economic unit, whether an individual, a company, a club, or a charitable organization, that chooses to do business with a financial intermediary and is willing to hold claims (e.g. a bank deposit) against a financial intermediary. For the moment we shall simplify by leaving the Government out of the picture. When a customer in a system of this kind acquires a new claim on an intermediary, he can do so only in one of three ways: (1) by gift; (2) by sale of some other asset, which may be (*a*) some other financial claim (which may be a claim against himself, as when he borrows from a bank), or (*b*) a 'real' asset; (3) by spending less than his current income (i.e. by saving). All this is as true of bank deposits as of claims against any other kind of financial intermediary. If the customer wants to add to his holding of such claims, he must go through one or other of these processes.

Remembering that we are leaving the Government out of account, we can now inspect these various methods whereby a customer can add to his financial assets, and see that all methods except one involve equal reductions in the financial assets held by others. The one exception is when financial intermediaries are (under 2*a*) adding to their lending to customers ('buying customers' bonds'). The change in capital value of financial assets is the outcome of a change in the flow of borrowing by customers. In such a society (no government money, no government bonds), this is the only way the *total* of financial assets can be increased; but to make this one hundred per cent. true, we must recognize (*a*) that financial intermediaries themselves can be 'customers', in the sense that they may borrow from and lend to other financial intermediaries, and (*b*) that in so far as 'customers' lend to and borrow from each other ('trade credit') they are acting as financial intermediaries.

The next step is to allow for the existence of a government (which can include a central bank) which, besides spending and 'earning' (by taxation) like anyone else, can persuade economic units (both financial intermediaries and their customers) to hold its own obligations. These obligations ('national debt' in the Radcliffe sense) are of two main types: cash (not bearing interest, and often referred to as 'money'), and bonds which bear interest. If now, looking at our list of the ways in which a customer may add to his financial assets, we include in 'spending' (in item (3)) the payment of taxes, and we include in 'income' the receipt of government subsidies, this list becomes a list of ways in which economic units—financial intermediaries and customers—can add to their individual holdings of claims against financial intermediaries *plus* government obligations. The *total* of all these financial claims, however, can only be increased (*a*) if economic units are willing to hold a larger total than before and (*b*) if either the financial intermediaries are willing to hold a higher total of claims against others or the Government is willing to issue more obligations (cash plus bonds) than before (i.e. to run an overall budget deficit, in the British sense).

The system to which we have found this rule applicable is in fact a highly realistic one: it is one in which there are government cash and bond obligations, both of which may be held by both financial intermediaries and customers, and in which financial intermediaries may have liabilities to other intermediaries, as well as to 'customers', and may hold among their assets both government and customers' obligations. Yet in this realistic model a growth of financial claims appears to be independent of the existence of any saving, whether the growth is in the liabilities of the Government (e.g. in Savings Certificates, long-term bonds, or notes issued by the central bank) or in the liabilities of the banks (bank deposits) or in the liabilities of other financial intermediaries (building societies, hire-purchase finance companies, &c.).

To find the connexion with saving, we have to look beyond the *total* of financial claims to the *distribution* of financial claims, and to remind ourselves that these financial claims will not exist at all unless someone is willing to hold them. And once we turn from the total to the distribution, we have to remember that economic units can add to their stock of financial claims not only by a purely financial transaction (e.g. borrowing from a bank or other financial intermediary) but also by spending on goods (capital goods as well as consumption goods) and services less than they are receiving in sales (including the receipt of income). Leaving aside transactions in capital goods, an economic unit can add to his stock of financial claims by saving, in the ordinary sense. As a man saves, he adds to his stock of financial claims, whether in cash, government bonds, or some other claims. When financial claims come into the ownership of people who want 'to hold their savings' in these particular forms, these claims have found firm holders. Firm holders are not, however, confined to individuals: many financial assets are firmly held by financial intermediaries, as part of their asset-structure to command the confidence of their creditors, but these creditors are themselves 'firm holders' of the intermediaries' liabilities because they (the creditors) choose to 'hold their savings' in this form.

All this is equally true if the financial intermediary is a bank, in which case the individual's asset is generally reckoned as money, and many people do indeed reckon to hold part of their savings in the form of money. But whether people look upon any part of their money balances (bank deposits or notes) as savings or not, the fact remains that they can add to these money balances only in the same ways as they can add to any other financial assets: i.e. by selling some other asset ('real' or financial) or by saving part of their income.

The difference between money balances and other financial claims is that the former are apt to change ownership much more frequently than do the latter. Any kind of financial claim may change hands, without the total in existence having changed: the saving and borrowing being done by some economic units is exactly equalled by the dissaving and repayment-of-loans being done by other economic units. This is, of course, what is happening every moment, and is mentioned here only to emphasize one likeness between money and other financial claims. Claims that people do not want to continue holding—in the sense that they see advantages in exchanging them for something else—will be exchanged. The something else for which the exchange is made may be (a) another financial claim, and this may have repercussions on the activity of a financial intermediary; or it may be (b) real goods and services, either for capital construction or for consumption. These are the possibilities that link the distribution of financial claims with the processes of generation of income; every disturbance in the holding of financial claims is a potential disturber of the generation of income.

Economic units are in fact continually disturbing their ownership of financial claims because they are continually saving, continually taking decisions about the advantage of spending on capital goods, and continually changing their views about the composition of their portfolios of financial assets (including money) and financial liabilities. At any given moment there is, in a very limited sense, a short-period equilibrium in the market for financial claims: all the existing assets (including the total stock of money) are owned by someone or other and bear some relation to the existing stock of all forms of wealth and the current flow of income. Equally, there is at every moment an imminent disturbance of this equilibrium for, quite apart from changes of view as to the relative attractions of various assets, in a growing economy net savings are being accumulated out of current income. If these savings were indeed handed over immediately through some genuine 'intermediary' to simultaneous spenders on capital goods, we should have no problem. Instead, in our complicated financial system, the accumulation of savings disturbs the balance-sheet position—the structure of assets and liabilities—of a variety of financial intermediaries, and these disturbances cannot in their results be distinguished from disturbances having other origins.

The complexity of the process of change in the structure of financial claims is largely due to the twofold nature of these claims. They have their *wealth* aspect: they are stores of wealth. They have also their *liquidity* aspect: they are more or less easily exchangeable for other forms of wealth, whether goods, services, or other claims. This liquidity attribute may be very slight, in which case the claims are regarded by holders as more or less 'permanent investments', or the liquidity attribute may be important, as in the extreme case of demand deposits which are held primarily as a stock of immediate purchasing power for everyday use. Traditional analysis of the process of credit creation and the generation of money income was comparatively simple because assets were assumed to take one or other of the two extreme forms: money, held for its ready exchangeability, and securities or capital goods, held as 'investments' or part of the stock of wealth. In fact, in a community with a highly developed financial system, especially when it is underpinned as in England today by the solidarity of a central banking system and by the political commitment to full-employment policies, the structure of financial claims does not fall thus easily into black and white, but is rather a spectrum of infinite gradation from greater to less liquidity and from less to greater stress on the store-of-wealth aspect.

In such an advanced community the process of getting richer by accumulation of capital, for the community as a whole and for many economic units of it, inevitably means that the total amount of financial claims is growing. As people save, they add to their wealth largely by adding to their holdings of financial claims. In deciding how to distribute these additional claims between those that are more liquid and those that are more fixed stores of wealth, they will have regard to their current income position and to their stock of wealth. As money income rises, whether this implies an increase in real income or not, they will want to hold more assets at the liquidity end of the spectrum. This is the truth on which the Quantity Theory of Money was founded; but in a community in which certain non-bank claims are regarded as highly liquid (and therefore merit the label 'near-money') we cannot assume that the enlarged demand for liquidity will be satisfied by proportionate enlargement of the stock of bank deposits. But as their *stock* of wealth increases by the accumulation of savings, people will want to hold more of a selection of financial claims; this selection may be heavily weighted by the attractions of the less liquid (but probably higher-yielding) stores of wealth. There is, however, no reason to suppose that an increased supply of liquidity will not be among the ways in which a man wants to enjoy the advantages of an enlarged stock of wealth.

We have therefore to conclude (1) that as money income grows, people want to hold more of a selection of financial claims, heavily weighted at the liquidity end but not confined to bank deposits; and (2) that as the stock of wealth grows by the accumulation of saving, people want to hold more of a selection of financial claims, heavily weighted at the *other* end of the spectrum, yet still including some at the liquidity end, and among them money itself.

II. *The Consequences of Changes in Financial Claims*

To illustrate the ways in which these disturbances can generate income and can have complex repercussions on the balance-sheets of a variety of financial intermediaries, we shall investigate the results of five examples. Of these five, the first two are cases in which an individual decides to save part of his income, and to hold this new saving in, in turn, each of two forms. In the third example, we consider what follows when an individual decides to switch his 'savings' (in his own description, referring to his existing stock of assets) from one form to another. In the fourth, we imagine 'savers' positions unchanged, but assume that a bank decides to lend more to its customers and to hold less government bonds. In the fifth example, we assume that the government runs a deficit which it finances by the issue of additional Treasury Bills. The detailed steps will, unless otherwise stated, assume an English framework, but the broad conclusions are of much wider validity.

(a) *Individual savings, held as Time Deposits in a bank*

Our first example is simple, and has often been mentioned in monetary literature. A person, who receives his income in the shape of demand deposits transferred from his employer's account to his own account at a commercial bank, decides not to spend the whole of his income. Further, he decides to hold his savings in the form of a Time Deposit at the bank: he simply instructs his bank to transfer part of the balance on his current account to a deposit account. Abstracting from everything else happening in the economic situation, there will have been no change in the total of financial claims existing in the economy. The total of bank liabilities, as of those of all other financial intermediaries, is unchanged, though a part has a different description. Similarly, the banks' assets, and their liquidity ratios, are unchanged, and they will therefore have no incentive to change their lending or purchases of bonds. The action of saving has thus been associated with no creation of credit, no channelling of funds into the hands of business firms eager to spend on the creation of capital goods.

Although, however, there has been no change in the total of financial claims, the decision on the saver's part to hold his deposit tightly instead of passing it on, by spending, does have effects on the economic system. These effects are a fall in the total flow of income, with the usual chain of deflationary effects; they are the effects that would follow a decision to hoard gold coin in an economy that used gold coin as its money, and the process of accumulating savings in the form of time deposits in the banks has therefore been appropriately described as 'hoarding'. Hoarding by itself has deflationary effects: the total of financial claims is unchanged, but the effectiveness of this total in generating and supporting the flow of income is reduced by the action of saving. Nothing has happened to encourage any creation of credit, or addition to the capital equipment of the economy. Nor even, until deflation has made the economy's stock of financial claims excessive in relation to the flow of income, is there any fall in the rate of interest to excite the generation of additional activity.

This is strictly true only in English conditions, where bank interest rates are sticky and the liquidity ratios, which guide banking activities, are related uniformly to the total of deposits. If these assumptions are not applicable, the action of saving-hoarding can, at least in theory, give some immediate impetus both to the creation of credit and to additional spending on capital equipment. If we imagine hypersensitive banks of the economist's smooth demand and supply curves, with perfect flexibility of competitive interest rates, the rise in the proportion of interest-bearing time deposits would prompt the bankers, in protection of their profits, to make a marginal reduction in the rates offered for time deposits. This would change the relative attractiveness of time deposits and other financial claims, prompting a chain of reactions on asset-portfolios through the economy, depressing interest rates generally and encouraging spending on capital goods. This, of course, is economists' modelling, far removed from the everyday realities of the financial world; but it may serve to remind us of underlying forces that could have effects in extreme situations or if they were really persistent.

More seriously, let us remove the English assumption that the banks' liquidity ratios take no account of the composition of total deposits. In the United States, as in many other countries, the ratio of cash reserve required against time deposits is lower than the ratio required against demand deposits. A transfer from demand deposits to time deposits, within an unchanged total, therefore frees some of the cash reserve: some 'required reserves' become 'excess reserves'. Each bank thus affected becomes free to exchange some of its cash reserves for advances or investments. In the absence of any offsetting action by the central bank, this will result (in the way shown in Chapter 1 above) in an increase in (1) total bank deposits and (2) total customer indebtedness to banks (advances) and/or bonds held by the banks, these displacing bonds held by the public. The saving originating the disturbance will thus have provoked a creation of credit, an addition to the total liquid assets held in the economy; in the hands of the public, more-liquid assets will have displaced some slightly less-liquid assets. To induce this change in the liquidity position, there will have been some reduction of interest rates and/or an increase in the availability of money to those wishing to borrow. In total, these changes will give an impetus to, and in part will be associated with, an increase in spending on capital equipment, and they may also prompt some expansion of consumption (dissaving). According to the traditional view of the relationship between income and the total of *demand* deposits, the generation of money income will continue until the level of money income has once more become appropriate to the new level of demand deposits which, with the time deposits, leaves the banks with no excess reserves. Whether this level of money income is higher or lower than, or equal to, the previous level of money income cannot be stated without knowledge of the actual figures of the ratios and other changes; it could be set out in an elaborate formula.

If, through the operation of this credit creation within the banking system, the deflationary tendency of the initial decision to add to time deposits is precisely offset, there is no further complication. But if the expansion of total deposits does not exactly fit the accumulation of time deposits, so that income shows a tendency to move to a higher (or lower) level than in the original position, there can be further disturbance due to the fact that the stocks of *other* liquid assets, near to money, will be out of line with the new level of income. The nature of these repercussions will become clearer when other cases have been discussed below; for the moment we can take it that they are, in this particular case, likely to be small, and indeed they have traditionally been assumed to be non-existent.

(b) *Individual savings, held as a share in a building society*

We now take the case in which the saver decides to hold his new savings in the form of a 'share' (i.e. term deposit) in a building society. The saver, instead of spending part of his inflow of demand deposits (say £1,000) for the purchase of consumption goods, transfers it to a building society which in return gives the saver a 'share', i.e. a claim to repayment of the capital sum plus interest.

The impact effect is that the total of financial claims in the community has increased by £1,000, in that, while the building society's liabilities are up by this amount, the total of bank deposits has remained unchanged. The ownership of bank deposits will have changed, £1,000 having been transferred from the saver to the building society. The building society then enlarges its lending to people wanting to buy houses; let us suppose that it lends out the whole of the £1,000 and does not hold any to 'reserve' in the form of bank deposits or government bonds. Many things can happen next: it is possible, for instance, that the seller of a house uses the proceeds, to the extent of the £1,000 borrowed (by the house purchaser) from the building society, to pay off a bank advance; then the total of bank assets and of bank deposits will be down by £1,000, with repercussions on the banks' liquidity ratios.

Let us, however, suppose that the borrower uses the £1,000 to buy a house that would not otherwise have been built. The £1,000 in bank deposits then passes, as an additional income stream, into the ownership of the people building the house; there is no change either in the total of bank deposits or in their composition. The act of building the house is the act of real investment which, in its effect on the income stream, exactly offsets the deflationary effect of the saving of £1,000 by the individual who transferred £1,000 from his current inflow of bank deposits to the building society. The final position is that bank deposits are unchanged and are still appropriate to the level of money income, which is unchanged although real income has been increased in the sense that the house-purchaser now enjoys occupation of his house; the real capital of the community is increased by the new house, and the total of non-bank financial claims is increased by £1,000, this being an additional asset of the man who saved and an additional liability of a building society. The building society in this case has, in common-sense terms, channelled the saving of one man into the hands of those who have transformed it into a real addition to the social capital (houses) of the community.

(c) *The individual switches from one asset to another*

If the saver regards his building society shares as a genuinely fixed investment and is content with the new distribution of his total wealth, and if the building society is content with the equal increase in its share liabilities and its mortgage loans, there is in a sense a new equilibrium and no impetus to further disturbance of the income stream. But if the process goes far, and either the saver or the building society, or, for that matter, the house-purchaser, who is in debt as well as owning a new house, regard their balance-sheet positions as having disturbed the desired relation between liquidity, income and stock of wealth, then further disturbance is entailed. The simplest (and perhaps most likely) example is that of the saver who regards a building society share as a highly liquid asset, not much inferior in convenience to an idle balance in his bank account. When he has added, say, £5,000 to his building society shares, he will feel not only much richer (a reason for holding rather bigger average balance in his bank account) but also a great deal more liquid. Let us suppose that the feeling of excess liquidity overbears the feeling that as a richer man he wants more money in hand, and suppose that he decides that, the building society shares being so easily cashable, he will hold £500 less in his bank account and earn the interest the building society will pay on it. In this circumstance the £500 transferred represents no saving, no reduction of the income flowing to the people who live on the rich man's spending. Nevertheless, the same train of consequences ensues: the building society pays the £500 back to people who will spend it so generating income; the total financial claims in the community rise, and so on. As money income rises, both spending and saving rise; the familiar multiplier analysis can be used to show that the total rise in money income will not be limited to the original £500 but will reach a much bigger sum which will be bigger the more people incline towards spending rather than saving an increase in their incomes.

All this generation of *money* income may or may not be associated with a rise in *real* income. If there was, at the outset, appreciable spare capacity, a rise in real income is likely; otherwise, the change in money income will have been reflected largely in a rise in prices. In either event, however, there will have been a rise in financial claims outrunning the original £500, for people will have saved, not exclusively in bank deposits, part of their additional incomes. How these additional claims will be distributed will depend on people's preferences for the various financial intermediaries, and it is not unreasonable to suppose that the building societies will have attracted part of the increase so that their liabilities and their lending will both have gone up by more than the original £500. There will, that is to say, have been a *multiple creation of credit* by the building societies, precisely parallel to the multiple creation of credit long recognized as occurring when banks receive an accretion to their reserves.

How far this generation of income and of financial claims can go will depend not only on people's disposition to spend or save increased income and on their preferences for various financial claims but also on whether the rules and policies of the monetary authorities allow any increase in the total of bank deposits. If they do not, this itself sets some limit to the inflation of income and claims.[1] But some

---

[1] A restriction not to an absolute amount of bank deposits but simply to the supply of liquid assets in relation to which the banks are subject to ratio control will limit the inflationary process, though not necessarily in the same way, for the banks may in the process either be able to attract or be forced to lose liquid assets to other financial intermediaries or their customers.

inflation there will have been: the income velocity of circulation of bank deposits will have risen. It is important to recognize that the expansion (inflation of incomes) takes place not because people have decided to spend more on goods and services but simply because someone decides that he will feel comfortable enough if he holds a smaller bank balance and a larger amount of building-society shares. His action sets in train an inflationary process because it enables the building society to lend more without compelling the bank to lend any less than before. The process he sets in motion is not merely one of generation of money income but also one of multiple expansion of the liabilities of financial intermediaries. The nearer these non-bank liabilities are to being regarded as money, the further can the process go and the less the velocity of circulation of bank deposits resists increase.

(d) *A change in the asset-structure of a bank*

We take next a quite different case, in which no decision to save, or to change the form of holding previous savings, is made by individuals or non-financial corporations. Let us suppose that a bank decides that it has been unnecessarily cautious and has been missing some good business, and that it will in the immediate future grant loans more readily so that its advances total goes up. To enable it to make these advances, consistently with maintaining its liquidity ratios, it sells government bonds: we assume, that is to say, the operation of the well-known advances/investments see-saw of English banking. We shall further assume, as in our previous examples, that there is no monetary action by the Government: the bonds sold by the banks have therefore to be bought by the non-bank parts of the private sector.

The banks can effect this change in the composition of their balance-sheets only by tempting people into matching operations: someone must buy the bonds, and someone must take the bank advances. The impact effect depends on exactly how people are persuaded to make these changes. Let us suppose that, by somewhat reducing the prices of bonds (raising their yield) people are persuaded to hold less in time deposits and more in government bonds; and that the banks can make the additional advances to people who were previously thwarted, by lack of finance, in their desires to spend on the expansion of the scale of their business activities. Then there is no change in the total of bank deposits, but a fall in time deposits is matched by a rise in demand deposits as the new borrowers at the bank make payments for goods and services. This expenditure, however, is not matching anyone's decision to save more, and the total of money income rises. There has been, as it has often been put, an 'activation of idle deposits', a rise in the income velocity of circulation of bank deposits.

As income increases, however, people do save more and, saving more, they want to add to their holdings of financial claims. To the extent that they want to hold additional time deposits, this will offset part of the inflationary impulse (as we have seen in the first example above) unless the monetary authorities in one way or another allow an increase in the total of bank deposits. Among the additional claims they will want to hold will be the liabilities of a variety of non-bank financial intermediaries —building societies, hire-purchase finance companies, and so on—and these intermediaries will then in turn lend more than before, so generating a further increase in incomes, out of which there will be further savings. The change in the disposition of bank assets will thus have set in train a multiple expansion of income, of savings, and of the assets and liabilities of financial intermediaries. The limits to the expansionary process will be set by (a) the inclination to save part of additional income, and (b) the inclination to place part of the additional savings with banks or other intermediaries whose expansionary powers are limited by rules, by limitation on the availability of reserve assets, &c. This last limitation will be the subject of later consideration; meanwhile it is important to notice that a multiple process of credit creation, associated with the generation of additional money income, can be set in train by a mere switch of banking assets, without any increase in the total of bank deposits.

(e) *A government deficit financed by issue of Treasury Bills*

Our fifth example of operation of the process of credit expansion is one of great importance in the English monetary system. The entire system centres on the cash which is non-interest-bearing debt of the government. It is by the issue of cash in exchange for other government obligations that the central bank keeps the system supplied with the cash desired for convenience, and the residuary debt operations, by which the Government keeps its own payments and receipts in step, take the form of operations in Treasury Bills. In fact, as we have seen in Chapter 5 above, the Government so plans its payments and receipts that it has practically every day a planned deficit to be covered by the issue of new Treasury Bills, although on a large proportion of days it afterwards relieves the shortage of cash by buying-in some previously issued Treasury Bills. The operation we are to examine in the following paragraphs is thus one which on a marginal scale is a regular feature of the English system; for the purpose of exposition, however, we shall think not of these marginal daily operations, nor even of the pronounced seasonal movement resulting from the regular unevenness of the inflow of taxes, but we shall suppose that the Government is running a deficit on an unusual scale and that, either by choice or by force of circumstances, it is covering this deficit by large additional issues of Treasury Bills. We shall suppose, moreover, that this deficit is not designed to prevent incomes from falling, but to promote an actual rise in incomes in the economy.

In order to make our analysis as realistic as possible, we

shall have to make some assumptions about the behaviour of interest rates. This is difficult, and we shall do best if we take as our starting-point an assumption that the Government neither chooses nor is forced to modify its policy on interest rates as a result of this operation in Treasury Bills. At the short end, it will be recalled, the Government sets the level of rates by its fixing of Bank Rate and its control of the discount market, and its choice of level is dictated primarily by the international monetary situation; at the long end, rates are greatly influenced by the authorities, but in general the authorities avoid alteration of the rates for the purpose of inducing, on any given day, a different scale of sales or purchases by the market.

We shall first depart from reality by assuming that Treasury Bills are held only by the banks and discount houses; later we shall take the realistic assumption that there are also 'outside' holders, though we shall continue to assume that these outside holders are within the English system, i.e. that they are 'residents' in the technical financial sense. (The complications that result from the fact that England is only one country in an international economy are ignored throughout this section of this chapter, but they are discussed in the next section.)

The position is, then, that the Government is having to transfer, to the people who are providing goods and services for government use, more bank deposits than are being transferred to the Government by tax-payers and purchasers of government products and services. Let us suppose that the excess (the deficit) amounts to £280 millions during one quarter of the year, and that the authorities provide initially by issuing during that quarter £2,280 millions instead of £2,000 millions of Treasury Bills. On our assumption that banks and discount houses are sole holders, and assuming no other bills or bonds are held as liquid assets, the customary £2,000 millions of Treasury Bills will be supporting a structure of £800 millions as the banks' 'cash in hand and at the Bank of

England' so making a total of 28 per cent. 'liquid assets'. Not all the £2,000 millions of Treasury Bills will be held by the banks themselves; some part will be held by discount houses, whose corresponding 'money at call' will however make up the banks' liquid assets to the £2,800 millions required to satisfy the 28 per cent. liquidity convention.

Into this situation the Government has to pay £280 millions more in deposits than it is receiving. In the way explained in Chapter 5 above, this is effected in the first place by cheques drawn on the Government's accounts at the Bank of England. These cheques, credited by customers to their accounts in the clearing banks and by the clearing banks to their accounts at the Bank of England, increase the total of bank deposits in the country by £280 millions, and the banks' cash reserves by £280 millions. This second change (in the banks' cash) is however precisely offset by the sale of the new additional Treasury Bills, which the discount market will have taken up at the weekly tenders spread over the quarter, and will have financed by borrowing more at call from the banks and/or selling Treasury Bills to the banks. The position of the banks before and after can be summarized thus:

POSITION I
(£ millions)

Liabilities				Assets			
Deposits	.	.	. 10,000	Cash			800
				Treasury Bills and Money			
				at Call . . .			2,000
				Other Assets . .			7,200
			10,000				10,000

POSITION II

Liabilities				Assets			
Deposits	.	.	·. 10,280	Cash			800
				Treasury Bills and Money			
				at Call . . .			2,280
				Other Assets . .			7,200
			10,280				10,280

The banks will now, however, have overshot the mark in absorbing Treasury Bills (either directly or by loans to the discount market). Although their liquid assets ratio is over 28 per cent., their cash ratio has fallen a trifle below 8 per cent.; this has to be corrected by the banks' calling on the discount market to repay loans, or reducing their own holdings of Treasury Bills, by £22·4 millions. Either of these operations is completed by the Bank of England which purchases the £22·4 millions Treasury Bills and holds them as additional assets in its Banking Department, against additional liabilities in the shape of Bankers' Deposits, these being part of the cash assets of the banks. In effect, the authorities find that while their total indebtedness has gone up by the full £280 millions deficit, interest on £22·4 millions out of the total is collected by their own operator, the Bank of England, because the cash ratio requirement forces the banks to hold an extra £22·4 millions of cash (interest-free government debt) against the £280 millions enlargement of their deposit liabilities.

This is by no means the end of the story. Although the Government will have paid its way, and the banks and discount houses will have balanced their assets against their obligations, three important effects will remain in the system to give impulses to further expansion. These are (1) the liquid assets ratio of the banks is now a little above the required 28 per cent.; (2) the public has now £280 millions additional bank deposits; and (3) the public's income has swollen by £280 millions in a quarter. Of these three changes, two are simple liquidity changes: the banks are more liquid, and the public is more liquid. With the repercussions of these changes we are already familiar. The banks will be disposed to lend more, and to buy bonds to the extent that they cannot reasonably lend. The public may want to spread some of its additional liquidity by 'investing' in some of the non-bank financial intermediaries, by buying some government bonds. To the extent that either the banks or the public buy government bonds, the Government will be able to reduce their issues of Treasury Bills, covering their deficit partly by the sale of bonds. To the extent that this happens, the additional liquidity threatened by the deficit is absorbed, and there is no impulse to further expansion, though both banks and public will be in a stronger financial position than before, *vis-à-vis* the Government. But to the extent that the banks lend money to spenders and the public lends to financial intermediaries that are free from bank reserve requirements, there will be further impulse to the expansion of money income in the economy.

We must now revert to the third source of disturbance remaining in the economy; the initial increase of £280 millions a quarter in the public's income. This growth in national income has complex direct effects on further income, and further effects on the liquidity position. To some extent this additional income, which is reinforced as the greater liquidity encourages spending (see previous paragraph), yields the Government more in taxes and in payments for additional imports, so reducing the rate of deficit and absorbing part of the increase in liquidity.[1] To some extent, again, the additional income gives rise to additional demand for liquid assets (especially bank deposits) to match the higher turnover; this does not (as the taxes do) reduce the issue of Treasury Bills, but it does mean that the increase in the supply of liquid assets in the economy is partially matched by an increase in demand for liquidity, and to that extent an impulse to multiple expansion of credit is avoided. To the extent that people want to use part of their additional income to build up their liquid assets, they are of course saving; but they may want to save beyond this amount, so that there will be some new demand for financial assets that have little

[1] On a simple assumption that additional payments to non-residents are absorbed by the Exchange Equalization Account (see p. 245 below) the effects of expenditure on imports are precisely the same as those of tax payments: they provide some of the Governments' sterling requirements.

liquidity attraction, being rather of the 'investment' kind. This decision to acquire even the less liquid financial assets will, as we have seen, have further repercussions on the liquidity position, and in the generation of additional income. Beyond all these 'leakages' of the additional income, there will remain some that will be used for additional spending, whether on consumption or on capital goods, and this spending directly creates more income, from which in turn there will be further 'leakages' (taxes, imports, additions to money balances and other saving).

If we can imagine a final restoration of equilibrium, the various impulses to expansion having been fully expended, it will be a position in which money national income will be higher than before, not just by £280 millions per quarter but by some multiple of this, the size of this multiple being smaller the sharper are the 'leakages' of taxation and saving. In this restored equilibrium, with higher income, there will also be a higher total of financial claims, of all degrees of liquidity. The way this new total is spread over various classes of claims, including bank deposits, will depend upon how people choose to distribute them having regard to two sets of conditions. The first set of conditions—the relative qualities of the various financial claims (interest yields, liquidity, &c.)—we suppose to be unchanged. The second set of conditions— the income and stock-of-wealth positions of economic units in the economy—will be different from what it was at the outset, and there is no certainty as to the resulting distribution of claims. There cannot be any assurance as to the relative demand for any particular financial claim, whether bank deposits or cash or anything else. Experience has, however, shown (though not to the degree sometimes supposed) that, in communities where bank deposits and notes are sharply differentiated from other claims, the tendency is for the community to restore the value of these claims to its original relationship to national income. That is to say, the income velocity of circulation of monetary assets has had some inherent stability. As financial development blurs the distinction between these and other financial assets, we should expect this stability to diminish, and there are indications that this is happening.

We now make closer approach to the current English system by removing our assumption that the banks and discount houses are the only holders of Treasury Bills, though we retain our (realistic) assumptions of interest-rate policy. Since about 1955 'outside' holders of Treasury Bills have become very important, the appetite of these holders having grown appreciably as the absolute level óf interest rates has increased. Apart from the long-term tendency of this demand to increase, the amounts of Treasury Bills so held from week to week appears to have depended largely on the size of the gap between the Treasury Bill rate and the Time Deposit rate paid by the banks. The Treasury Bill rate is the higher of these, and the bigger the gap, the greater has been the outside demand for the bills. But this interest-rate gap is decided in the main by government policy from week to week, having regard to the international monetary situation and not with any view to stimulating (or discouraging) the outside demand for bills.

It follows from these circumstances that an enlarged issue of bills (e.g. the £280 millions we have assumed to be required to finance a government deficit) does not meet, at the impact, any enlargement in the outside demand. The whole increase has therefore to be absorbed by the banks and the discount houses, and what has been said in the earlier paragraphs of this section applies without change.

This is true, however, only of the initial impact. As the bank deposits in the ownership of the public increase, and as the further repercussions on financial assets and on income occur, the bank deposits coming into the hands of outside holders (or potential outside holders) of Treasury Bills are likely to increase. They are likely to respond to this situation by buying more Treasury Bills than before. To the extent that they do this, the effect is precisely parallel to a purchase of government bonds by the public: the Government is able to finance its deficit without enlarging the liquid assets base of the banking system. There will still, nevertheless, have been an increase in the liquidity of the economy, in that the outside holders regard their Treasury Bills as highly liquid assets, virtually as liquid as bank deposits. To the extent that Treasury Bills are diverted from the banking system in this way, 'multiple expansion of credit' (in which the banks can engage because of their reserve ratios) is avoided, but this does not mean that there are no repercussions in the creation of further credit. A company that has an enlarged holding of Treasury Bills may, for example, be ready to extend trade credit more generously to its customers. It is with good reason that Treasury Bills are regarded as an engine of inflationary finance.

III. *The Leaks in the Process of Expansion of Credit*

(a) *A classification of leaks*

When an initial change (an increase of the liquid assets reserves of the banks, to take the most familiar example) sets in motion an expansion of the supply of financial assets (the 'credit structure'), total eventual expansion cannot be deduced directly from the reserve ratios. We cannot, for example, deduce from the 28 per cent. liquid assets ratio in the clearing banks that a £28 millions increase in the supply of those liquid assets will cause a £100 millions increase in bank deposits. The expansion is limited, short of this point, by 'leaks' of the reserve assets into other parts of the system, where they may or may not give rise to multiple expansion of other financial claims. In this section we investigate this process of leakage, and we shall, unless other warning is given, be thinking in terms of the current English system. At this stage of our analysis we shall make a closer approach to reality, in that we shall take account in a simple way of the existence of external transactions. We shall think, that is to say, of the English economy as part of an international economy. We shall assume that the rate of exchange between English money and foreign money is fixed by the willingness of the English Government (the Exchange Equalization Account) to pay foreign money (or gold) in exchange for English bank deposits or English bank deposits for foreign money (or gold) at a fixed rate, the Government providing itself with bank deposits by selling Treasury Bills as required, buying back Treasury Bills when it has a surplus of bank deposits (a realistic assumption). We shall assume that neither Treasury Bills nor English bank deposits are held externally (i.e. by nonresidents): this is an abstraction from reality.[1]

The leaks that follow an initial impulse to expansion are of several kinds, which may react on each other. Our first broad classification is into (1) leaks that result directly from decisions of economic units to redistribute their financial claims, and (2) leaks that result from an increase in income induced by the expansion of financial claims. The first kind of leak occurs because the initial change disrupts the equilibrium between the relative supplies of financial assets and people's preferences for the various assets. The second kind of leak occurs only when the disturbance in the supply of financial assets (the increase in the liquidity of the economy) has generated an expansion of income. (The reader may remember that in the process of expansion of income there is a similar brake operated by 'leaks' that reduce the income multiplier, but in the

---

[1] In reality, sterling being an international currency, some sterling claims (in practice, working balances of bank deposits plus, in the main, Treasury Bills) are held outside the U.K. (principally by monetary authorities of the Rest of the Sterling Area). Excess payments to such holders have the impact effect of causing the R.S.A. instead of U.K. residents to hold Treasury Bills or other sterling claims.

case of credit expansion the motivation governing the leaks is different.)

The second classification to make refers to the *direction* of the leaks; it cuts across our first classification. The leak may be either (1) to the Government (the public sector), or (2) to the outside world. Either kind of leak may occur through the desire to adjust the distribution of assets or through the expansion of income. On our assumption as to how the foreign exchange market is managed, the impact effect will be the same, whether the leak is to the Government or to the outside world; but they are analytically distinct, and a persistent leak of one kind would provoke in government policy reactions quite different from those provoked by persistent leak of the other kind.

(b) *Leaks consequent on redistribution of assets*

First we investigate the disturbance of the holdings of financial claims that occurs when the Government runs a deficit, financed by issue of additional Treasury Bills. In order to avoid the complications of expanding income, we shall assume that the deficit does no more than prevent a fall in income; we assume also that the banks are enabled, by the increase in liquid assets, to make advances more freely but that business men are so gloomy that this easing of bank credit has no immediate effect in accelerating enterprise and so generating additional income.

One leak we have already encountered: the banks will find the cash component of their liquid assets deficient, and will have to rebuild their cash ratio by reducing their holdings of Treasury Bills. This is a leak to the Government (cash being a liability of the central bank), and there is no further disturbance: all that happens is redistribution of the composition of the liquid assets of the banks, while the Government finds that part of its deficit finance is being obtained free of interest.

Next, what happens because some business men, previously denied advances, are now able to get bank advances? On our assumptions, they are likely to require these advances to pay off trade debts. Their suppliers find that trade credit is being paid off, and these suppliers' holdings of bank deposits increase. These additional bank deposits (the result of the banks' 'creation of Credit') may now have found, for the time being, a settled home: the creditor firms may be glad enough to hold larger balances, in the shape of bank deposits. If this is all that happens, there will be no leaks; but the whole system is more 'liquid' than before, and will expand the more readily as soon as the creditor firms take a less gloomy view of the business situation.

But suppose that some of the creditor firms decide to hold their increased liquidity not as bank deposits but as Treasury Bills or government bonds. This is a leak to the public sector: the Government will find itself receiving more bank deposits than it is having to pay out, and will reduce its sales of Treasury Bills to the banks. The process of credit creation would then have to be partially undone, until a new equilibrium was reached with the banks holding part of the additional Treasury Bills and some firms holding the rest (or government bonds replacing the Treasury Bills), and other firms holding the additional bank deposits created against (*a*) the additional Treasury Bills and cash held by the banks and (*b*) the amount of new bank advances related to these bank-held Treasury Bills, and *not related to the total additional Treasury Bills and cash*. The multiple creation of credit by the banks will thus have been limited by the leakage; but it must be remembered that the liquidity of business firms will now have been increased not only (1) by the increase in bank deposits held by some of them but also (2) by the additional Treasury Bills and bonds held by some firms, all these assets being more 'liquid' than the trade credit which these assets have displaced. The balance-sheet position of other firms will have been changed by bank advances displacing the trade credit they were previously having to take; this

R

is not so obviously an increase in liquidity, but it does have this character, in that the firms have preferred the new position as one in which they have more room for manœuvre.

There are many variants of this case. One variant we must notice is that in which firms decide, when they find their financial position easier, to 'transfer some of their funds abroad'. This is not an altogether fanciful case: the firms may have associated companies abroad, they may be under pressure for prompter payment to foreign suppliers, or they may simply prefer U.S. Treasury Bills to British (abstracting from foreign exchange restrictions). To get the foreign exchange, the firms have in effect to pay English bank deposits to the Exchange Equalization Account. This is a net reduction in the cash needs of the Government, which therefore has to issue less Treasury Bills to the banks. As long, that is to say, as the U.K. Government has some foreign exchange to sell, the decision of firms to hold some of their increased assets in this form constitutes a leakage in the process of credit expansion. In effect, it is a net reduction in the Government's deficit, in the sense that the Government has financed its needs partly by selling, to English firms, some of its claims on other countries (i.e. its 'foreign-exchange reserve').

Now take a quite different case. Suppose that the firms that are more liquid choose neither bank deposits, nor Treasury Bills or bonds, nor foreign exchange. Suppose that they decide to hold part of their additional funds in the form of building society 'shares'. Then there is a further process of credit expansion, as explained on pp. 231–3 above. There is, on the face of it, no leak in the process of expansion of bank deposits. But suppose—and this is a realistic assumption—that the building societies do not lend on house mortgage all the additional funds they receive; instead, they hold back 15 per cent. as a 'reserve of liquid assets', the assets they choose for this purpose being government bonds. Then the government is able, consistently with its general policy in debt management, to sell more bonds than before, and therefore is able to pay its way without issuing to the banks quite so many Treasury Bills. The banks find their liquid assets down somewhat: there has been a leak in the process of expansion of bank credit, which must therefore be smaller than the expansion when building societies lend to customers 100 per cent. of their additional resources. Although, in this way, the leak has limited the expansion of bank deposits, the liquidity of the economy will have been increased by the increase in building-society assets and liabilities. If (as we have supposed) the reserve ratios of the building societies are lower than those of the banks, the rise in building-society liabilities will, in absolute amount, exceed the amount the leak cuts off the expansion of bank deposits.

The case we have just examined may be stated more generally: if the redistribution of claims is towards financial intermediaries that hold as reserves the government liabilities in any way substitutable for those held by banks, the expansion of non-bank liabilities will force some reduction in the extent to which bank liabilities are expanded by a given initial impulse. The smaller such reserves held by non-bank intermediaries, the less narrowly will the expansion of bank deposits be restrained; the greater, that is to say, the total increase in liquidity. Also, of course, the less favourably the other financial intermediaries are regarded as compared with the banks themselves, the less likely are people to redistribute their assets in favour of the non-banks, and therefore the smaller are any leaks, and the less is the secondary expansion of liquidity. If the banks have unique attractions, they need fear no loss of business. If, on the other hand, people think almost as highly of non-bank intermediaries, the fact that bank deposits are not 'lost' by transfer to those intermediaries does not mean that the banks are unhurt: it means instead that the expansion of liquidity on a given base is so much the greater (because non-banks have lower reserve requirements) and the banks will feel the pinch when (as a result of the great inflation of credit) their money costs begin to soar.

If the government deficit, reinforced by the increased liquidity it engenders, causes an increase in the flow of money income (and sooner or later, this result must be expected) there will be further additions to the stock of financial claims. For people will want to use part of the increase in their incomes not for spending on currently produced goods and services but for adding to their wealth in the shape of financial claims. The assets they choose to hold will include some money and some other liabilities of financial intermediaries. Part of the additional money balances they want to hold, now that they have a higher level of income, may be cash—actual notes and coin— and the rest will be bank deposits.

These two requirements, for cash and bank deposits, can for the moment be regarded as a single requirement for bank deposits, after which we can make a correction by supposing that the public wants to exchange some of its bank deposits for cash. To the extent that the rise in income induces a demand for more bank deposits (bigger 'transactions balances', reflecting the higher level of money income) the newly created bank deposits will be absorbed without giving any impulse to further expansion of credit. Use of increased money income for the purpose of building-up money balances thus avoids any multiplier effect in the expansion of income *and* avoids any multiplier effect in the superstructure of liquidity, beyond the effect in bank deposits.

To the extent that people want to hold their increased balances in the form of notes, even the multiple effect in the banking system is avoided. For if people choose to exchange some of their increased bank deposits for notes, the banks must get additional notes from the Bank of

England. They can do this only by letting their other liquid assets run down (reducing either direct or 'indirect' holdings of Treasury Bills). The Government is not deprived of any means of paying its way, for notes are wanted in replacement of Treasury Bills. The Government will thus be financing the same deficit but incurring lower interest costs. The banks will have expanded their assets and their liabilities rather less, and the public will have saved— by accumulating these non-interest-bearing government bonds called bank-notes—to cover part of the government deficit. To the extent that this happens, *all* multiplier effects, including those within the banking system itself, will be avoided. This can of course put only a *partial* brake on the process of expansion, for it is not conceivable that the public would devote *all* its increase in income to the building-up of its stock of bank notes, plus the other leaks (payments to non-residents, payment to the tax-collector, and net purchases of government securities).

iv. *The Growth of Financial Claims*

The multiplier effects in the expansion of financial claims are caused by the *intermediary* nature of many of the economic units—both banks and others—with which others 'place funds', and by the fact that such intermediaries do not have to hold a 100 per cent. reserve of claims on more central financial institutions (the central bank for the clearing banks, the clearing banks for building societies, &c.). Intermediaries can attract funds (i.e. induce customers to hold claims against the intermediaries) by offering net advantages which include interest payments, security, and facilities for repayments. The last of these advantages is often dependent on some holding of 'reserves' of claims upon some more central financial institution, and it is an advantage that can be developed into a major attraction: the extreme case is in a clearing bank. The other attractions—

interest and security—depend upon efficiency in lending; it is usually by developing a new lending service that a new type of financial intermediary gets a hold. As the advantages of interest, security, and repayment facility can be developed in an infinite variety of combinations, we may expect a continuing increase in the range and variety of financial intermediaries. This increase in the variety of financial intermediaries is of course one of the main characteristics of the financial development of an economy. As the financial intermediaries develop, the possibilities of multiple expansion of credit increase: the economic units of all kinds become more liquid.

The process of capital accumulation, in such a system, also implies a growth of financial claims. Although capital can accumulate exclusively in the ownership of the Government, or exclusively in the form of real assets remaining under the control of those who did the saving (as when a small shopkeeper builds a storage shed at the back of his own little shop), the tendency is for the developing attractions of financial intermediaries to cause people and corporations to accumulate some capital in the shape of financial claims. To the extent that this accumulation of claims has reflected an increase in the real capital goods, there is an increase in 'net worth' of all economic units in the economy, added together. But beyond all this change in the real capital position of the economy, the developing attractions of financial intermediaries—and people's responsiveness to these attractions—prompts a multiple growth of financial claims; and in relation to this growth, the appearance of a financial asset is always paralleled by the appearance of an equal financial liability.

The fact that, aside from real capital growth, liabilities grow as fast as assets, does not mean that there is no growth in liquidity. Although the values (in terms of the unit of account) are matched, the liabilities of the intermediaries are more liquid than the assets: otherwise the intermediaries could not make a living. This is a rule that applies to banks, and it applies also to other financial intermediaries. The activities of some of the non-bank intermediaries may not add importantly to liquidity in the economy, but they always add a little. In their nature some are remote from the banks, while others are close to them, and tend to become closer as the growth in the range of their business and in their reputation makes it possible for them to offer attractions more closely approximating those offered by the banks.

This growth in liquidity, despite the parallel growth in liabilities as assets expand in financial intermediaries, is not unlike what happens when a new financial claim is matched by the growth of real capital. In this latter case also, the claim is usually more liquid than the capital asset itself; this is, after all, one of the main reasons for joint-stock company organization. The 'investment' element (i.e. the income and security aspects) in such a claim may be very high; but there is still a liquidity aspect. This liquidity aspect is accentuated as stock markets develop, and as joint-stock companies become larger, less personal, and more like investment trusts: a 'blue chip' industrial share approaches, in the balance of its attractions, some liabilities of financial intermediaries. Thus original association of a financial claim with the construction of a capital asset does not mean that the existence of this claim is unconnected with the liquidity situation of economic units in the economy. All financial claims have some bearing on the liquidity situation, whatever their origin. How relevant they are to the monetary situation does not depend upon their original association with, or independence of, capital accumulation; their degree of monetary relevance —their potential influence on the pressure of spending— depends upon the balance of attractions offered by the debtors, the balance between interest, security, and facility of exchange. It is because banks generally outdistance other financial intermediaries that their liabilities (bank deposits) are most obviously relevant to the monetary situation. Equally, it is because a change in the structure of interest rates can disturb the relative attractions of various financial claims that such a change is associated with the availability of loans from various financial intermediaries.

v. *Rates of Interest, Debt Management, and Monetary Policy*

The title of this section might well be taken for a treatise, but we shall confine ourselves to the aspects that are most immediately related to the preceding discussion of the nature of credit and the expansion of the structure of financial assets and liabilities. A financial claim is attractive to holders for a combination of interest yield, security, and exchangeability, and some financial claims offer more of one attraction, some of another. The bank balance on current account is most exchangeable but offers no interest at all. It follows that a change in rates of interest alters the balance of attractiveness between different financial claims. People can, as we have seen, adjust their asset portfolios to such a change in the balance of attractions, quite independently of what is happening in the way of accumulation of capital. This adjustment will leave the structure of financial claims in the economy less heavily weighted by the exchangeability attribute than before, if interest rates have risen; more heavily weighted by exchangeability, if interest rates have fallen. These changes do not depend on any change in the flow of money national income: it is well known that a rise in interest rates is usually associated with a fall in the stock of the most liquid financial claims (e.g. bank deposits) relatively to national income or, as it is labelled, a rise in the income velocity of circulation.

This is one particular illustration of the interdependence of money income, stocks of wealth, and the various attractions of financial claims, and the impulse to change can equally well come the other way round. If, for example, the flow of money income rises, the exchangeability quality in financial claims may become more important, and this will force some rise in interest rates as non-bank financial intermediaries seek to maintain their business.

This theory of the interdependence of the structure of financial claims, the level of interest rates and the flow of money income is what lies behind much of the importance attached to the management of the national debt, as well as the importance attached to other aspects of interest-rate policy. A government that does not want inflation to get out of hand is prepared to commit itself to paying high rates of interest for many years on bonds, because sales of long-term bonds allow it to reduce its dependence on Treasury Bills that provide a basis for expansion of credit both in the banks and outside. The help this gives to government economic policy (in putting it in a position to restrain inflation) does depend, it must be emphasized, on the difference between the quality the public attaches to the bonds and the quality attached to the Treasury Bills. It is rightly argued that Treasury Bills can, and long bonds cannot, qualify as part of the banks' liquid assets reserves (the 28 per cent. requirement), and that the re-placement of Treasury Bills by long bonds ('funding') therefore makes the system less liquid. But if the Treasury Bill issue is reduced simply by forcing local government authorities to borrow at short-term in the market, and former outside holders of Treasury Bills regard the local authority debts as just as good (for their purposes) as Treasury Bills, there is no effective reduction in liquidity.

To the extent that government debt operations do in-duce the market to absorb less liquid instruments, it is done in the main by paying higher interest, whether this higher interest is paid by the central government or by the local ratepayers. Theoretically this higher rate of interest will, in so far as the rates of interest at which

intermediaries operate are sticky, make loans by them less
readily available; and, when the rates are at last adjusted,
cause the ultimate borrowers (who want to spend on capital
development, or on consumption beyond income) to drop
marginal projects, as explained in Chapter 9. The authorities can thus, in a system of the English kind, exercise
a restraining influence through the monetary system in
several ways:

1. They can raise the short-term rates of interest which
   are directly or indirectly under their control: this
   operates both as a disincentive to capital spending,
   and disturbs the equilibrium between financial
   intermediaries, hindering lending by those whose
   rates are relatively rigid.
2. They can press funding of the national debt: that is
   to say, they can make long-term bonds more attractive to lenders, thereby enabling themselves to
   reduce the availability of the short-term government
   debt (e.g. Treasury Bills, cash, local authority short
   debt) that serves as a liquidity reserve for banks and
   other financial intermediaries. This will reduce the
   availability of loans generally; exactly where the
   pressure falls will depend, among other conditions,
   on whether the authorities make their long bonds
   more attractive by raising their yields or by other
   means (e.g. by influencing market expectations).
3. They can run an overall government surplus, so
   making possible a net reduction of the national debt.
   This reduction can be concentrated at the short end
   (e.g. Treasury Bills) to secure the maximum monetary effect. Contrariwise, if the Government happens
   to run a surplus at a time when it wants to avoid
   monetary restraint, it can concentrate the reduction
   of debt at the long end.
4. They can exercise their authority (by legal powers
   or 'moral suasion') to require higher reserves of liquid

assets in the banks and/or other financial intermediaries.
5. They can exercise their authority (of either kind)
directly to obstruct lending by the banks and/or
other financial intermediaries.

The choice between these courses must depend to some
extent upon the Government's attitude to manipulation,
by fiscal measures, of its budgetary position; it will depend, too, on how persuasively it can operate a funding
policy. Within the limits set by such considerations as
these, its remaining choice is between an emphasis on
raising interest rates and an emphasis on direct interference with the banks and other financial intermediaries,
by raising liquidity ratio requirements and/or direct
restraints on lending. In an extreme situation, it may be
necessary to resort to all these measures, but in a less
extreme situation the authorities may choose between
them. What considerations should guide their choice?
The answer depends partly on the responsiveness of the
business world to changes in interest rates. If there is a
major disincentive effect on capital spending, and if a rise
in interest rates sharply disrupts the operations of financial
intermediaries so interfering with the availability of loans,
there is much to be said for moving interest rates, although
this will involve more expensive service of the national
debt. It is generally believed that the United States
economy does work in this fashion; but in Britain there
are grounds for believing that the disincentive effect is
slow to operate, and that the financial intermediaries fairly
rapidly adjust themselves to a movement of interest rates.
Interference with the banks and/or other financial
intermediaries obviously has great potentiality, but the
authorities may have to face the awkward choice between
administrative cumbersomeness on the one hand and in-
equity and inefficiency on the other. The fewer the firms
that have to be regulated, the easier it all is: hence the

temptation, in Britain, to regulate the banks alone. And, since the banks are, from the viewpoints of most borrowers, much the most convenient quick lenders, interference with the banks gets the maximum quick effect. But if the restriction has to be prolonged, the disadvantages multiply. As intending borrowers are denied the funds they want, there appear opportunities for other financial intermediaries to step in and do the business, *especially if the borrowers are not deterred by the higher interest that has to be paid to non-bank lenders.* Thus (*a*) the restriction becomes ineffective, (*b*) borrowing and lending is forced into channels that are, for many purposes, less efficient than the banks, and (*c*) the banks are subject to disabilities while their competitors are allowed to thrive. How serious these disadvantages are depends upon how easily the non-bank intermediaries can step into the shoes of the banks. In a system in which the banks are so peculiar that nobody would regard other claims as at all competitive with bank deposits, the disadvantages would be slight. But as a financial system develops, other financial institutions become more closely competitive with the banks, and this tendency is accentuated as the trade cycle is flattened and as the protecting cover of central bank support broadens out through the financial structure. In such a highly developed system, the disadvantages of direct interference with the banks alone grow rapidly if the interference is prolonged, and this applies equally to interference by liquidity ratio control (as is usual in the U.S.A.) and to interference by 'requests' to limit bank advances (the more usual method in Britain). In either case, prolonged interference gives rise to justifiable argument that the control should be widened to cover other financial intermediaries.

VI. *The Determination of the Volume of Bank Deposits*

Enough has been said in this chapter to show that the relationship between bank deposits and other financial claims is so complex that there can be no simple answer to the question, what determines the volume of bank deposits at any given moment? To say that it is a multiple of the reserve assets of the banks is a part of the answer, but the whole truth is very much more intricate. We shall not attempt to give a precise answer to the question, but we shall, in summary of parts of the discussion in this chapter, simply list some of the more important factors that affect the volume of bank deposits in the English system, indicating in which direction a change in each factor tends to change the volume of deposits. The relevant factors are:

1. The volume of national debt of all kinds (including cash, Treasury Bills, and short and long bonds) created by the Government (more created, more bank deposits).
2. The public willingness to hold cash (more cash outside the banks, less bank deposits).
3. The public's willingness to hold Treasury Bills and other government obligations, short *and long* (more held, less bank deposits).
4. The willingness of the discount houses to hold short bonds (the more willing, the less effect will reduced availability of Treasury Bills have in restricting the banks' liquid assets, since the banks can lend to enable discount houses to hold short bonds).
5. The cash and other liquidity ratios of the banks (higher ratios, lower bank deposits).
6. The public's relative preferences for bank deposits and claims on other financial intermediaries (higher preference, more bank deposits).
7. The public's relative preferences for borrowing from banks or from other financial intermediaries (more from banks, more bank deposits).
8. The liquidity reserve requirements of non-bank intermediaries (higher requirements of government obligations, lower bank deposits).

At least some of these factors are influenced by the rate of interest policy followed by the authorities. If all interest rates are raised, this increases the relative attraction of all interest-bearing assets (including time deposits) as compared with cash and demand deposits. If the *structure* of interest rates is changed, long rates rising relatively to short, the public's preference for long bonds will be increased, and their preferences as between the banks and other intermediaries, both as borrowers and as lenders, may be changed. Another aspect of this relates to the influence of the cash position: the English authorities *choose* to maintain a certain fairly steady relationship between Bank Rate (the rediscount rate) and the Treasury Bill rate. This implies a willingness to interchange cash and Treasury Bills freely at the steady rate, which makes the supply of Treasury Bills rather than the supply of cash the influential quantity under Item 1 above.[1]

The list begins with national debt—the total obligations of the Government—because some of these obligations are both the basis of the credit structure and the Government's final means of meeting its residuary financial requirements. In this sense, the present structure of financial claims has been governed in large degree by the history of government finance. It also means, more immediately, that a residual government deficit—after paying the wages of its servants, the cost of adding to the equipment of the nationalized industries, and the cost of adding to its international reserves of gold—adds directly to the credit base. This addition is neutralized only if the Government can at the same time persuade people to buy more government bonds *and not regard them as a liquidity reserve*. In the absence of such persuasion, there is certain to be an increase in the volume of bank deposits; but how great an increase cannot be told without precise quantification of all the factors in our list—and these items are themselves summaries of complex webs of financial mechanism.

[1] Cf. Section V of Chapter 5.

11

BANKING AND MONETARY POLICY IN THE UNITED STATES: A COMPARATIVE STUDY

1. *Commercial Banking*

THE banks in the U.S.A. may properly be said to form 'a banking system' in the important sense that all are linked directly or indirectly with the New York money-market and all look to one central bank, although that central bank is federal in organization and has its chief seat of government in Washington, 200 miles away from the New York money market. But there is no dominance of the system by a few gigantic banks, as the English system is dominated by the 'Big Five'. In England the same six or seven banks appear in almost every town, and they are doing much the same kind of business as in any other town. This is not unlike the position in the State of California (a country in itself) but over the remainder of the United States the banking scene is quite different. There are about 14,000 banks in all, and they vary so greatly in size, type of business, and outlook that it is difficult to generalize in describing the banking services available to the public. This variety also makes the technical problems of central banking quite different from those in England and most other countries.

Despite the concentric forces that have been felt in American banking, as elsewhere, the system is still overwhelmingly one of 'unit banks', not branch banks; but in this also there is wide variation. The development of nation-wide branch banks has been prevented by law, and still more by the traditional feelings in which the legal restrictions are deeply entrenched. These feelings are derived to some extent from the historical fear of the newer west for the money power of the older east; they also express the more general feeling in every region against remote control, and the distrust of any incipient monopoly of finance. The laws restricting branch banking are essentially those of the fifty States, and they vary from one State to another. In fourteen States (including California) branches extend over the State; in sixteen, branches are allowed, but are limited to relatively small areas; in the remaining States, branches are in general not allowed. No bank may open a branch outside the State in which its head office lies.

Within these limits, branch banking has grown quite rapidly since 1930, and particularly since 1945, but the position still contrasts sharply with that in England. The eleven London clearing banks have between them some 13,000 branches; of the 13,800 American banks, three out of every four have no branch at all, and the remainder (3,140 banks) have between them only 16,000 branches. Even among those having branches, it is exceptional to find more than two or three branches, and these branches are often in the same town as the head office. Only about 500 banks have more than five branches each; very few have more than 100 branches each. California is the State where branch banking has gone farthest: here the Bank of America, the largest bank in the world, has over 800 branches, and five other banks have between them 1,000 branches. In New York City there are 49 banks with 695 branches (end-1965). At the other extreme, Chicago City has 84 unit banks which are not allowed to have branches at all.[1] Elsewhere there is great variety; in so far as there is a norm, it is the 'unit' or single-office bank serving

---

[1] In Chicago many of the routine services normally available at banks are provided by 'currency exchanges'. These offices (to English eyes, a clumsy device) help Chicago to make do with extraordinarily few banking offices.

its small local community. The fact that there are 13,800 banks therefore does not mean that it is a highly competitive business; the large number of banks reflects the large number of towns, and many towns have only two or three banks, or sometimes only one. In the great centres, especially New York, there are of course many banks, and these do compete with each other as keenly as bankers compete anywhere. The governmental bodies charged with enforcement of the laws restricting mergers inquire closely into the degree of competition, and their reports indicate that competition is a reality in towns of any size, and especially for the larger customers.

The picture of a great number of small banks is to some extent illusory, for large-scale organization plays a large and increasing part. 'Groups' or 'chains' of banks, under substantially common ownership and some degree of common control, have developed to defeat in effect the restriction of branch banking. There are no reliable figures, but 427 banks are believed to be under the control of forty-six holding companies. In terms of deposits, much the biggest group is the Transamerica, with ten banks spread over six States; there are also big groups in Minneapolis and New York State. The scale of bank organization has also been greatly modified in recent years by an amalgamation ('merger') movement affecting some of the largest banks in the country, including the New York giants and big banks in Pittsburgh, Boston, Dallas, Kansas City, Baltimore, Washington, D.C., and elsewhere. This merger movement has been going fast enough to arouse discussion, and the English arguments of 1917–18 (when the 'Big Five' emerged) have been echoed across the Atlantic. The degree of concentration of banking in many of the large cities is now very high, and it is no longer possible to describe the United States, even outside California, as a country of small banks. What is still lacking, outside California, is the wide network of branches. The United States remains predominantly a country of local banks.

In general, the American people prefer it that way; but times are changing.

The structure, and the sentiments that lie behind it, pose problems of control quite beyond anything existing in a compact system of the English type. In England, banking opinion can crystallize among a group of men small enough to sit round a small table, and the wishes and intentions of the authorities can be made known to such a group without anyone crossing more than a street or two from his own office. In the United States there are several thousands of men who are entitled to call themselves 'bankers'; they are scattered over a huge area and do not acknowledge New York bankers as their spokesmen or Washington authorities as their political masters in any but the most limited sense. An important consequence is that the central banking weapon of 'moral suasion' is of little use. The organization of banking opinion is a serious business, and the American Bankers' Association accordingly has a liveliness and importance far beyond any analogous body on this side of the Atlantic.

The business of the American banks is primarily to hold deposits and to effect the transfers of deposits (the 'ledger-clerk function') and to make short-term loans to firms and individuals. Among the deposits, Time Deposits are important: the 'savings' aspect of banking business is generally weightier than in England. On the other side of the balance-sheet, their lending to firms includes a sizeable proportion of medium-term loans, and to individuals and firms there are some mortgage loans; in both these particulars American banks are more openly committed than are English banks. Consumer credit-business has become important in recent decades. Both short- and medium-term government bonds are held, in important amounts, as in England. There is no precise parallel to the London loans to the discount market, but the great city banks do a variety of loan business with a variety of financial specialists, while smaller banks have, as their second-line defence, deposit balances with other banks.

This business of inter-bank deposits has historically been, and continues to remain, of great importance. Before the establishment of the Federal Reserve System the balance of a country bank with its 'city correspondent' served as its reserve in the fuller sense as well as being a working balance for clearing purposes. The city correspondent bank would allow its country correspondents various facilities as banker to customer; the relationship was very much that between the country banker and the 'London agent' in nineteenth-century England. With the development of the Federal Reserve System these 'correspondent' links would seem to have lost some of their purpose, as member banks may look to the Federal Reserve Banks for many of the most important facilities. Nevertheless, the habit remains, and inter-bank business is substantial. 'Country banks' hold balances with their big brothers in the various financial and regional centres, and most of these in turn hold balances with New York banks. These inter-bank deposits now form about 6 per cent. of the total deposit liabilities of all banks: two-sevenths of this total is at New York banks. The correspondent relationship is used to facilitate clearing of cheques and remittance business generally; much of this work of the correspondent has been taken over by the Federal Reserve System, but it remains by no means negligible.

The huge number and geographical dispersion of the American banks necessitate elaborate arrangements for clearing and remittance business. To English eyes these arrangements inevitably look cumbersome, but their efficiency is constantly being increased and mechanical methods are more and more used. Nevertheless, the work remains heavy, and it is not surprising that the American customer has to pay much more in commissions for the 'ledger-clerk service' performed by his bank. These costs of using demand deposits check the spread of the banking habit, and in much of the country this is no further developed than in England. In many places, however, the banks have been very lively and enterprising in their efforts to attract new classes of customer, and the number of demand accounts is prodigious.

Time Deposits are received at rates of interest varying according to the periods for which they are fixed, in contrast to the English single seven-days category. These time deposits amount to over half of total deposits. But once we begin using such figures, we must remember the variety among the thousands of banks: some banks have much higher proportions of Time Deposits, and approximate to the habits of the mutual savings banks. In catering for the small savers the banks vary a good deal: most of them deliberately seek such custom as a means to develop custom more generally.

Under laws enacted after the great banking crisis of the early nineteen-thirties, most accounts, whether Demand or Time, are protected by insurance with the Federal Deposit Insurance Corporation (F.D.I.C.), a government agency financed by a tax on all insured deposits. The protection is limited to $15,000 for each depositor in a bank, enough to cover all ordinary personal balances though not of much account to the big commercial corporations. An insured bank has to submit to inspection by the F.D.I.C., a provision that brings into the Federal government's supervision many banks that would otherwise escape its eagle eye. (The F.D.I.C. is only one of many authorities having inspection powers in American banking, but its writ runs further than the others.)

Turning to the function of the banker as a lender to business and investor of surplus funds, the outstanding feature is, as in English banking, a strong preference for the very short-term commitments. What the banker really likes is a customer who wants finance for purely seasonal expansion of stock of a commodity in regular consumption, not subject to the whim of fashion or the vagaries of the weather; but neither American nor English bankers expect this ideal to be approached except in a small minority of cases. But they do have a very strong preference for the *temporary* loan, financing fixed capital only until other and permanent arrangements can be made by the industrialist. Alongside this basic similarity, there is sharp contrast in the formal arrangements whereby banks lend to the generality of business customers. In England agreement by word of mouth is often deemed sufficient, or there is a simple exchange of letters. In the U.S.A. a formal document of contract is usually drawn up; the lawyers are much more prominent and much more active in American banking. The credit invariably takes the form of a loan in the U.S.A., while in England the overdraft is much the most usual, though not the invariable, form.

As in England, commercial banks in the United States have in the present century experienced a relative shrinkage in the demand for bank credit of the traditional kind: the development of markets for industrial securities, the cash-payment habit in retail trade, and the development of credit relations between firms have undermined the bankers' market. The inadequacy of outlets was particularly felt in the years of slack trade before 1939, when the supply of reserve money was increased out of all proportion to contemporary requirements, and after the war, when government inflation further increased the lending power of the banks. In these circumstances of money-glut the banks broadened their ideas in lending policy; the most important, though not the only consequential developments were the *term loan* and *consumer credit*.

The term loan is granted for a period of years—three, five, or even ten years—with specific provision for its reduction by regular periodical payments.[1] It is used by

---

[1] The maximum period tended to increase in the long period of easy money, and tended to shorten in the tighter conditions of the mid-fifties. Sometimes arrangements are concerted with insurance companies, who

small firms as well as large. Particularly it is favoured by firms that are too small to make an issue to the bond markets, and by corporations (notably public utilities) that wish to anticipate investment of undistributed profits and can reasonably expect to make the repayments as the profits emerge. Banks normally 'syndicate' term loans for all but small borrowers: that is, they agree among themselves to contribute jointly to the borrower's requirements and to share correspondingly in the repayments. The banks like this business so much that they do it at rates of interest only $\frac{1}{4}$ or $\frac{1}{2}$ per cent. above the corresponding rates for business loans. In amount the term loans with other loans fixed for more than one year now represent about one-third of the total of the banks' loans to business; in the eastern states, term loans are more like one-half of total business lending. English banks sometimes have with borrowers arrangements analogous to those of the term loan, but the proportion of such business is probably smaller in England than in the U.S.A.

The other big development of the latest generation is in the financing of instalment purchases by consumers. About half the bank loans for this purpose are made to specialist finance companies and sales organizations which do the final lending to the consumers. Even so, the amount of direct credit to consumers is very large: about a seventh of total bank loans, and two-fifths of all instalment credit. Some banks make a special line of it: they have a separate part of the counter where buyers of cars, refrigerators, &c., go to arrange an instalment loan from the bank, and the service is pressed on the public by vigorous advertising. The banks go to great expense to obtain information on the credit-worthiness of these customers; this keeps the charges quite high, although bad debts have been extraordinarily slight. Banking opinion is not wholeheartedly in favour of this kind of business, but many bankers regard it

take the later maturities while the banks are paid off in say the first five annual repayments.

as the most effective way of attracting customers who will eventually make wider use of banking services. Terms of lending in this class have sometimes been directly regulated by the Federal Reserve System.

The banks are also quite openly in the business of loans on real estate mortgage. Some they handle directly, but they also sometimes lend to other financial organizations who lend to the property-owners. This is a business English bankers prefer to leave alone, and there are misgivings in the U.S.A. The freedom with which banks engaged in this business was certainly one of the elements of instability in the boom of the late twenties; the question of selective control by the Federal Reserve authorities has been much discussed. Experience of that same boom has also been responsible for the control of bank lending to the securities markets; this is a class of lending that was once very big indeed. Its amount now is trivial in relation to total bank lending, though not insignificant for the New York banks which do most of it.

In addition to his loans to customers, which the banker rightly regards as a chief justification of his existence, the U.S. banker has to hold 'cash' reserves which are authoritatively specified either by the Federal Reserve System or (in the case of non-member banks) by State law; these 'required reserves' include cash in vault. There is one other bulky element among his assets: his portfolio of securities, principally U.S. government bonds. Nearly two-thirds of the banks' holdings of government securities are within five years of maturity, and nearly all are within ten years. This implies a shorter average life than that of an English bank's portfolio of government securities, but in this respect English and American habits have been becoming more alike—in England the average 'life' has been shortening while in the U.S.A. it has been lengthening.

In considering every aspect of their lending and indeed of all their other operations, it is essential to remember the immense variety among American banks. In New York City, at the one extreme, the banks' portfolios consist of genuinely short-term loans and substantial 'term-loans' to trading and industrial corporations, with some very short loans to financial operators of one kind or another; their loans to agriculture are relatively small. At the other extreme, some country banks may have as much as half their money out on real estate or in poorly secured loans to local farmers, and the rest largely in government securities. Between these two extremes, every possible variety is ranged: there is no standard balance-sheet in American banking. Variety of business makes for some variety in costs, and this is reflected in varying charges to customers, especially where competition is weak. In England the same kind of borrower pays the same kind of rate on his loan, whether he is in London or in a little market town in the North, and the rate he pays is not much higher than that charged to the big customers; costs are spread over the whole country. In the predominantly unit structure of the U.S.A., on the other hand, costs tend to stick where they fall, and the small country bank lending to the small borrower is apt to charge much more than a great city bank charges to a big customer whom it is afraid of losing to a rival bank. The variety of assets-structures has also its implications for the technique of control by the central bank; before pursuing this, we must look in some detail at the New York money-market which has important bearing both on the behaviour of the commercial banks themselves and on the technique by which the central authorities seek to control them.

II. *The New York Money-market*

Among the many changes that have occurred since the first edition of this book was written, none has been more striking than the development of the New York money-market. Gone are the days when the market was primarily concerned with very short loans by banks to the Stock Exchange. Stock Exchange firms can still get these short loans from the banks, but this business is largely done on a negotiated basis. The weight of money-market activity is now in the hands of a relatively small group of dealers, both banks and non-bank dealers, who are chiefly concerned with very short government paper and with day-to-day balances at the New York Federal Reserve Bank. Like the London foreign-exchange market, the New York money-market is essentially a network of telephone lines, linking among themselves the Federal Reserve Bank (which also acts as agent for the U.S. Treasury), the five great dealer banks, and about a dozen non-bank dealers clustered in the Wall Street area, but also linking them with other dealers in securities, a variety of miscellaneous financial institutions, and with the larger banks throughout the country.

There is still a market in the older instruments, notably *commercial paper* and *bankers' acceptances*. The commercial paper consists of short-term promissory notes, originating in some 350 firms in all sorts of business all over the country. The notes have lives of three, four, or six months; their main use is for seasonal finance and their nearest parallel in London is the inland bill of exchange. This commercial paper, as also the similar paper created by finance companies, has revived slightly in recent years, and represents for industry and trade a source of finance competitive with the ordinary bank loan. Bankers' acceptances, comparable with fine bank bills in London, have also revived somewhat, but they show no sign of returning to the importance they had in the nineteen-twenties, much less of assuming that central place in the monetary system that was once intended for them. The really important business of the market is in neither of these instruments but in Treasury Bills and other short government paper, in 'Federal Funds', and in very short loans to dealers against their holdings of government securities, in finance paper and in Certificates of Deposit.[1]

In the short government securities, the five 'dealer banks' (two of them from Chicago) and the non-bank dealers all operate very much as do London stock-jobbers, in that they stand ready to buy or sell at any time, irrespective of their momentary holdings or their desire to hold any security. They necessarily hold a 'stock-in-trade'; the non-bank dealers operate with funds far exceeding their own capital, borrowing from the big New York banks and from 'out-of-town' sources against some of the securities that happen to be in their portfolios. At the short end of the market (in which the Reserve Bank most continuously operates), there is a very active business in Treasury Bills, most of which run for 3, 6, or 12 months. They are broadly similar to British Treasury Bills and are issued in weekly batches by tender. The tenderer for London Treasury Bills has the option of taking them up on any day in the following week, whereas the New York issue is for one fixed day only; in this detail the more flexible London system probably makes for smoother markets. In London the tender is dominated by the syndicated bid of the discount houses, while the great English banks do not tender at all; this does not by any means imply a non-competitive market, though competition is much less sharp than in New York. There the competitive bidders are the big and medium-size banks (including many out-of-town), the dealers, and non-bank buyers (financial institutions and other large businesses) who tender through the agency of the big New York banks and non-bank dealers. Non-competitive bids are allowed, having been introduced in order to popularize the Treasury Bill among small banks who cannot be expected to be expert in fixing a price. New York dominates the tender—about two-thirds of the weekly issue goes first into New York hands, though much of this passes into out-of-town hands.

[1] For Certificates of Deposit see p. 286 below.

The New York dealers take up large amounts not to hold but for quick resale to non-bank buyers, small banks, and even to large banks when these have been unsuccessful at the tender. The whole business is more complex than in London, and the greater heterogeneity of the New York market almost certainly makes for conditions closer to Marshall's perfect market.

Once issued, U.S. Treasury Bills continue to enjoy an active market. The dealers (including dealer banks) establish bid and offer prices; they deal as principals, making their profit out of the 'turn'; there is virtually no broking. Even the large banks sell as well as buy, unlike the London banks, which are ordinarily only buyers of Treasury Bills. The Federal Reserve Bank is always active in this market.

If banks, after making what adjustments they wish in their portfolios of commercial paper, acceptances, and government securities, are short or long of cash, they can operate in the Federal Funds market before being reduced to borrowing at the Federal Reserve or holding excess reserves (according to whether they are short or long of cash). This market in Federal Funds is something for which London has no precise parallel, the nearest to it being the bidding by the discount houses for their marginal funds before they resort to the discount office ('the front door') of the Bank of England.[1] The demand for Federal Funds (balances at the Reserve Bank) is a demand by banks and by dealers in government securities. The supply of Federal Funds is mainly by banks, the big New York banks again predominating, though out-of-town banks increasingly put funds into this market instead of carrying barren excess reserves. There are also non-banking sellers, such as dealers in government securities

---

[1] In the 1960's a direct 'inter-bank market' has developed in London, and this has some similarity to the Federal Funds market, though non-participation by the London Clearing Banks limits this new market to narrower scope than the Federal Funds market.

after they have sold bills to the Reserve Bank, and agents of foreign banks who have by some means or other come into possession of balances at the Reserve Bank. The market is extremely active and a free higglers' market if ever there was one, and the tighter monetary conditions of the middle fifties drew into its vortex temporarily surplus bank-cash from all over the country. Banks outside as well as inside New York act as dealers, maintaining a wide network of contacts through which they buy and sell Federal Funds. One Wall Street brokerage firm has been prominent in centralizing transactions and more or less making the price; and the big banks both deal directly with each other and act as brokers. Since there are always some banks willing to borrow at the Reserve Bank, and the required eligible paper (nowadays effectively government securities) is always available, the price of Federal Funds cannot rise much above the Reserve Bank's discount rate; but since 1963 the System has kept the market on a fairly tight rein and the Federal Funds rate has tended to keep closely up to, and frequently above, the official discount rate.

Besides Federal Funds, which are balances standing to the credit of banks in the books of the Reserve Bank and are transferable on the day on which instruction is given, the market deals also in 'Clearing House Funds'. The latter are cheques drawn on New York banks and passed through the Clearing House; since they do not go through the Clearing House until the following day, they are 'money tomorrow'. Federal Funds being 'money today', an exchange of Federal Funds for Clearing House Funds is in effect a loan overnight.

The dealers, who need money to enable them to hold securities, search for both these classes of 'money'. Normally, the New York banks only provide the dealers with Clearing House Funds, but banks outside New York provide Federal Funds. In addition, the dealers secure part of the money they require by 'buy-backs' from non-bank operators, whereby a spot sale at a fixed price is linked with a forward repurchase, also at a fixed price but slightly higher in order to allow the other party to gain what is in effect interest on a short loan. This device has become very important since the war; in rather tighter form, and known as 'sale-and-repurchase agreement', it is used by the Reserve Bank as a way of putting cash into the hands of the dealers when markets are tight and the authorities do not wish to force more bank borrowing at the penal rate 'at the discount window'.

The entire market is highly competitive. There is an immensely complicated criss-crossing of transactions, with both non-bank dealers and the New York banks competing for the spare cash of out-of-town banks and of the whole gamut of firms both inside and outside New York. Development of the market along these lines makes for more complete use of the spare cash of one bank to meet the shortage of cash in another bank and for economizing the cash holdings of non-bank operators. The system is in this respect becoming more like that of London, where 'spare cash' is virtually eliminated by the operations of the discount market. But the number, variety, and geographical dispersion of the American banks make it rather unlikely that the extreme position of London will ever be reached; for the present, certainly, America's central bankers have to work on the assumption that at any given moment some banks will be short of cash while others have excess.

III. *Control of the Quantity and Price of Credit*

Responsibility for controlling the American banking system is settled by the laws of the federal union and of the fifty component States. A bank can be registered under federal law, in which case it is called a 'national bank', or under the law of the State in which it is situated, when it is a 'State bank'. State laws vary appreciably, and they vary from federal law, but all prescribe elaborate conditions banks must fulfil. Chief among these are provisions relating to the capital of a bank, its cash reserves, its accounts, and the inspection of the bank by officers of the government (State or Federal) concerned; there are also generally restrictions on the amount of lending to any one customer. Except for the regulation of cash reserves, these restrictions have no parallel in contemporary English banking; they have some importance in a unit banking system, but would hardly be appropriate in a highly concentrated system of the English type. The more important controls are exercised through the Federal Reserve System. All national banks are obliged to be members of the System: State banks have the option to be members, and enough of them are members to bring the total of member banks up to 6,221 (end of 1965) having 83 per cent. of total bank deposits. Supported by the restrictions imposed by State laws on non-member banks, the weight of these member banks in the entire banking system is sufficient to allow the Federal Reserve System to exercise effective control over the supply of money. The methods whereby the Reserve System exercises this control are the prescription of reserve ratios, operation as lender of last resort, open-market operations, and 'selective credit controls'.

The power of the Federal Reserve System is substantially based on the fact that it is virtually the sole source of cash. Six-sevenths of the actual currency in circulation consists of Federal Reserve notes. The remainder consists of small notes and coin and certain vestigial forms of currency, all of these being issued by the Federal government in much the same way as coins are issued by the Royal Mint in London. Balances at the Federal Reserve Banks, like Bankers' Deposits at the Bank of England, are exchangeable into notes or coin as required by the banks and the public. The law requires all member banks to hold reserves, consisting of balances at the Reserve Banks plus vault cash, bearing certain minimum ratios to their own deposit liabilities to the public. The ratios are fixed by the

Board of Governors of the Reserve System, and are variable within a wide range set by law in 1935. Against Time Deposits one ratio (in 1966, $5\frac{1}{2}$ per cent.) is set for all member banks.[1] In relation to Demand Deposits, different ratios (in 1966, $16\frac{1}{2}$ and 12 per cent.) are set according to the situation of banks in Reserve Cities or elsewhere (the latter being classified as 'Country banks'). For non-member banks, reserve ratios (on the whole, more generous to the banks) are fixed by the various State laws under which these banks operate, and over these ratios the Federal Reserve System has no authority. Thus all banks, whether inside or outside the Reserve System, have clearly defined reserve requirements, and this implies, as we saw in earlier chapters, that the body with power to create or destroy reserve balances has very great influence over the creation of bank money throughout the country. This body is of course the Reserve System itself, for the Reserve Banks can create (or destroy) reserve balances (standing in its own books in favour of banks) by buying (or selling) securities.[2]

The pivotal position of this Reserve Bank cash depends upon the interest the commercial banks have in keeping their reserve ratios reasonably close to the prescribed minima. At most times the profit motive is sufficient for this, given that the banks can look to the Reserve System as a lender of last resort.[3] When, as in the nineteen-thirties, extraordinary circumstances lead to the persistence of 'excess reserves' on any great scale, the Reserve System can reduce these excess reserves at a stroke by raising the required minimum ratios; more usually, excess

---

[1] There may be a lower rate (in 1966, 4) for certain classes of small Time Deposits; and Time Deposits made by foreign central banks bear unrestricted rates.

[2] 'Securities is used here in the widest sense, to include not only such instruments as bankers' acceptances (bills of exchange) and U.S. Treasury Bills and bonds, but also (1) gold certificates issued by the U.S. Treasury to importers of gold, and (2) I O U's of banks on which they borrow from the Reserve Banks at 'the discount window'.

[3] Cf. p. 101 above.

reserves on a moderate scale can be attacked by open-market sales of securities by the Reserve System.

It is of course in the interest of the Reserve System as the controller that excess reserves should be kept within moderate bounds. For this purpose, as well as for the important purpose of preventing the collapse of the banking system in a crisis, the Reserve System has to be the lender of last resort. A member bank finding that its reserve (balance at the Reserve Bank) is falling below the prescribed ratio can buy Federal Funds or borrow from the Reserve Bank. It borrows either by rediscounting one or more of its customers' 'notes' (I O U's of some form) or by giving its own I O U to the Reserve Bank; normally nowadays it gives its I O U, pledging short-term government securities as cover. The rate charged is the Reserve Bank's published discount rate.

This operation of the Reserve System 'at the discount window' has important features differing from those of the corresponding operations of the Bank of England. Most obviously, whereas the English banks obtain reserve cash only indirectly by forcing the discount houses to borrow at the Bank of England, the American banks borrow directly from the Reserve System. Given the unit structure of American banking and the huge area of the country, direct access to the discount window implies the necessity of a wide spread of Reserve Bank offices. For its service as lender of last resort the Bank of England could perfectly well be confined to a single office, as indeed it is for this purpose. But the Reserve System of the U.S.A. must be a *Federal* Reserve System: a network of Reserve Banks and Branches, totalling thirty-six offices in all, spread over the length and breadth of the country. This dispersion of the System's offices is especially important having regard to another Anglo-American contrast arising from the direct access to the lender of last resort: the power of the Reserve Banks to look into the business of the member banks. The action of a Reserve Bank as lender of last resort is not, in ordinary circumstances, a right to which member banks are automatically entitled; it is regarded rather as a privilege they enjoy if they fulfil certain conditions. In general, a member bank is expected to borrow at the Reserve Bank neither continuously nor in amounts large in relation to the general scale of the member bank's total resources.[1] The Reserve Bank is entitled to inquire into the operations of a member bank that wants to borrow, and these inquiries are pressed if the borrowing threatens to become continuous or unduly large. It follows that the organization of the Reserve System must be such as to allow close contact with banks all over the country. It also follows that when member-bank borrowing is increasing, the Reserve System is increasing its power to inquire into, and to enforce objection to, the conduct of member banks. This is a very important power, to which there is no parallel in the English system. The Bank of England acts as lender of last resort to the discount houses alone, and there would be little point in telling them that their difficulties were due to excessive lending by the commercial banks.

The discount rate is in form fixed by each of the twelve Reserve Banks separately. There are arrangements for co-ordination, though not for complete centralization, of these decisions: the individual Reserve Banks 'establish' their rates which have to be 'reviewed and determined' by the central Board of Governors in Washington: in effect this means that regional views, if strongly held, have considerable weight, and the twelve rates do not necessarily move in unison when a situation is open to conflicting interpretations. The discount rate is not a penal rate; it is usually above the Treasury Bill rate, but it is below the general run of loan rates and the real check to borrowing lies not in its cost but in the considerations mentioned in the previous paragraph.

[1] This convention against continuous or large borrowing is not entirely one-sided; there is still reluctance on the part of some (not all) member banks themselves, a reluctance rooted in the tradition that dependence on another bank was a sign of weakness.

In contrast to its work as lender of last resort, the open-market operations of the Reserve System are completely centralized. Directions governing these operations are decided by the Federal Open Market Committee in Washington, and are executed by the Securities Department, known as 'the Trading Desk', of the Reserve Bank of New York. The most frequent operations are outright purchase or sale of Treasury Bills, but there are small dealings in Bankers' Acceptances, and since 1961 there have also been important dealings in longer-dated government paper. The Trading Desk also grants loans, for a maximum of fifteen days, to the dealers in government securities. These loans, known as 'repurchase agreements', take the form of a sale of short government paper by a dealer to the Reserve Bank, with simultaneous forward repurchase. The initiative is with the Reserve Bank, which is not considered to be under any obligation to give automatic relief in this way. The difference in the spot price for the one transaction and the forward price for the other allows the Reserve Bank interest on the effective loan, and the arithmetic is normally based on the official Discount Rate of the New York Reserve Bank.

The impact effect of these open-market operations, whatever form they take, is precisely parallel to the first impact effect of open-market operations by the Bank of England: a purchase of securities by the Reserve Bank adds to the cash reserves of member banks, and a sale of securities reduces the cash reserves of member banks. But what happens after that is different.

The difference arises partly from the varied assets-structures of American banks. At any moment some banks will have excess reserves (i.e. reserves exceeding the legal requirement plus essential working cash) while others will be in debt to the Reserve Banks. On balance the excess reserves of (some) member banks somewhat exceed the total borrowing by (other) member banks; this margin of 'net free reserves' is closely watched by the Reserve

System. If the margin is unusually wide, credit conditions will be 'easy' and money-market rates will tend to be clearly below the Reserve Bank's Discount Rates. Suppose that at this stage the Reserve System, thinking that a boom is threatening to get out of hand, decides to tighten credit: its action will be to sell securities to absorb cash. The impact effect, spread over the system, will be that banks with excess reserves will find these shrinking, some banks will be forced to begin borrowing at the Reserve Banks in order to maintain the required reserve ratios, and banks previously borrowing will need to borrow more and will encounter more nagging from the Reserve Bank. Money-market rates will rise, as banks generally will be less willing lenders. The further the process is pushed, the rarer will excess reserves become, the more banks will be forced to 'the discount window', and the higher open-market rates will rise. The Treasury Bill rate is particularly sensitive to the position of bank reserves, and if the Reserve System persists in keeping the banks' reserve position 'tight' in this way, the rise in interest rates will spread, and 'the prime rate' for lending to the best commercial and industrial customers may eventually be changed if the movement in the market is pronounced. Such a movement of market rates used to precede a change in the Reserve System's own official Discount Rates, but in recent years the System has sometimes raised its official rates, so signalling its views to the market, at an early stage in the process.

Correspondingly, if the Reserve System wishes to ease credit (fearing trade recession), it will buy securities, so helping banks to shake themselves free from borrowing at the discount window and adding to excess reserves in banks already comfortable. Open-market rates fall and banks lend more freely. Again, the Reserve System may emphasize easy conditions by reducing Discount Rates.

There are many points of contrast with conditions in London, where Bank Rate changes are traditionally much more important, and open-market operations are regarded primarily as a device for enforcing Bank Rate. The difference is due in part to the unique historical power of London's Bank Rate (a glory, alas! departed), but it is also related to the compressibility of cash in the American system. In London the cash ratio is rigid and the discount houses stand as a buffer between the central bank and the commercial banks; in the U.S.A. the Reserve System can make cash scarcer, with the effect of making all banks feel less comfortable and bringing some of them under direct pressure as borrowers at its own offices.

In the exceptional conditions of the 1930's, when the excess reserves were very large indeed and gigantic open-market sales would have been necessary to bring the member banks to heel, the Reserve System was able to tighten conditions by raising the required reserve ratios, wiping out excess reserves by a stroke of the pen. Correspondingly, it was able to ease the credit situation spectacularly by reducing required ratios. But this is a weapon regarded by the System as appropriate only to extraordinary circumstances; ordinarily the amount of spare cash in the system as a whole is small enough to allow the authorities to rely on open-market operations alone.

With the rapid development of the New York money-market, particularly the market in Federal Funds, the American system is becoming rather less unlike the English system. As dealers scour the banks and other bodies all over the country for spare cash, excess reserves dwindle; if they completely disappeared, open-market operations would produce their effect simply on member-bank borrowing at the Reserve Banks, and *gradual* changes in the credit climate would be less easy to keep under control. But the system would still be unlike the English in that the Reserve Bank would still have direct contact with borrowing banks.

In addition to (but never in complete substitution for)

the general control of the credit situation, the American authorities have since 1934 made some use of 'selective credit controls': restrictions on the availability of credit for particular purposes. Much the most important and continuous control of this kind has been that on lending for speculation in the Stock Exchange. During the 1941–5 war there was a control of instalment credit, and this was revived for a time in 1951–2 in the belief that variations in consumer credit are a peculiarly unstable part of consumers' expenditure. In 1950–2 there was temporary regulation of lending for 'real estate construction'; this again was designed to check undue expansion of demand in a particular direction. There also was during this Korean period a system of 'voluntary credit control' under which banks and other important groups of lenders agreed principles on which they would curtail credit facilities in particular directions. These selective controls were the American counterparts of English controls that were operated, on an informal basis under 'requests' from the Chancellor of the Exchequer, during the long cheap-money period. Since 1952 the United States authorities have in general reverted to quantitative and general methods of credit control: selective controls have never been forgotten, and from time to time there are proposals to revive or develop the measures taken in 1950–2.

The regulation of stock market credit has, however, remained in force continuously.. It was inspired by the fantastic lengths to which stock market speculation went, to some extent on the basis of bank credit, in the Wall Street boom of 1927–9. The Federal Reserve System is authorized to curb excessive use of credit for purchasing or carrying securities by setting limits to the amount that brokers and dealers in securities, banks, and others may lend on securities for that purpose. (Note that the System's power extends far beyond the banks themselves; also that bank lending on securities for purposes other than for stock-market speculation is unhindered.) The restriction is enforced by prescribing minimum percentage customer's margins. The customer's margin is the difference between the amount a bank (or other lender) lends to the customer for the purpose and the market value of the security. The higher the percentage of customer's margin to market value, the lower is the dependence of the speculation on borrowed money. Thus by raising the percentages the Federal Reserve can discourage speculation, and by dropping the percentage it can encourage speculative buying at a time when stock-market prices are falling too rapidly for the health of the economy. In recent years the margin prescribed (as the customer's share) by Federal Reserve regulation has varied from 90 per cent. to 50 per cent.; at present (September 1966) it stands at 70, to which level it was raised (from 50) late in 1963.

The early 1960's saw a decided shift of emphasis in American monetary policy. The international balance of payments had turned adversely to the United States, and the American authorities have had to look over their shoulders at the gold and foreign exchange position, a concern from which they had been free for a generation. The detailed response to this new situation was effected by closer co-ordination of U.S. Treasury actions with Federal Reserve policy, and involved some weakening of adherence to the 'bills-only' doctrine of open-market operations. While internal economic conditions seemed to demand lower interest rates and easier credit conditions, the weakness of the balance of payments pointed to the desirability of firmness in the short-term interest rates which are most immediately relevant to international capital flows. The authorities sought to deal with this dilemma by keeping the market well supplied with Treasury Bills, so keeping short rates up, while maintaining bank reserves in a fairly easy state by buying medium-term and longer-term government bonds. This at least put back into the banks through the long market the reserves that were taken out by sales within the short market. Whether this shift in the composition of the outstanding government debt made very much difference to the structure of interest rates is a matter of opinion, but at least the Americans were willing to modify their doctrinal position in an effort to get some reconciliation of the conflicting requirements of the domestic and international aspects of their monetary situation.

An interesting aspect of this development was the part played by the U.S. Treasury. Hitherto the Americans had laid great stress on the distinction between monetary action, as the business of the Federal Reserve System, and the management of the national debt, as the business of of the U.S. Treasury; and this distinction, with corresponding emphasis on the political independence of the central bank, suited their system of political organization. But it so happened that in this episode the Treasury came round to the view that the domestic situation needed stimulus, before the Federal Reserve was convinced, and it also happened that in the Kennedy Administration the Treasury got into hands well versed in market operations. The real breach in the bills-only doctrine was therefore made by the Treasury, which began operating on a large scale in the bond market; and though the Federal Reserve came in fairly quickly and was soon itself operating on a large scale outside the bill market, and although information was fully shared and the details of market operations were throughout carefully co-ordinated, the episode naturally left the Treasury rather more interested than previously in the business of formation of monetary policy.

Another development associated with the authorities' concern with the balance of payments has been the raising of the ceilings set, under Federal Reserve Regulation Q, to the interest rates the commercial banks may pay on Time and Savings Deposits. For reasons arising from the banking experiences of 1927–33, these interest rates have since that time been narrowly restricted, and this tended directly, and indirectly through the influence on other short rates, to make New York a relatively unattractive international centre for the deposit of short funds, as interest rates rose in the outside world. For the sake of protecting the gold reserve, and as part of the policy of keeping short rates up for external reasons while keeping bank credit easy for domestic reasons, there was clearly a case for raising the ceilings. This case was reinforced by the dissatisfaction of the New York banks with an international development that had resulted from the artificially low rates paid on time deposits in New York: to take advantage of the gap that had opened out between these rates on dollar balances and the rates that foreign banks could afford to pay for dollar balances, the 'Euro-dollar' market developed in London and other centres. This business in dollar balances has now taken such a strong hold that it seems likely to persist even though some of the original impetus has been removed by the concession by the American authorities of greater freedom to their own banks in the rates they may offer for certain classes of Time Deposits.

This raising of the ceiling on deposit rates, because it was not made general to all classes of deposits, gave great impetus to the development of yet another monetary instrument—the marketable Certificate of Deposit. This is a device whereby a deposit fixed for, say, a year can change ownership at any time within the year. These Certificates of Deposit were at first used only in very large denominations, but certificates down to $10,000 each are now in use. The total outstanding has grown to some $17,000 millions, an appreciable proportion of the total liabilities of the banks. By these and similar devices, as well as exercising their freedom to offer more attractive rates, the banks have become more competitive with the non-bank financial intermediaries, to which they had been losing ground, and New York has become more attractive to internationally movable funds consistently with the maintenance of moderately easy credit conditions domestically.

Another notable innovation of the 1961–2 period was the great extension of Federal Reserve operations in the foreign exchange market. Since the major currencies of western Europe became convertible, the transfer of funds between one centre and another has become comparatively easy and, with uncertainties about exchange rates as well as international political upsets, New York as well as the other international centres have been exposed to large and sudden movements of funds. A forceful example of what could happen—and of how it could be dealt with—occurred in March 1961, and since this crisis the American authorities have been willing to co-operate with other monetary authorities in absorbing at least part of these international monetary shocks. Partly because foreign exchange had been the U.S. Treasury's business in the 1933–5 episode, the Treasury took the first responsibility, but the Federal Reserve co-operated from the start and it is notable that the official reports of the Federal Open Market Committee regularly record decisions on foreign exchange operations just as they record decisions on domestic monetary operations. The operations themselves are simply sales or purchases of balances in the central banks of about eight countries whose currencies are convertible. The American authorities have agreements with their opposite numbers in the countries concerned. These agreements ensure that the buying and selling of the currencies promotes and does not conflict with the underlying principle of absorbing some of the shock of swings of private funds from one centre to another. The agreements also specify the limits to which one country will go in helping another over such difficulties, and the negotiation of the agreements therefore provides opportunity for each country to air its views on how other countries should behave if they want to avoid strain on the foreign exchange markets for their currency.

In this matter of foreign-exchange operations, as in the development of domestic open-market operations, it is notable that the former distinction between the roles of the Federal Reserve and the Treasury has been breaking down; in fact, just as the 1950's saw the American banking system and the New York money market become technically less unlike the English system, so the early 60's have seen the political aspects of the American monetary system become much less unlike those of the English system. Partly this has been a matter of personalities, partly it has been a logical development of the widened political interest in the behaviour of the economic system. But it has also been partly due to the weakening of America's balance of payments, and to the recognition by responsible Americans that they must try to solve their economic problems without wrecking the world economy. Because of all this, the old idea of a complete separation of powers has gone—and, an Englishman may be permitted to think, gone for good.

12

PROBLEMS OF MONETARY ORGANIZATION IN THE EMERGENT COUNTRIES

THROUGH most of this book the problems and their solutions have been generally stated in terms which apply directly to the highly developed banking systems either of the English type or of the American type. I would emphasize once more that this preoccupation with English and American conditions reflects no notion that those conditions are the ideals from which those of other countries show unfortunate aberrations. Rather our special concern with English and American banking is based first on the fact that these conditions are likely to be of most direct interest to the majority of readers of a book written in English, and second on the fact that the systems of other countries do appear to be developing along similar lines—indeed, they are frequently being forced to develop along similar lines. Nevertheless, there are problems peculiar to other systems, and these are worth studying both because they are important to the countries concerned and because, when we see how banking institutions work against a different background, we are more likely to understand what is fundamental and what is superficial in the more developed banking systems. In the post-1945 period special interest has been attached to economic growth in the underdeveloped countries and therefore to the influence and adequacy of their banking systems in facilitating economic growth.

It is important to emphasize at once that the term 'banking system' itself, borrowed from the more developed countries, is not realistic in most of these countries: penetration of the entire economy by an integrated structure of banking institutions is characteristic only of the countries of the West and the Dominions that have absorbed British populations and British institutions. In other countries, both inside and outside the Commonwealth, it is more usual to find some 'expatriate banks'—outliers of the great European and American systems—operating in a few centres where trading connexions with the outside world are important, and then some indigenous banks—often small and isolated—scattered more widely but still leaving great tracts of the country unprovided. This position is, however, changing fast, especially where central banks have been established for any considerable period of years and have made a determined effort to encourage the growth of a system rather than a scattering of banks.

With banking offices few and far between, and the banking habit little developed, the use of cash is necessarily more prominent; 'cash' in most cases means paper money issued by the government or by a central bank. At the banks there are both Demand Deposits and Time Deposits; in many countries all bank deposits are interest-bearing. Demand deposits and the cheques for transferring them are used only by business firms and a few of the richest individuals. Time Deposits are held by these customers too, and are frequently the only financial assets held as investments. In so far as small people are attracted into the banks, it is mainly as depositors, on Time Deposit, of their savings, and it is largely by the spread of this savings-bank business, with high interest rates and other attractions, that the banks are gradually becoming more widely known and more widely used for all kinds of business. From this relative importance of cash transactions, the concentration of much of total deposits in a few groups of large customers, and the efforts that are being made by the banks to attract new customers as depositors of their savings, it follows that a rise in the total of bank deposits can have quite different significance from the inflationary significance it normally has in the more highly developed systems. In an under-developed country, a rise in the total of bank deposits may simply denote a spread of the banking habit, if it is associated with a decline in the total of notes used in the country. Or again it may mean that, though total national money income has changed little, some distorting circumstance has transferred wealth from those who use notes to those who hold their balances in bank deposits. Similarly, a great rise in the demand for cash need not mean that there is a great inflation of money incomes, but simply that numbers of small-savings depositors have suddenly lost confidence in the banks.

A second relevant characteristic of these countries is the virtual absence of a capital market, in the sense of an active market in long-term loans and shares in industrial and commercial firms. There are, it is true, government bonds; these are held by financial institutions such as banks and insurance companies (sometimes there is an element of compulsion in these holdings) and by large trading corporations, but there is virtually no 'market' in the active sense, nor is there any possibility of borrowing on such instruments by private enterprise. Nor is there any *short* capital market—a 'money-market' that is to say, although, as we shall see, there has been something of a fashion for trying to establish money-markets.

In the absence of capital markets of the advanced 'western' kind, the wealth of the richer people is generally confined to real estate and gold. In real estate there is usually a thoroughly active and competitive market, and there is much renting of property on varied tenure systems. The market in gold is also very active, coins, ingots, and jewellery all being important, sometimes with almost daily variations in prices. Industrial ownership is rarely dissociated from management, and expansion of business operations beyond the range of family wealth is normally dependent on borrowing at the commercial banks.

Until the middle decades of the twentieth century these countries characteristically had no kind of central bank. Now, following in the steps of Australia, New Zealand, Canada, and other countries that 'emerged' somewhat earlier, one emergent country after another has established its own central bank, and it is important to consider how a central bank can operate in an environment so different from the countries in which central banking first developed. The relevant contrasts are by no means confined to the financial scene itself. Most of these countries have comparatively uneducated populations working in subsistence economies; but their detachment from the currents of outside markets is sometimes overrated, and a huge traffic through the great trading centres links the mass of the people with the vicissitudes of world trade. These vicissitudes can be of great importance, especially because the exports usually comprise few commodities and those of the kind most uncertain both in local output and in world prices. The international trading position can therefore be of immense importance to the central bank in its efforts to make local monetary conditions conducive to the kind of steady economic development that is so obviously desirable.

In such circumstances foreign-exchange policy becomes of great importance: the automatic system of fixed exchange rates, with the country's currency tied to some international standard (whether gold or the currency of some international financial centre), is unlikely to be always appropriate. For fixed exchange rates would leave the country exposed to the full inflationary force of an unusually favourable balance of payments or the full deflationary force of an unfavourable balance of payments. And once an automatic system is rejected, there is a task for some central monetary authority which can appropriately enough be the central bank; this task is the management of the foreign-exchange arrangements coupled with the role of technical adviser to the government on foreign-exchange policy. As long as exchange rates with some international banking centre are fixed, the business of foreign exchange can be effectively managed by overseas banks operating in that international centre; this was the essential part of the system of British colonial territories, though attention was often concentrated on the note-issue arrangements of the Colonial 'Currency Boards'. But if there is any question of manipulation of exchange rates, or of any elaborate system of exchange control, some other machinery is required, and this provides an opening for an independent central bank.

If a country establishes, in some such way as this, an independent monetary system, it does not thereby escape all the effects of movements in its balance of international payments. The impoverishment implicit in a fall in world demand for its export products still has to be borne; inflation of the incomes of export producers still follows a bumper year of production of the export crops. What may be modified, in some degree, is the secondary deflation or inflation that occurs in an unregulated system when the commercial banks respond to the weakening or strengthening of their balance-sheets by the change in the balance of payments. To secure any such modification of deflationary or inflationary pressures, the liquidity of the commercial banks must be brought under the control of the central bank.

For this purpose of controlling the liquidity of the commercial banks three steps are usually taken: (1) the note-issuing powers of the commercial banks are either abolished or severely restricted; (2) the commercial banks are required to maintain, at the central bank, balances ('reserves') bearing a certain relation to their deposit-liabilties to the public; and (3) the central bank is constituted lender of last resort. Of these three steps the third and the less radical form of the first are absolutely necessary. The second and the more stringent form of the first are advantageous in that they help to provide the central bank with an income: for purposes of control they are mere embroideries. Even when the country's financial structure is extremely rudimentary, these powers should be taken by the central bank, for banks grow quickly once they get a start, and it is desirable that the commercial banking of the country should grow within a framework of effective central banking control.

The constitution of the central bank as lender of last resort is fundamental in that it removes from the commercial banks all responsibility for providing reserves against an abnormal loss of cash. The commercial banks can then (subject to the reservations explained in earlier chapters) be relied upon to minimize consistently their cash reserves in order to maximize their profits. The plan of obliging them to hold certain minimum-ratio balances at the central bank, apart from the central bank's advantage noted above, merely serves to give point to this expectation that their reserves will bear a constant ratio to their deposit liabilities. Restriction of their note-issuing rights prevents them from adding to their cash by printing more notes.

Taken by themselves, these restrictive powers do not allow the central bank to do much towards damping down the economic fluctuations to which these countries are subject. A favourable balance of payments, though it can be reduced by exchange rate manipulation, will still have an automatic effect in enlarging the reserves of the commercial banks; and vice versa with an unfavourable balance. If the central bank is to offset, or 'sterilize', variations of this kind, it must have further powers. In a highly developed financial system, open-market operations can be used for this purpose; but where there is no effective market in securities, whether short or long, there is no hope in this direction. (A new central bank should, nevertheless, be given the appropriate powers; the Canadian experience in the middle decades of this century showed how rapidly open-market operations may become a major weapon of a new central bank.) In the absence of such opportunity, it is important that the central bank should have power to vary the required reserve ratios. An inflation of bank reserves can then be sterilized by a raising of reserve ratios, and correspondingly a drain from bank reserves can, by reducing the required ratios, be prevented from forcing a secondary deflation. Further support can be given by budgeting for a government surplus and using the proceeds to build up the Government's balance at the central bank, when disinflationary measures are called for; the Government's balance can later be run down when the authorities want to reduce the deflationary elements in the system. This kind of manipulation of government balances, causing a converse movement in commercial bank reserves, of course calls for co-operation between the finance ministry and the central bank; but such co-operation is in any case always desirable, even though it does not always exist in an imperfect world.

Importance is often attached to the fixing of a rate of discount by the central bank; as we have seen in earlier chapters, there are good reasons for the stress laid on interest rates in the more developed systems. In countries such as we have been describing, however, the central bank's discount rate can have little significance although, if the bank actually operates as lender of last resort, it is forced to have some sort of policy on rates of interest. But we have assumed that there is no capital market in the ordinary sense, and no short money market; and there is not in most cases any point in considering the possibility of influencing international short money movements. Such rates of interest as prevail in the country—the yields on government bonds, the rents on real estate—are not the rates of active markets, and they often seem to have little connexion with the rates of interest paid and charged by the commercial banks. Moreover the banks, especially if they are powerful overseas banks, are not likely to be borrowers at the central bank; even for purely domestic banks, borrowing at the central bank is likely to be too small to impinge seriously on their peculiar structure of interest rates. In all these circumstances, there is little to hope for in the interest-rate powers of a new central bank —but it is always well to remember that today's new central bank will not be so new to-morrow.

Thus far we have been thinking in terms of what a central bank can do to influence the economic conjuncture at any time, and throughout it has been apparent that the strength of its weapons is limited by the rudimentary nature of the country's financial structure. From the points of view, however, both of long-term economic growth itself and of the development of the central bank's own influence, there are other ways in which the central bank can meet the conditions peculiar to an emergent country. The central bank can *provide or supplement* the ordinary banking facilities of the country. In exceptionally favourable conditions it may be able both to supplement existing commercial banking and to encourage its independent development.

If a central bank has offices in the right places it may be able to provide useful banking services, of the ordinary kind, for the general public. There is nothing about a central bank's nature that makes such business impossible, and even in developed countries some central banks have ordinary customers. Against this there is a growing opinion that the central bank, however technically competent it is to do ordinary banking business, should leave it to separate institutions. This opinion, however, is always supported by arguments that assume that there are already in existence commercial banks covering at least a large part of the field. There is, for instance, the argument that as the commercial banks are obliged to keep balances at the central bank without earning interest on these balances, the central bank should not compete against banks who have to go to some expense to obtain deposits. Such competition, if it is even suspected, is at once dubbed 'unfair competition'; and if the central bank alienates the commercial banks in this way, its use of the 'weapon' of persuasion will have small success. There is also the argument that, when the central bank acts as an ordinary banker to the public, transfers of money from a commercial bank's customer to a central bank's customer (or vice versa) disturb the supply of money. These arguments collapse entirely if there exists no commercial bank, and lose most of their force if the commercial banks cover only a small part of the field. But the former of these arguments does imply a further proposition: that the development of independent commercial banking may be discouraged by central-bank invasion of the field. The central bank should encourage the growth of ordinary commercial banks rather than invade the field itself, though there are likely to be special fields, such as medium- and long-term lending, for which the central bank may appropriately establish its own subsidiaries.

There are three possibilities of encouragement. The first is provision and encouragement of the use of rediscounting facilities. The second possibility is the administration by the central bank of a subsidy for newly established commercial banks. The third is a complex system of subsidies for particular classes of loans.

The development of rediscounting is important in a new banking system in that it enables banks to economize their till money without increasing the risk of being broken by a 'run' for cash. Since cash is a non-earning asset, economizing cash reserves implies increasing earning power. Growth of rediscounting facilities therefore acts in the same way as a subsidy; but it has the additional advantage of developing contacts between the various parts of the banking system and making it easier for the central bank to enforce its policy. The central bank can do much in this way by selecting (and possibly securing the adaptation of) any suitable credit instrument already in use in the country (the *hundi* in India is an example), and offering favourable rates for cash obtainable on deposit of these instruments with itself. Sometimes there is room for reduction of stamp duties on such instruments, and then the central bank should do its best to persuade the Government to sacrifice revenue for the sake of promoting the development of the banking system. In these countries the central bank must also be prepared to open numerous branches (or attractive agencies) in order to provide assistance quickly and easily to new local banks. Unfortunately there is almost universal prejudice against rediscounting, as it has often been regarded as a sign of weakness. The central bank should make it its business to persuade bankers that rediscounting is not necessarily an evil practice.

If the Government is willing to bear the expense, the outright subsidy method may be employed. If so, the central bank is the obvious agent for administration of the subsidy: for compulsory inspection powers would be a decided advantage in developing its contacts with newly established banks. It might be difficult to discriminate between new banks and those already well established without encouraging the growth of a unit-banking system rather than a branch-banking system; but I believe this difficulty could be overcome.

The third line of attack is more complicated. For liquidity reasons bankers prefer short 'self-liquidating' loans, and it may be economically justifiable, and highly conducive to economic development, to encourage by subsidy some extension of lending on less liquid, less conventional lines.

In giving official encouragement—possibly at some expense—to the development of commercial banks, and of any other financial intermediaries, it is important not to lose sight of the real contribution that such financial institutions make to the functioning of the economic system. Apart from the facilities for making payments— a service that can be provided in other ways—financial intermediaries (including banks) contribute to the real flow of goods and services because they make saving more attractive and because they influence the distribution, between potential spenders on capital construction, of the resources the economy has decided to withhold from immediate consumption. Unless a financial institution is helping, directly or indirectly, in one or other of these ways, it is parasitical. From this point of view, some case (perhaps not a very impressive case) can be made for the existence of the London Discount market, as was shown in the Radcliffe Report. But it is a case depending very much on the international business of the London money market, and does nothing to justify the vogue for encouraging (in effect at the expense of the taxpayer) the establishment of short-money markets in countries where they have not grown naturally from opportunities afforded for real help to the banks. It is sometimes supposed that new financial intermediaries are useful if they can 'mobilize idle funds' in the sense of enabling the banks to reduce their cash reserves. If this reduction of cash reserves is made possible by a government offer of interest on Treasury Bills, no one gains except the intermediary who gets a margin out of the Treasury Bills, and he gets it at the expense of the taxpayer. There is only a real contribution to social income if actual saving is made more attractive and/or if the banks (or the lenders) are, because of the new instruments and new institutions, able to become more efficient lenders to industry and trade. These conditions were certainly met by the London discount market in the early days when it contributed so much to the integration of a curiously stunted system of banking in England; it is arguable that they are in a very indirect way met by the London discount market today; but it is very difficult to see how the conditions are met in some of the countries that have recently boasted the acquisition of a short-money market.

This hothouse development of short-money markets is only the latest phase of a not very happy tendency for the less developed countries to follow too closely the patterns of financial structure seen to exist in the more highly developed centres. If progress in the development of financial institutions is really to contribute to economic growth, it must be based on a thorough understanding of the problems rather than on a slavish imitation of what now exists in the countries whose financial institutions developed first. The 'new' countries alone cannot be held responsible for their misunderstandings: they have often taken British or American advice based more on familarity with the City and Wall Street than on fundamental analysis of banking problems. Since 1929 we have both lived and learned—but not, perhaps, learned quite enough.

APPENDIX 1

THE LONDON BANKERS' CLEARING HOUSE

[The following description is based on an article in the 'Three Banks Review', June 1954, but was rewritten in 1963 for the sixth Edition of this book. We acknowledge with gratitude the courtesy of the Three Banks and of the Clearing House officials in preparing and allowing publication of this authoritative description.]

As most of the domestic banking business of England and Wales is spread over the eleven clearing banks' numerous branches, and almost every part of the country has branches of at least two or three of these banks operating in it, it is inevitable that a large proportion of cheques should be paid in to banks other than those on which they are drawn.

For payment to be obtained these cheques must be presented to the branches on which they are drawn, and as the majority of cheques are drawn on the clearing banks they have developed their own clearing system, centred on the London Bankers' Clearing House, for the exchange and settlement of cheques drawn on each other.

The clearing banks also receive from customers cheques drawn on banks, Government departments, &c., and Scottish and Irish banks which are not members of the Clearing House; these cheques are presented for payment direct, through separate channels, but more often than not the end result is a transfer from one clearing bank to another via the Clearing House.

The Clearing House is situated in Post Office Court, at the Mansion House end of Lombard Street, within easy walking distance—as it needs to be—of the clearing banks' main London offices. It is managed by the Committee of London Clearing Bankers (see p. 73), on which each of the 11 clearing banks—Barclays, Coutts, District, Glyn Mills, Lloyds, Martins, Midland, National, National Provincial, Westminster and Williams Deacons—is represented. This Committee delegates to a Chief Inspector the responsibility for the day-to-day working of the clearings. For clearing purposes the Bank of England also has a seat in the Clearing House, but it takes no part in the administration of the Clearing House.

The operations actually performed in the Clearing House fall into three parts—Town, General, and Credit. The Town Clearing covers nearly 100 London offices of the clearing banks which between them handle the main business of the financial institutions and other firms in the City. Cheques drawn on branches of the clearing banks outside this area go through the General Clearing, except for a small proportion which is exchanged under local arrangements. The third part of the Clearing House work is the Credit Clearing, instituted as recently as April 1960. The contrasting character of the Town Clearing, covering mainly 'financial' business, and the General Clearing, covering general business of the whole country, shows in the totals of transactions in 1962:

	Number of 'articles'	Total Value
Town Clearing . .	20 millions	£224,246 millions
General Clearing . .	438 millions	£48,604 millions

The Town Clearing

This deals only with cheques and other claims (e.g. maturing bills of exchange) drawn on, and paid into, 'Town Branches' of the clearing banks and the Bank of England, and is in effect a 'local' clearing for the City of London. To be a 'Town Branch' an office must be within the Town Clearing Area, stretching roughly from St. Paul's in the west to the junction of Aldgate High Street with Minories in the east, and from London Wall in the north to the Thames in the south. Any clearing bank new branch opened within the defined area automatically becomes a Town Branch.

The essence of the Town Clearing is speed, since very large sums are involved and many very important transactions are effected comparatively late in the day but have to be settled on that same day. For this reason there is a Morning Session and an Afternoon Session each day, but the latter is restricted generally to items of £2,000 and over so that the volume of work handled during this session is kept at a reasonably low level without materially affecting the total cleared.

For ease of handling the following items are excluded from the Town Clearing and must be presented direct to the offices at which they are payable:

(i) Standing Orders (Original Bankers' Orders).
(ii) Coupons and Warrants subject to deduction of Tax.
(iii) Articles with any attachments other than:
    (a) Bankers' Payments or cheques drawn in favour of draft (or bill, &c.) attached.
    (b) Articles with receipts which must be no larger than the articles and securely gummed at all edges.
    (c) Special presentations or wrongly delivered articles with tickets attached.
(iv) Travellers' cheques.
(v) Bank of England Dividend and Redemption Warrants, unless delivered as a separate charge.
(vi) Documentary Bills of Exchange.

It is a rule of the Clearing House that all other 'clean articles' (i.e. cheques or other claims without documents attached), drawn on Town Branches of the clearing banks must be presented through the clearing and may not be presented for payment direct to the office of the paying bank by another clearing bank.

The Morning Clearing is from 9 to 9.30 a.m. and the Afternoon Clearing from 2.30 to 3.45 p.m. (or on Saturdays 11.30 to 11.55 a.m.).

The Morning Clearing deals with cheques of less than £2,000 that are drawn on and have been paid into Town Branches the previous day, and cheques for larger amounts which might have been passed through the previous day's Afternoon Clearing but, for some reason or other, missed that Clearing. Special Collections for any amount may also be included.

Items which pass through the Afternoon Town Clearing are restricted to:

(i) Cheques, &c. of £2,000 and over—£5,000 and over on Saturdays;[1]
(ii) Clean bills of exchange of any amount;
(iii) Payments of any amount in respect of 'Walks' clearings and of special collections of articles drawn on clearing banks' branches outside the Town Clearing;

[1] Where a 'fate' is required the cheque may be passed through the Afternoon Town Clearing with a ticket attached indicating that it is a special presentation. A fate is information for the presenting bank as to whether the cheque will be paid or not.

(iv) Credit Clearing transactions of any amount, including payments given by clearing banks to non-clearing banks and Scottish and Irish Banks;

(v) Clearing vouchers issued by the Bank of England in payment of dividend and redemption warrants;

(vi) Payments of any amount in respect of Scottish and Irish cheques clearings.

In each session the procedure is simple. Each clearing bank has its own desk to which other members deliver cheques drawn on its branches. Each delivery of 'charge' is machined and agreed as soon as possible by the staff which each member provides—at the peak period over 100 are busily engaged in machining, agreeing, and sorting—and the cheques are sent by messenger to the branches on which they were drawn. When all the totals have been agreed after the afternoon session (the morning's totals having been carried forward) the Daily Settlement takes place. Each bank has a 'Balance Sheet' on which it makes a summary of the balances due to be received from or paid to the other member banks in respect of the day's operations in the Town Clearing and of the previous day's operations in the General Clearing and in the Credit Clearing. After adding adjustments for differences, and items returned unpaid or wrongly delivered, each bank strikes a net balance, which is the amount it is due to receive or pay. A transfer ticket is made out, checked and signed by one of the Inspectors and a representative of the Bank of England who attends daily for the settlement, and this authorizes the amount to be transferred to or from the bank's account at the Bank of England. Thus the whole day's clearing transactions, which often top the £1,000 millions mark, are settled.

Into this very tight schedule the operations at the branches themselves have to be closely geared. The banks close their doors at 3 p.m.—at most City branches the busiest time for customers paying in is between 2.30 p.m. and 3 p.m.—and articles for that afternoon's Town Clearing must be sorted, machined, and delivered to the Clearing House by 3.45 p.m., machined there and sorted by the paying banks ready for messengers to hurry back to branches. These messengers leave the House at 3.55 p.m.–4.0 p.m., carry the cheques to the paying branches, and must be back at the House by 4.30 p.m. with any items being returned unpaid.

In this way the tradition of the Town Clearing is maintained and customers of Town Branches of the clearing banks know that if a cheque for £2,000 or over is paid in by 3.0 p.m. it will be cleared the same day through the Town Clearing provided of course that it is drawn on a Town Branch. Moreover the fate of the cheque— whether it is 'good' or 'bad' money—will be known a few minutes after 4.30 p.m.

The General Clearing

This covers cheques, &c., which may not be passed through the Town Clearing or cleared by local arrangements. It includes cheques drawn on certain non-clearing banks, as well as those on many non-Town branches of the clearing banks, and cheques paid into Town Branches but not eligible for the Town Clearing. Inside the Clearing House the procedure for handling all these is not quite the same as for the Town Clearing. The number of items included in the General Clearing is so huge that the banks deliver the actual cheques, &c., not to the Clearing House but to each other's Clearing Departments. Totals are then agreed between them at the Clearing House at 9.30 a.m. the following day so that these may be included in that day's Settlement. (Saturday's clearing is combined with the following Monday's, with settlement on Tuesday.)

The Clearing Department of each bank will have received the cheques from branches of that bank, the branches having sent the cheques off on the day they were paid in. The Clearing Departments sort and amalgamate these remittances into bundles of cheques, which are then delivered to the Clearing Departments of the banks on which they were drawn, the totals being noted for agreement at the Clearing House (as described above). To a Clearing Department receiving such a bundle, it is 'in' work; this has to be agreed, sorted into branches, and posted off to the branches the same day. On arrival there, usually by first post the next day, the cheques are examined and paid. Any returned unpaid are posted back direct to the branch of the bank where paid in, so that in the ordinary course of events and in the absence of postal delays, which fortunately are few, the fate of a cheque is known on the third business day after the day of pay-in.

For example, on Monday a cheque drawn on the Penzance branch of Bank B is paid into the Newcastle branch of Bank A which posts it to its London Clearing Department the same afternoon. On Tuesday morning Bank A's Clearing Department delivers the cheque to Bank B's Clearing Department, which sends it off to its Penzance branch to arrive on Wednesday. If the cheque is unpaid it will return direct from Penzance to Newcastle, arriving by midday on Thursday, i.e. on the third business day after the day of pay-in.

The Credit Clearing

This clearing, handling credit slips instead of debit items, was instituted in 1960 to facilitate exchange and settlement of vouchers originated under the Credit Transfer Scheme. In 1962 77 million such vouchers, representing over £6,000 millions, were passed through the Clearing House.

Any member of the public, whether having a banking account or not, may pay in funds to any branch of a clearing bank for credit of another person's account at a branch of any bank in the United Kingdom. A small handling fee is charged for the service, and generally the recipient's account is credited two business days later. One of the most important features of the system is that such transfers represent 'good money'—there is no question of vouchers being returned unpaid. With this exception the Clearing is operated on similar lines to the General Clearing, transactions between the clearing banks being included in the Daily Settlement at the Bankers' Clearing House.

Walks Clearing

Items handled include cheques, &c., drawn on the offices in the City and West End of the merchant banks, Scottish banks, the single Irish bank with a London Office, the industrial bankers, certain Government Departments, and private firms. For payment to be obtained these cheques, not being drawn on branches of the clearing banks and therefore not eligible to pass through the Clearing House, must be presented direct to the offices on which they are drawn.

The City and West End is divided into areas so that the work of delivering the cheques may be carried out more quickly. Walks items received from branches are sorted into the respective banks, &c., and made up into charges, i.e. bundles of cheques with a listing attached to each. The charges are then sorted into the different

Walks areas and delivered to the various banks by clerks or messengers. Charges are normally delivered daily, during the morning, and the clerks return early in the afternoon to receive a cheque or bankers' payment in exchange. It is a rule of the clearing banks that payments for Walks charges must be made either by bankers' payment or cheque drawn on a Town branch of a clearing bank, so that clearance may be effected the same day, or in cash.

Where a cheque is drawn on a non-clearing bank's office in the provinces, the clearing bank sends it to its nearest branch for presentation.

Scottish and Irish Clearings

It is the general practice to lodge cheques, drawn on branches in Scotland, at the London office of the Scottish bank concerned, which sends them to its Head Office in Scotland for presentation to the various branches. Payment through the London Office is made in due course.

The Bank of England sends all Scottish cheques to the Edinburgh Head Office of the Royal Bank of Scotland for collection through the normal Scottish clearing channels.

Irish cheques are either lodged with a London agent, payment being made on an agreed settling date, or remitted to an agent or subsidiary in Ireland for collection and settlement through agency accounts.

Provincial and Local Clearings

It is general policy that, where possible, the clearing banks should exchange and settle cheques drawn on each other's branches in the same localities. This procedure saves clearing time and ensures that essential items only are remitted to London Clearing Departments for presentation through the General Clearing.

In twelve large centres—Birmingham, Bradford, Bristol, Hull, Leeds, Leicester, Liverpool, Manchester, Newcastle, Nottingham, Sheffield, and Southampton—the Banks have long-established Clearing Associations. During 1962 these centres handled 13 million items representing over £2,750 millions. A clearing is held each morning—Liverpool also having a second exchange each afternoon—at a central point where articles drawn on the respective branches within a relatively small radius are exchanged. Settlement is effected through the member bank's accounts with the local branch of the Bank of England at the Birmingham, Bristol, Leeds, Liverpool, Manchester, Newcastle, and Southampton centres. In the other five towns, where there is no branch of the Bank of England, the work of collating claims and establishing the amount of balances due is undertaken by one of the member banks. Settlement is usually effected by the issue of bankers' payments on London or Agents' Claim Vouchers which are remitted to London and passed through the Clearing House there.

APPENDIX 2

THE ULTRA-CHEAP MONEY OPERATIONS
OF 1945-7

In the episode briefly referred to on p. 207 above, the U.K. Government sought to enforce a policy of very low interest rates by holding the shortest rates down, by seeking to revise public expectations, and by absorbing securities unloaded by holders who were sceptical of the endurance of very low rates of interest. The open-market operations that formed part of the official measures were a special case of operations discussed, from a 1966 viewpoint, in Section v of Chapter 5. The episode remains of some special interest, partly because the Government's policy failed, and the account of it given in earlier editions of this book has therefore been retained here. The analysis of the processes of the open-market operations is here given in terms applicable to the 1945-7 episode; the essentials of these processes remain unchanged, though some of the details here given are no longer topical and have therefore been ignored in the more general account of open-market operations given in Chapter 5.

For the purpose of absorbing securities unloaded by sceptical holders in the private sector, the Treasury were able to use the resources of the 'Public Departments'. Among these are the funds of the Post Office Savings Bank, the trustee savings banks, and the great social insurance funds, all of which are entrusted to a body called 'The Commissioners for the Reduction of the National Debt'. These National Debt Commissioners, as they are commonly called, are a separate body established by Parliament for another purpose very many years ago; but they include the Chancellor of the Exchequer and the Governor and Deputy Governor of the Bank of England, and their policy in distributing their resources can be trimmed to suit the exigencies of Treasury operations. The most important of the 'Public Departments' is, however, the (accounting) Issue Department of the Bank of England; in the nineteen-fifties it was primarily by varying the securities held in the Issue Department that the authorities operated on the gilt-edged market. Altogether these funds by 1945 totalled thousands of millions, and constituted a formidable *masse de manœuvre*. The authorities could, to the extent that Treasury Bills were held, unload the Treasury Bills on to the banks, using the ordinary bank deposits received in payment to take up medium-term and long-term securities previously held by the public. Thus the buying pressure desired by the authorities to push up market prices of medium- and long-term securities (i.e. push down the rates of interest) could be manufactured.

It is important to appreciate that this manœuvre was possible only if the banks played their part, which was to absorb the Treasury Bills unloaded by the Public Departments. They had an incentive to do this as long as they could obtain more cash for reserve, since they would receive interest on the additional Treasury Bills held. Under the 'ever-open-back-door' system then operating, the Bank of England would in fact provide them with as much cash as they required to enable them (consistently with maintaining their 8 per cent. cash ratio) to hold all the Treasury Bills offered. Indeed, the back door was held open on the understanding that the banks would see to it that the Treasury Bills were absorbed. The authorities derived further power from the existence of 'Treasury Deposit Receipts', war-time instruments which were in effect unmarketable Treasury Bills which the banks were compelled to buy and hold.

The process was thus thoroughly reliable, as far as the creation of the buying pressure for medium- and long-term securities was concerned. (The efficacy of this buying pressure in causing a fall in interest rates is another part of the story). It depended upon (1) the willingness and ability of the authorities to lengthen the average life of securities held by the Public Departments, &c.; (2) the willingness of the banks to expand their Treasury Bill holdings provided they were allowed more cash; and (3) the willingness of the Bank of England to create more cash for the banks without raising the short-term money rates.

The process will perhaps be more readily understood if it is set out in balance-sheet terms on the same schematic plan as has been used in this book. In the following paragraphs and tables, the figures used are not quite the actual figures of the 1945–7 episode, but are simplified figures, based on the real ones and not so very different from them. The use of imaginary figures is designed partly to ease the reader's arithmetic, but partly also to avoid the complications due to (*a*) the former practice of 'window-dressing' the banks' cash ratios, and (*b*) the simultaneous operation of other factors such as the rise in the demand for ordinary bank advances. (We have no precise information of the changes in securities held by the Public Departments.) The following figures must be regarded as imaginary though not very far from being a picture of what actually happened during the fifteen months November 1945 to February 1947.

POSITION I

(£ millions)

Bank of England

Note and Deposit Liabilities to Commercial Banks .	400	Government Securities .	500
Public Deposits . .	100		
	500		500

Commercial Banks

Deposits . . .	5,000	Cash in hand and at the Bank of England . .	400
		Money at Call, Treasury Bills, and T.D.R.'s .	2,200
		Other Assets . . .	2,400
	5,000		5,000

Public Departments

Treasury Bills	2,000
Medium- and Long-term Securities	2,000
	4,000

Then we will suppose that the Public Departments buy medium- and long-term government securities to the amount of £500 millions, and that the banks are expected to take up the Treasury Bills sold by the Public Departments. The public have to be paid by drafts on Public Deposits at the Bank of England, and these Public Deposits are replenished by the sale of Treasury Bills to the commercial banks. Then we may imagine, as an immediate impact result of the transactions of the Public Departments:

POSITION II

(£ millions)

Bank of England

Notes and Deposit Liabilities to Banks:	Government Securities	500
400 + 500 (a) − 500 (b) = 400		
Public Deposits:		
100 − 500 (a) + 500 (b) = 100		
500		500

Commercial Banks

Deposits:	Cash, &c.:	
5,000 + 500 (a) = . 5,500	400 + 500 (a) − 500 (b) = 400	
	Money at Call, T. Bills, and T.D.R.'s:	
	2,200 + 500 (b) = . 2,700	
	Other Assets . . . 2,400	
5,500		5,500

Public Departments

Treasury Bills: 2,000 − 500 (b) 1,500
Medium- and Long-term Securities: 2,000 + 500 (a) . . 2,500

4,000

Notes

1. Changes marked (a) arise as Public Departments buy from the public securities to amount £500m., paying by cheque on Public Deposits at the Bank of England; the cheques are credited by the banks to their customers, and used to increase their own balances at the Bank of England.

2. Changes marked (b) arise as the Public Departments sell Treasury Bills to the commercial banks, which pay for them by cheque on their balances at the Bank of England, these cheques being credited by the Bank of England to Public Accounts.

3. The cash ratio of the commercial banks in Position II is about 7¼ per cent.

The commercial banks now have to rebuild their cash ratio to 8 per cent. They can do this by unloading on to the Bank of England part of their very large holding of Treasury Bills, either directly or by calling loans from the discount houses who in turn have to unload Treasury Bills on to the Bank of England, through the ever-open back door. In either case we can summarize the resulting position thus:

POSITION III

(£ millions)

Bank of England

Note and Deposit Liabilities:			Government Securities:		
400+40 (c) = .	.	440	500+40 (d) = .	.	540
Public Deposits	.	100			
		540			540

Commercial Banks

Deposits	. . .	5,500	Cash, &c.:		
			400+40 (c) = .	.	440
			Money at Call, T. Bills, and T.D.R.'s:		
			2,700−40 (d) =	.	2,660
			Other Assets	. .	2,400
		5,500			5,500

Public Departments
(as in Position II)

Notes on figures in Position III

(c) Denotes a change due to payment by the Bank of England to the commercial banks for Treasury Bills passed into the former through the open back door.

(d) Denotes transfer of Treasury Bills from the commercial banks (or discount houses who thereby are enabled to pay off Money at Call) to the Bank of England.

Thus in effect the £500 millions of Treasury Bills unloaded by the Public Departments has been taken up as to £460 millions by the commercial banks and as to £40 millions by the Bank of England—this proportion of 92 to 8 reflecting the commercial banks' requirement to hold 8 per cent. in cash and 92 per cent. in earning assets against the additional £500 millions of bank deposits acquired by the general public as the latter unloads its securities on to the Public Departments.

Fundamentally the depression in interest rates is dependent on the willingness of the banking system to create additional deposits, and this (given the 8 per cent. cash ratio) implies willingness of the

Bank of England to create additional cash. But as the increased supply of liquidity (bank deposits) by the banks is, in accordance with their principle of preferring short assets, made only against short assets (additional Treasury Bills), the pressure of the increased liquidity upon long interest rates can become effective only by the intervention of some body willing to transmute the short loans offered by the banks into a pressure of long term loans, so relieving the public's desire to unload long-term securities as their yields fall. As rates of interest fall, the public (being sceptical of continuance of the fall) 'go short'—they exchange securities for cash. Someone must 'go long' in order to absorb the securities offered. The banks will create more deposits, but they are not willing to 'go long' enough. The Public Departments step into the breach, and 'go longer' in the composition of their own portfolios, replacing Treasury Bill holdings by medium-term and long-term securities.

A closer study of Positions I and III above will reveal that the operation results in a higher percentage of money-market assets among the total assets of the commercial banks, for the entire increase in assets is in cash and money-market assets. As Treasury Bills were, at this time, exchangeable for cash on demand at the Bank of England's ever-open back door, this rise in Treasury Bills would not be resisted by the banks on account of any loss of liquidity. On the other hand, they might think that a small proportion of their increase in resources could safely be invested in long-term securities. To the extent that they did this, the complicated process just described could be short-circuited; the action of the banks in taking the long-term securities offered by the public would reduce the extent to which the Public Departments had to redistribute their resources between Treasury Bills and longer-dated bonds. We might, for instance, arrive at an alternative position, which we shall call IIIA:

POSITION IIIA

(£ millions)

Bank of England

Notes and Deposit Liabilities	440	Government Securities	.	540
Public Deposits . .	100			
	540			540

Commercial Banks

Deposits			5,500	Cash, &c.			440
				Money at Call, T. Bills,			
				and T.D.R.'s			2,560
				Other Assets (including			
				long-term Government			
				Securities)			2,500
			5,500				5,500

Public Departments

Treasury Bills	.	.	.	.	.	.	.	.	1,600
Medium- and Long-term Securities		.	.	.	.	.		2,400
								4,000

Here, because £100 millions of the securities on offer by the public (at the prices bid by Public Departments) are taken up by the commercial banks, only £400 millions of Treasury Bills have to be replaced in the Public Departments by securities bought from the public. These £400 millions are taken up as to £360 millions by the commercial banks and £40 millions by the Bank of England—the £40 millions being (as in the other case also) the amount of additional cash necessary as a basis for the £500 millions addition to the total of bank deposits.

It might be supposed that the commercial banks, pursuing their ordinary liquidity rules, would in fact be prepared, in the way we have just seen, to add somewhat to their holdings of medium-term and long-term securities as their cash and money-market assets expand. On the other hand, the commercial bankers might be infected by the general investing public's scepticism about the future of the rate of interest. If the banks, like the public, think that the prices of government securities are going to fall, they are unlikely to add to their own holdings. They, like the public, will be inclined to 'go short'—i.e. to increase the average liquidity of their asset portfolios. This is the case we have shown in Position III above, where the amounts of cash reserves and money-market assets are increased while other (longer) assets are maintained at the same absolute amounts as in Position I. The banks may indeed go farther in this direction, and themselves unload the longer securities on to the Public Departments, taking up more Treasury Bills in exchange. This, though it increases the necessary lengthening of

the Public Departments' assets, does not require further enlargement of the cash basis. This peculiarity arises from the fact that
the desire of the commercial banks for greater liquidity is satisfied
by the enlargement .of their holdings of Treasury Bills, whereas
we have supposed that the public's desire for greater liquidity
could be satisfied only by additional bank deposits. If the public
would be content to hold Treasury Bills, a mere exchange in the
portfolio of the Public Departments of long securities for Treasury
Bills would meet the case, without any creation of bank deposits.[1]

In general we may say that the public's pressure to hold shorter
assets as rates of interest fall must be matched by a corresponding
lengthening of the assets held somewhere else in the system or by
a 'shortening' of the whole Debt by substitution of short for long
bonds. To the extent that the banking system itself will undertake
this 'lengthening' of its assets, the need for any intervention by
a special public agency (in this case the 'Public Departments' in
their capacity of an investor of funds) is reduced. In the actual
historical experience of 1945–7, the Treasury did issue short bonds
in replacement of long bonds and the commercial banks did add
somewhat (about £200m.) to their 'Investments', in spite of the
rising demand for Advances (which rose by over £100m.). The
banks were encouraged to do this by the great inflation of their
liquid assets caused by the operations of the Public Departments;
and to the extent that this increase in bank 'Investments' occurred,
the need for the Public Departments to take up medium-term and
long-term securities was reduced.

When such large resources were at the disposal of the authorities
and when they were supported in some measure by the commercial banks (despite the danger of infection of bankers by the
public scepticism), why did the 'ultra-cheap-money drive' of
1945–7 fail? For fail it did: in the first months of 1947 the long-
term and medium-term rates began to creep upward again, the
long-term rate passing 3 per cent. before the end of the year.
Fundamentally the failure was due to the market's conviction,
backed by very large-scale willingness to exchange securities for

---

[1] In this episode the Treasury Bill Rate was held at virtually the same
level as the banks' Deposit Rate, and the outside public had no incentive
to hold Treasury Bills. From 1955 onwards the Treasury Bill Rate has
sometimes been appreciably higher than the Deposit Rate, and 'outside'
holdings of Treasury Bills have therefore become both large and variable.

money, that $2\frac{1}{2}$ per cent. was, in the circumstances of high demand for real capital investment and scarcity of resources, an unnaturally low rate that could not be expected to last.

It was obvious that, in the prevailing economic circumstances, even 3 per cent. was an unnaturally low rate, defended only by the stringent physical controls of capital investment. But 3 per cent. had, after all, been held for years, and it was the attempt, the patently juggling attempt, to press it down yet farther, flying in the face of basic conditions, that the market found so difficult to swallow. The distrust felt by the weighty investing institutions and by other important operators (who were most influential in formulating the market demand schedule for government securities) was perhaps heightened by the tone of the propaganda speeches of the then Chancellor of the Exchequer. At any rate, the demand curve for money (in exchange for fixed interest securities) proved both flat and unstable.

The instability of the position to which the authorities drove the securities market in 1946–7 is due to the influence of speculation. This has been explained by Professor F. W. Paish (*The Post-war Financial Problem*, pp. 19–21):

So long as interest rates are falling and prices of securities are rising, the movement will be assisted by those who hope for capital profits from its continuation. The incentive to look to capital profits rather than to income is increased by high rates of taxation on incomes without corresponding taxes on capital profits. This incentive reaches almost absurd levels in the case of the very rich man paying surtax at maximum rate, for whom sixpennyworth of capital appreciation is worth a pound of gross income. But as soon as the rise is checked, and security prices look as if they are more likely to fall than to rise farther, speculation works in the opposite direction. When interest rates are low, it takes several years even of gross income to make up for the capital loss due to a small rise in interest rates, while with high rates of tax the number of years of net income lost by capital depreciation will be very much larger. If we take a $2\frac{1}{2}$ per cent. rate for irredeemable securities, and $\frac{1}{2}$ per cent. as the gross rate obtainable on deposit account at a bank, the difference in annual net yield, with income tax at 9s. in the pound, is only £1. 2s. 0d. The capital loss from a rise of only $\frac{1}{4}$ per cent. in the rate of interest from $2\frac{1}{2}$ per cent. to $2\frac{3}{4}$ per cent. is just over £9. Thus even this small rise in the rate of interest would wipe out the whole of the net yield on the securities for over eight years, and if an investor expected a rise in interest rates of even this magnitude within the next eight years it would pay him better to keep his money on deposit at a bank. For a very wealthy man, paying the maximum rate of surtax on part of his income, the net yield is only 1s. 3d.

per £100 or 1s. per £100 more than on bank deposit. At this rate it would take him over 180 years to make good the capital loss due to a rise of ¼ per cent. in the rate of interest. Thus a surtax payer cannot afford to take the risk of capital depreciation unless it is balanced by an at least equal chance of appreciation. The result of this is that as soon as a further fall in interest rates becomes unlikely, surtax payers and, to a somewhat smaller extent, income-tax payers, must take their profits, even if it means getting only ½ per cent. interest on bank deposit for years together. Thus a high level of security prices, reached with the help of speculative purchases, may prove very difficult to consolidate once the rise ceases.

Under this influence, once the top of the market seemed to have been reached, it began to wobble, and the authorities had to pump more and more deposits into the system in exchange for securities unloaded by the public on to the Public Departments. The amount of new money ran into figures that became alarmingly high—£900 millions, a 20 per cent. addition to the previous total of deposits, in little more than a year. At this stage the authorities got cold feet. Given market sentiment, creation of bank deposits on an enormous scale would have been necessary for holding the 2½ per cent. line; the only alternative was retreat. Support was withdrawn and the long-term rate slipped back to 3 per cent. and beyond, although short rates remained pegged until 1951.

ADDENDUM

RECENT CHANGES IN THE LONDON
MONEY MARKET
(SEVENTH EDITION)

DURING the three years since the Sixth Edition of this book was written, there have been in Britain minor changes in the policies and techniques of the monetary authorities, and in the general business of the banks; most of these changes have been taken into account in the textual amendments that have been made in the book for its Seventh Edition. In the money markets of London, however, the changes even in these few years have been so radical as to demand special attention, and it is to these major developments, and their consequences for the conventional parts of the monetary system, that this Addendum is devoted. The beginnings of this revolution—for recent developments amount to this— were already visible in the late 1950's, and were remarked upon in the Sixth Edition, in Chapter 7, especially in its fifth section; but the repercussions of those beginnings were by 1963 already spreading more widely than was recognized in those summary remarks.

There has already been a hint, in the opening words of the middle sentence above, of one important aspect of the changes that have been occurring. Whereas it used to be reasonable (though it was only in an approximate way) to speak of 'the London money market', there is now no escape from the plural, 'the money markets of London'. The London discount market, dealing in bills and short bonds and borrowing from the banks, used to be the London money market in the ordinary sense, though purists would sometimes insist that there was a market for 'bills' and a market for 'money'. Now, by contrast, the money markets in London include, in addition to the traditional discount market, the Euro-dollar market, the local authorities market, and the inter-bank market. To distinguish between the markets in this way is to over-simplify the structure of markets, for there are important connexions as well as obstacles between the various markets, and there are also important channels of business—as in the hire-purchase finance houses—that spill over beyond this classification.

It is also important to recognize that the developments in all directions have sprung from three sources: (1) the extraordinary opportunities of dealing in dollar balances, (2) policies on capital finance for local government authorities, and (3) the restrictions, whether by governmental policy or by their own conventions, limiting the activities of the clearing banks and the discount houses. New intermediaries (not always unconnected with the clearing banks and discount houses) have arisen to do business with borrowers who were encountering obstacles in conventional channels.

Among the earliest of these changes was the rise of the Euro-dollar market. This was symptomatic in that it was a new development of the activity of London as an international centre. The rapidity of the revival of London as an international centre has been one of the most surprising features of the post-war period, which opened with a presumption that the structure of fixed exchange rates would be protected from erratic international capital movements. The Euro-dollar market is also symptomatic in having been instrumental in the movement towards integration of foreign exchange and domestic monetary operations, which has been characteristic of London as a financial centre in these latest years.

The Euro-dollar is an ordinary dollar balance in the books of a bank in the U.S.A. (ordinarily in New York); what is extraordinary is that it is lent out, as a dollar balance, by the depositor (this depositor being not a resident of the U.S.A.), and that the borrower of the dollars comes to this market in London although the obvious place to borrow dollars is New York. The market has developed in London because there are owners of dollar balances who can get better interest by lending them in London than they could get from the New York banks, and the borrowers of Euro-dollars can get the dollars more easily, and sometimes more cheaply, than they could borrow in New York. These advantages in borrowing and lending rates arise from the restrictions on rates paid in the U.S.A. and the willingness of lenders in the London market to lend to particular large borrowers on easier terms than would be charged to them in New York. Such favourable conditions are naturally limited to very large transactions; in fact, most of the lenders are actually banks, and the transactions can be regarded as wholesale dealing in dollars outside the bounds of the officially regulated U.S.A. monetary system.

The banks dealing in these dollar balances include the clearing banks, the British overseas banks, and many important European and other foreign banks, with or without their own offices in London. Oddly enough, they include London branches of American banks, for the transactions of these branches are not subject to some regulations that restrict the terms of business in their parent banks in New York; the growth of Euro-dollar business has been one of the major elements in the recent growth of these American banks in London. The Canadian banks are also very active, both as lenders and as borrowers, and Japanese banks have been among the largest borrowers in the market. Certain British overseas banks and accepting houses have been very active in developing the market; their foreign exchange departments are among the most important intermediaries, although their transactions are necessarily confined within the British foreign exchange regulations.

The mechanism of the market is simple enough. A typical lender is a European bank which has come into the possession of a demand deposit in a New York bank, as a result of its ordinary business of collecting for a customer (e.g. a European industrialist) the proceeds of the sale of goods exported to the U.S.A. (Dollars are being collected in this way all the time; most are paid away quickly in settlement for imports *from* the U.S.A., but with the U.S.A. running an adverse balance, dollars have tended to accumulate in European ownership.) The European bank offers the dollars as a loan to some broker in the Euro-dollar market in London; the broker marries the offer to the requirement of some bank (e.g. another European bank, or a Japanese bank) or an international trading organization or other undertaking requiring the use of a dollar balance. Transactions are ordinarily in units of a million, or at least half a million, dollars. The period of loan may be as short as two days, or for as long as two or three months, at the end of which time the borrower is under obligation to repay by cheque drawn on a bank in the U.S.A. The first borrower may re-lend, again in dollars and for repayment in dollars; ordinarily he would expect a slightly higher interest rate when he lends, because he loses the use of the dollars but remains liable to make repayment, whether or not he duly receives repayment by the second-line borrower.

There has been some outlet for these loans in dollars to large American business firms, for although one would ordinarily expect such firms to borrow from banks inside the U.S.A., they have sometimes been able—if their names were well known internationally—to secure slightly better terms in the Euro-dollar market. Thus the London market has enjoyed the profit of borrowing balances in U.S.A. banks and lending them out to the customers of U.S.A. banks. Not all the profits so earned fall into British hands, however, for among the intermediaries in the Euro-dollar market are the American banks in London, as well as Canadian and other overseas banks. Nevertheless, it has been encouraging to see the extent to which the London market could find profitable opportunities in what is basically American domestic business as well as in genuinely international banking business.

In the 1960's a 'retail' side has developed in the market, in that the American banks in London—and recently some purely London financial firms also—have been issuing Euro-dollar certificates of deposit (parallel to the ordinary U.S. certificates of deposit referred to in Chapter 11) for amounts of $25,000 upward, to run for periods of one to six months.

A U.K. 'resident', in terms of U.K. foreign exchange restrictions, cannot ordinarily enter into an obligation to repay a loan in dollars, and therefore cannot borrow Euro-dollars. The forward foreign exchange market, however, provides the link whereby funds from the Euro-dollar market can percolate to domestic borrowers. If, for instance, attractive rates are being offered by an English local government authority, for say one month, an operator can borrow Euro-dollars, sell dollars spot, receiving sterling in exchange, and simultaneously buy dollars forward (a 'swap' transaction) so that he can lend sterling to the local government authority, while ensuring that he has a known amount of dollars available at the end of the month, when he has to repay the dollars he has borrowed in the Euro-dollar market. Opportunities of this kind imply a link between interest rates in the two markets, but a link which itself depends on the rate at which forward dollars can be bought. If the cost of the 'swap' operation in the foreign exchange market is very low, foreign money can flow easily through the Euro-dollar market into the local authority loan market, or indeed any other market in sterling loans.

The market in short loans to local government authorities operates only in sterling. It developed rapidly from 1956 onwards and since the early sixties has become, in terms of the sums traded, probably the largest of the money markets. The borrowers are the local government authorities, and the lenders are (in roughly equal proportions) banks (mainly 'outside banks'), other financial institutions, industrial and commercial companies, and other miscellaneous lenders such as charitable trusts. The minimum sum dealt in is usually £50,000, and blocks of £500,000 are not uncommon. The main business of the market is in deposit loans, of which about £1,800 millions were outstanding during 1966. More than half this total is at 7 days' notice, an appreciable amount is at 2 days' notice, and a small amount is overnight money; these three classes of very short money have recently covered at least two-thirds of the total. The remainder is fixed for periods of 1, 3, 6, or 9 months but to continue after these periods subject to 7 days' notice. Several firms operate as brokers (never as dealers) in this market: a few Stock Exchange firms, a few foreign exchange firms, and two or three specialists. The specialist firms have a large share of the total business, with turnovers of many millions every week of the year. The transactions are fixed by these brokers usually by telephone, constant contact being maintained with the larger local authorities and the more active sources of funds.

Besides their business in deposit loans, the specialists are also every day negotiating the placement of local authority mortgages and bonds, mostly for periods of 11 months to 10 years, but occasionally running up to 15 or 20 years. There is great variety in renewal provisions, break clauses, etc. in these transactions, each one being tailored to the lender's specification. Here also, as in the short deposits, the minimum is generally £50,000, with £100,000 and £200,000 the most common sums, but sometimes running up to £500,000 or £1,000,000, and exceptionally amounts below £50,000. The firms in this market also take much interest in the market inside the Stock Exchange for 'yearlings', the one- or two-year bonds the local authorities are now allowed to issue with Stock Exchange quotation. The larger local authorities also make stock issues through the London new issue market, these stocks having lives trimmed to the stock market's appetite, and commonly running for 10, 15, or 20 years, and occasionally longer.

The activity of all parts of this market, the great variety in choice of repayment dates available to lenders (from overnight loans to twenty years or more, with the 'population' of maturity dates thickly spread right through the range), and the absence of any risk of default, are conditions making this market unusually effective in keeping interest rates in close relationship with each other. This does not mean that long and short rates cannot diverge from each other: they can still do this, as expectations change (a matter discussed in the second section of Chapter 9), but a disturbance in one part of the market very rapidly produces its full repercussions (whatever they are) in other parts of the market. During 1966 there has been a pronounced tendency for the various rates to move into a narrower bunch (around $7\frac{1}{4}$–$7\frac{1}{2}$ per cent. at the end of the year). This has been due in the main to crystallization of the dominant view that short rates are more likely to come down than to go up in the first half of 1967 but that there is unlikely to be any large fall in the average level of interest rates during the next few years. The narrowing of the spread of rates may, however, have also been partly due to the increasing perfection of the market: as both lenders and borrowers are able to shift easily from one maturity to another, differences between rates can be expected to lessen, provided that there is no very pronounced belief that a big change in rates is just round the corner.

Another new development has been the appearance of the 'inter-bank market'. This is a market for lending and borrowing between banks. The participants are banks outside the clearing: Scottish banks, merchant banks, British overseas banks, and foreign banks, which do not have their own clearing house but are themselves customers of the London clearing banks and make payments to each other by drawing cheques on their accounts at the clearing banks. There are a hundred or more of these 'outside banks' in London, and it is believed that nearly all of them sometimes deal in this new inter-bank market, and that many of them are dealing every day. The clearing banks do not, it is understood, participate in this market, presumably out of tenderness for the discount market the disappearance of which they are unwilling to contemplate.

The transactions in the inter-bank market are usually but not always arranged by brokers. Besides a few specialists, these brokers include members of the foreign exchange market; here again, as in the local authority market, it is significant that there are close contacts between a new money market and the foreign exchange market. £100,000 is the unit most frequently traded, but occasionally there are transactions in £50,000, and larger deals ranging up to £500,000 or £1,000,000 are common. The *Midland Bank Review*, in an informative article (August 1966), mentions £1,000 millions as the possible size of these loans outstanding, and £50–£100 millions as the size of the daily turnover. In contrast to the normal business in the London discount market, loans in the inter-bank market are all unsecured, the lender depending entirely on his knowledge of the borrower's ability to repay at the due date. Loans may be simply overnight, or for periods up to six months; generally it is only a matter of days.

The discount market is inevitably the loser by the development of new markets, especially the inter-bank market which in effect provides outside banks with an alternative to the discount market as a user of surplus cash which must be available at very short notice. Unlike the discount houses, banks borrowing in the inter-bank market cannot go directly to the Bank of England for 'lender-of-last-resort' help to enable them to repay loans falling due. This difference, bearing on the theoretical liquidity of loans, perhaps accounts for part at least of the differences between the rates commanded by loans from the same bank in the two markets: certainly rates in the inter-bank market are consistently above those ruling in the discount market.

The discount market has also suffered during these years from the great reduction in the total issues of Treasury bills. This reduction has been partly due to the policy of the central government in forcing local government authorities to do their own borrowing, so that the local ratepayers have had to pay the higher rates ruling in the new markets instead of paying (through the Exchequer) the lower rates paid on Treasury bills which are held in the classical discount market. There have, however, been a number of other factors influencing the volume of Treasury bills available for the discount houses. The heavy fall in the U.K.'s international gold reserves in 1964–5, especially, reduced issues of Treasury bills, in the way explained in Chapter 6. Also, at the recent high levels of interest rates, the government broker has been able to sell unusually large amounts of medium- and long-term government securities whenever (as has happened from time to time) interest rates have looked like falling; and these large sales have enabled the Exchequer to reduce its resort to Treasury bill issues. Against these factors depressing the availability of

Treasury bills for the discount market has been the decline in the demand by industrial and commercial companies for such bills; as the local authority market has developed, with higher rates of interest, companies have tended to use Treasury bills less, and the newer markets more, as an outlet for their temporarily surplus funds. On balance, however, the total of Treasury bills available for the discount market has greatly declined.

While the discount houses have been suffering from a sharp reduction in the supply of Treasury bills, they have enjoyed a compensating increase in their business in commercial bills; and these have the advantage of being on the whole more profitable than Treasury bills. Some of the discount houses have for many years been trying to foster the use, by industrial and commercial firms, of bills of exchange of the traditional kind, and during the ten years from 1955 circumstances played into their hands. The restriction of bank advances for many normal trading purposes has been almost continuous and, even when the control has been relaxed, firms have seen advantage in opening or maintaining alternative avenues for borrowing, so that they should be safer when restrictions came on again. For some time the authorities were content to regulate bill finance by sending to the accepting houses and banks requests, parallel to those relating to ordinary bank advances, to restrict the volume of bills accepted. This left untouched the growth of trade bills (which bear no acceptance by a bank or recognized accepting house) and it is not surprising that there has been a sharp revival in the use of this instrument of business finance. In 1965–6, however, the authorities instituted a tight control, by 'requests' to the discount houses, whereby the purchases of trade bills by the discount houses, and their purchases of other bills ('bank acceptances') are rigidly limited by reference to a base period. The loophole in the control has thus been completely blocked—by action which includes, to the great inconvenience of the discount houses, a double regulation of bank acceptances—but fortunately for the discount houses the stoppage of further growth was made effective only after their holdings of bank acceptances and trade bills had risen to a comfortably high level, more than compensating them for the scarcity of Treasury bills.

During the last ten years, 'external convertibility'—that is to say, the freedom of non-residents to transfer money from the country—has been established both in London and in most other countries important in the financial universe. This external convertibility has been an essential condition for the development of a very extensive Euro-dollar market, and for other Euro-currency markets such as the Euro-sterling market in Paris (similar to, but much more limited than, the London market in Euro-dollars). With this greater freedom of movement for balances, and with the protective use of forward markets in foreign currencies there has been a decided internationalization of short-money markets. In these circumstances one would have expected the Bank of England, which has been under the necessity to watch the gold reserves very carefully, to make its control of short interest rates even stricter than before. Oddly enough, the opposite has occurred. The interest rates most relevant to the international short capital flows are those ruling in the local authority market, which has attracted considerable sums from non-residents, who protect themselves by hedging in the forward exchange market. The Bank of England does not, it is understood, ever intervene in any way in this market, although of course it can bring about major movements in its rates by moving Bank Rate by the usual fairly big jumps up or down. In the bill market, where the discount houses, the clearing banks, and the Bank of England have all continued to play their traditional roles, the Bank of England's control has remained absolute, though in 1966–7 the Bank has been exercising its control more flexibly by modifying its rules of operation as lender of last resort. It has continued to rely on this absolute control of the Treasury bill market (a control that includes the exercise of the Bank Rate weapon) to exercise influence indirectly on the new money markets. More importantly, however, it has adopted the practice of operating in the forward exchange market, a device that had been long debated among experts and long resisted by the authorities. Since non-resident holders of funds are willing to employ their funds in any London market only after protecting themselves in the forward exchange market, the authorities can influence the relative attractiveness of London by altering the cost of forward exchange cover, instead of enforcing a change in relative interest rates. This kind of control device could become much more useful if the foreign exchange markets became less subject to abrupt changes in international confidence in major foreign exchange rates.

The tendency of the various financial centres of the world to become more closely interlinked, despite fears of currency devaluations, is also to be seen in the spreading of the tentacles of particular banks and banking groups across national frontiers. While in the main the London clearing banks have held to their principle of transacting international business for their customers through 'correspondent' relationships with independent banks in other countries, there have been important developments of closer relationships and even of the establishment of their own branches abroad. The Midland and Barclays especially have developed in this way. Barclays, which already had Barclays D.C.O. as an important subsidiary, now habitually refers to itself as 'The Barclays Group', with 4,341 offices of which 2,772 are in the U.K. The Midland has a 45 per cent. interest in 'Midland and International Banks Limited' (the other shareholders are banks in Australia, Canada, and South Africa) and has close connexions with Dutch, German, and Belgian banks.

As well as having greatly developed their activity in overseas business, the London clearing banks have made an important change in one of their traditional attitudes in domestic business. This has been the break from the cartel on deposit rates; they have been driven to this departure by the cumulation of new opportunities that have been opening since 1950 for customers wanting to place money on deposit for short periods. For two generations these banks had worked under a very strict mutual agreement on deposit rates, the only terms offered to the public for time deposits (balances on 'deposit account') being for deposits at seven days' notice, the agreed rate of interest being ordinarily (since 1951) 2 per cent. below Bank Rate. During the 1950's two circumstances combined to put strain on this agreement. First, the banks for several years stood aside from the development of hire-purchase finance, and specialist firms that grew up to do this business were able to offer rates for time deposits well above the cartel rate. Secondly, the sophistication of company financial officers had far advanced since the days when Treasury bill rates had last been much above the banks' deposit rate, and when in the 1950's rates on Treasury bills settled to $1\frac{1}{4}$ or $1\frac{1}{2}$ above this cartel rate, much company money began to go from bank deposit accounts to Treasury bills. Stung by the competition of hire-purchase finance houses and the Treasury bill, some clearing bankers were already, before 1958, wondering whether they should compete more actively for 'big money'. At that time, however, the banks were still 'underlent', in the sense that their advances ratios were much lower than they would have liked, and most bankers saw little point in raising the cost of deposits if the money was only to be re-lent to the government. Many were even more sceptical about the idea of competing for deposits, and when the Radcliffe Committee questioned the representatives of the clearing banks, these witnesses clung to the cartel system. Since that time, however, there has been the tremendous development of local authority borrowing, by methods outlined above, and from these absolutely safe borrowers big lenders have been able to get rates well above the Treasury bill rate, and that much higher still above the cartel rate on time deposits. The gap that had been $1\frac{1}{4}$ or $1\frac{1}{2}$ per cent. was widened to 2 per cent. This competition was too much for the banks; all of them now compete for large deposits, at rates only slightly below the local authority rates. They do the business only in large amounts, and at the side door, not at the front door. The large depositor, that is to say, puts his money with a subsidiary of his bank, knowing that the security is identical and fixing the period of his deposit at some limit suiting his own needs. Meanwhile, the small depositor continues to be received at the front door at the cartel rate. The figures involved in this book-keeping operation are large, in relation to the total deposits of the clearing banks, and the change has laid traps for the users of some of the new series of financial statistics which have been appearing in recent years.

This change in the London clearing banks has tended to accentuate the importance of the interest rates in the new money markets of London, and correspondingly to reduce the importance of the traditional structure of Bank Rate, Treasury bill rate, and highly stereotyped overdraft and deposit rates. It is not surprising that the banks have been changing somewhat their practice on overdraft rates, particularly by increasing the dispersion of effective rates round the traditional norm of 'Bank Rate plus one'. Further developments may occur as the banks react to the changes that are occurring in their world. Until now the banks have been relatively free from pressure to change, as high interest rates have boosted their gross earnings and as they have been denied, by government fiat, the opportunity to raise their advances ratios to levels unknown for forty years. They have also been able to plan much more economical operation of their routine business, with the adaptation of computers to their needs: a rapidly growing proportion of accounts is now covered by computers, enabling the banks to reduce their employment of women and to look forward with reasonable confidence to the transition to decimal accounting in 1971. There are, however, other factors pulling in different directions: the growing competition from trustee savings banks and building societies, and the planned introduction of a governmental giro payments system. Altogether, the environment in which the banks have to do their business is changing rapidly, and looks like continuing to change. The ways in which they adapt themselves to these environmental changes are bound to have repercussions on the structure of money markets in London and on the inter-relations of the various groups of financial institutions; and so also will changes in the international monetary scene have effects on London's financial structure. If monetary policy is to play any appreciable role in the future, the techniques of control will need to be adapted, perhaps more radically than hitherto, to all these changes, present and future, in the nation's financial structure and particularly in the London markets which form its hub.

January 1967

INDEX

Acceptance of bills, 54.
Acceptance credit, 48, 163.
Accepting Houses, 43, 45, 48–52, 69, 85 n.
Accepting Houses Committee, 73.
Accepting Houses credit intelligence service, 49.
Agricultural interests, U.S., 79, 270.
Amalgamation of banks, 25, 26, 189.
Amalgamation of discount houses, 59.
American Bankers' Association, 264.
'Announcement effects' of monetary measures, 129.
Anti-inflation policy, 189, 191.
Argentina, 134, 143.
Australia, 6, 19, 135, 292.
Authorized dealers in foreign exchange, 145.
Authorities and governmental actions concerning, accepting houses, 52.
  banks, 14, 26, 51, 94, 95, 123, 188, 193, 264, 270, 298.
  capital accumulation, 252.
  cash supply, 94, 95, 105, 107, 223, 237, 240, 274, 290, 318.
  central bank, 67, 70, 72, 77.
  discount houses, 59, 61, 62.
  economic activity level, 217, 256, 257.
  exchange regulation, 133.
  finance, 125, 168, 260.
  gilt-edged market, 309, 310.
  inflation, 150, 151, 255, 295.
  interest rate structure, 38, 151, 208, 209, 215, 238, 256, 257, 260, 285.
  liquid assets supply, 34, 127, 172, 223, 240, 241, 251, 259.
  market operations, 116, 219, 222, 235, 238, 241.
  Special Deposits, 125–7.
Availability of loans, &c., 187, 198, 201, 215, 217, 231, 256, 257.

Bagehot, Walter, 102.
Balance of convertible currencies, 146.
  payments, 127, 136 n, 138, 140, 141, 146, 149, 151, 192, 208, 284, 288, 292, 294.
  trade, 41, 143, 144.

Balances at Post Office Savings Banks, 154.
Baltimore, 263.
Bank of America, 262.
Bank of England:
  and Accepting Houses, 51, 52, 85 n.
  Acts (1694), 68.
    (1844), 100.
    (1946), 68–71, 126.
  aims, 111, 113.
  Annual Report, 74.
  assets, 84, 85, 93–95, 108, 109.
  'back-door operations', 84, 105, 107, 109–11, 149, 312, 313.
  balances, 87, 99, 312.
  a bankers' bank, 12, 86.
  Bankers' Deposits, 28, 29, 33, 34, 83, 84, 86–89, 91–99, 107–10, 119, 120, 123, 124, 135, 146, 240, 276.
  Banking Department, 57, 84, 98, 109, 110, 118, 240.
  bills taken by, 104, 105.
  bond market operations, 123.
  branches, 308.
  business for private customers, 83, 85, 104.
  and circulation, 91.
  and clearing house, 301, 304.
  control of, 69, 71, 72.
  control over other banks, 39, 45, 72, 82, 87, 88, 93, 94, 95, 101, 103, 112, 113, 117, 122, 123.
  control over other financial institutions, 127.
  conventions, 70.
  Court of Governors, 69, 104, 124.
  Deputy-Governor, 68, 69, 73, 309.
  direct operations with clearing banks, 105–7.
  'Directions', 71–72.
  directors, 68–70, 73.
  and Discount Houses, 59, 60, 104, 122, 123, 182.
  Discount Office, 273.
  'Discounts and Advances', 84, 93.
  Discounts operator, 115.
  dividend and redemption warrants, 303, 304.
  and export credits, 194, 195.

REPRINTED LITHOGRAPHICALLY IN GREAT BRITAIN
AT THE UNIVERSITY PRESS, OXFORD
BY VIVIAN RIDLER
PRINTER TO THE UNIVERSITY